AF328684

# RAISING THE ROOF

CODE2

AGATA TOROMANOFF

# RAISING THE ROOF

## WOMEN ARCHITECTS WHO BROKE THROUGH THE GLASS CEILING

PRESTEL

MUNICH · LONDON · NEW YORK

# TABLE OF CONTENTS


006 INTRODUCTION

008 OLAJUMOKE ADENOWO

014 AMALE ANDRAOS

018 GAE AULENTI

022 SANDRA BARCLAY

026 DEBORAH BERKE

030 TATIANA BILBAO

036 LINA BO BARDI

040 CAROLINE BOS

044 ALISON BROOKS

050 SARAH CALBURN

054 FERNANDA CANALES

060 LUCÍA CANO

064 ODILE DECQ

070 ELIZABETH DILLER

076 JANE DREW

080 FRIDA ESCOBEDO

084 YVONNE FARRELL & SHELLEY McNAMARA

090 DORIANA FUKSAS

094 JEANNE GANG

098 EILEEN GRAY

102 ZAHA HADID

106 ITSUKO HASEGAWA

110 ANNA HERINGER

114 FRANCINE HOUBEN

120 ROSSANA HU

126 LOUISA HUTTON

130 KRISTIN JARMUND

134 AMANDA LEVETE

140 INÊS LOBO

144 ELLEN VAN LOON

150 DORTE MANDRUP

156 NORMA MERRICK SKLAREK

158 MARTA PELEGRÍN

162 CARME PIGEM

166 CARME PINÓS

170 SAMIRA RATHOD

178 SU ROGERS

182 NATHALIE ROZENCWAJG

186 DENISE SCOTT BROWN

190 CRISTINA SEGNI

194 KAZUYO SEJIMA

200 ANNABELLE SELLDORF

204 ALISON MARGARET SMITHSON

206 BENEDETTA TAGLIABUE

212 XU TIANTIAN

218 MONICA TRICARIO

224 NATHALIE DE VRIES

228 BETSY WILLIAMSON

234 ADA YVARS BRAVO

238 CAZÚ ZEGERS

244 INDEX

252 ARCHITECTS' WEBSITES

255 PHOTO CREDITS

# INTRODUCTION

P. 2
CARME PINÒS
CUBE II OFFICE TOWER,
GUADALAJARA, MEXICO 2014
P. 7
FERNANDA CANALES
CASA BRUMA
VALLE DE BRAVO, MEXICO, 2017

The history of architecture, as in many other disciplines, has been largely written by men. Women in the discipline have been mostly marginalised or ignored, such as Marion Mahony Griffin, the first woman in the world to be officially licenced as an architect, who was Frank Lloyd Wright's first employee and was not given much recognition for her large contribution to his residential projects, or Anne Griswold Tyng, who remained in the shadow of Louis Kahn. Until recently male architects happened to be those most often favoured with major and prestigious commissions around the globe and those most often awarded the highest honours. It is difficult to believe that when Zaha Hadid won the Pritzker Architecture Prize in 2004, it was actually the first time in the award's 25-year history that a woman had won. Statistics continue to show that more than half of students enrolling in architecture schools are women, although only a relatively small percentage start a professional career in the discipline.

The situation is evolving gradually, however, and to foster the change, the discourse must be altered as well. It is time to consider the history of architecture as a discipline created by both genders, without constantly emphasising the gaps, which are visibly decreasing. The number of women entering or establishing their own practices, who and successfully juggling their professional and family lives, is steadily growing. Prestigious events, like the Venice Architecture Biennale, are less rarely curated by women. In addition, since 2004 the Pritzker prize has seen a couple of female winners. Women win major international competitions, design large-scale projects, and are credited for their work. Whether within big firms, partnerships, or individual architecture studios, they have become an integral part of architecture and should be treated as such. The profession is not to be divided into male or female, and the aim of this book is definitely not to create a parallel, "feminine part of the story". The selection of projects is also not, at any rate, a presentation of so-called feminine architecture. Gender may affect an architect's approach or way of working but surely should not be a criterion to discuss the style. It is also not a "special mention" but an insight into architects' unique visions, which contribute to the fascinating complexity of architecture. My goal is to celebrate the great buildings that create our landscapes and bring innovation into the way we live today all around the globe.

To avoid focusing on clichés of gender disparities and marking long-overdue changes in the discipline, the presentations of architects in this book deliberately omit lists or awards that pay tribute exclusively to women. The intention is to encourage fair discourse and to advocate the vision of an equitable architectural scene. The situation is largely improving thanks to the many women architects who speak up for their rights and fight against discrimination by teaching and holding significant positions, and are thus role models and mentors for others. The best idea would be to provide more opportunities and support to young architects, treat women as equal partners, and finally stop making distinctions between the genders, whether in categorisation or in awards, among other issues. In the same spirit, this book offers a glimpse into a handful of inspiring careers.

Featuring 50 architects from all over the world and their key works, this survey encompasses practitioners with well-established careers, who run their own studios or are equal partners, as well as young, emerging architects. The number of both is growing. In addition to professionally active architects, there are also portraits of late figures like Gae Aulenti, Lina Bo Bardi, Eileen Gray, and Zaha Hadid, as any picture of women in architecture would be incomplete without them. The aim of featuring a selection of their designs is simply to celebrate their impressive visions, full stop. They all are, or were, great architects, not women architects. Enjoy the journey through their inspiring biographies and their innovative and aesthetically enthralling architectural realizations.

# OLAJUMOKE ADENOWO

One of the strongest African voices in architecture, Olajumoke Adenowo (b. 1968), is one of the most influential and inspiring Nigerian architects. Influenced by family trips to Europe in early childhood, she knew she wanted to become an architect. Adenowo's truly impressive path started at the age of 14 when she enrolled to study Architecture at the University of Ife, where she also completed her postgraduate studies, gaining an MSc in Architecture. While aware of global traditions and history, she creates independently of formal western training. "My work is to evolve architecture rooted in my Nigerian heritage, which the global north can respect, learn from, derive value and fresh insights from," she explains. The mission of her professional career is to promote Nigerian architecture, particularly examples that draw from local culture but have global perspectives.

Adenowo started her first job at an architectural studio when she was 19 and designed her first building four years later. At the age of 26, in 1994, Adenowo founded AD Consulting Limited, of which she is the Principle Partner. The firm's portfolio includes more than 70 buildings, many of which were commissioned by the world's biggest brands. The architect's approach to architecture is complex and multileveled, however some aspects seem to play critical roles. First, creating buildings that are naturally sustainable, whether thanks to selected materials or ingenious solutions. Second, the way the architect works with natural light, how the shapes and window layout interact with the rays of sunlight, which generously fill the interiors. Dynamic layouts, even when enclosed in a static shell, make the spaces very narrative. Adenowo remarks that her buildings go beyond three dimensions to a fourth dimension, which is time. "It reflects my approach which is to draw from my heritage to understand the future," she says.

Parallel to her ground-breaking architecture career Adenowo is also a philanthropist with a long-distance philosophy of implementing changes. 1999 marked her establishment of the Awesome Treasures Foundation which is an intercontinental philanthropic foundation recognised by the United Nations and focused on supporting women and youth. "We have global summits from Nigeria to Accra, New York, and London. We are raising transformational leaders, helping people find their purpose and deploying their purpose to impact their communities and the globe," she explains. Adenowo is also the author of several books and the host of a radio show called "Voice of Change"; reaching over 15 million people per broadcast, the show has been on air for nearly a decade. The University of Ife (now Obafemi Awolowo University), which Adenowo graduated from with distinction, not only honoured her as an Ambassador of Excellence for outstanding achievements in architecture, but also commissioned her to design a new senate building for the university campus, originally designed by Bauhaus graduate Arieh Sharon. A fellow of Nigerian Institute of Architects, in 2018 Adenowo was recognised by the Royal Institute of British Architects (RIBA) as one of the most inspirational women in architecture today. When profiled by CNN she was referred to as "Africa's Starchitect".

# "I'm rooted in my heritage, I'm global in my frame of reference."

In one of your interviews, you mentioned that, together with your parents, you travelled a lot in your childhood, especially across Europe. Has this experience influenced your way of looking at architecture? Is that when the architect in you was born?

Travelling as a toddler definitely broadened my mind precociously. The defining moment in my decision to become an architect was touring the Palais de Versailles at the age of three. It affected me on two levels: first as an architect and also my vision of leadership. I could see as young as I was, though I couldn't quite crystallize my hypothesis very vividly, the consequences of the failure of leadership, in the end of the royal family who once held court in the chateau. The sheer opulence and scale of the chateau as viewed through my toddler eyes and the monuments, castles, piazzas, and parks of Paris, Hamburg, Amsterdam, Edinburgh, and other cities we toured made me fall in love with form and space, and that is when my desire to become an architect was born.

You enrolled to study architecture at the University of Ife at the age of 14 (!), started working as an architect five years later, and got an opportunity to design your first building when you were only 23 years old. Two years later you established your own firm, AD Consulting. Throughout this impressive beginning of your career, did you ever experience any gender related issues? Has being woman in architecture ever impacted your professional path?

My career in architecture would have been markedly different if I were not a woman especially in the patriarchal space in which I work. The decision-makers on huge budget items like architecture are not women, and the real decisions are made in Boys' Clubs which exclude women or are not women-friendly environments. Things are changing slowly but the token women we have in decision-making still seem to be in the process of getting over the Queen Bee syndrome; consequently for myself

and for many women in male-dominated industries the terrain is inequitable. I probably have had to work five times as hard as the men simply to get a foot in the door. I have come this far in spite of being a woman and not because of being a woman. I get commissions when the client has considered all other options, rises above nepotism, chooses the path of meritocracy, and decides it's in their enlightened self-interest to work with me. This seeming adversity can be an advantage because by the time a client is working with me, they are fully persuaded that I am the best architect for them. For decades I therefore have never lost a client.

You have designed and executed over 70 buildings so far. Sustainability, the use of light, and the element of surprise are some of the most important aspects of your realizations. What do you find most challenging in architectural practice?

Bringing my vision to reality as envisioned is the greatest challenge. It is like swimming against the tide in an environment where even the elite struggle to discern between buildings (as shelter) and architecture, the art and science of design. This is why I work with discerning clients who know the difference. Those who know that architecture is beyond mere function – it's about distinction. In a climate where developers or budgets actually drive the construction market and the value of good design as the return on investment has not yet been clearly appreciated, it is challenging to be a thinker, to produce seminal work. This is why I celebrate our clients like in the Reeve Road project where I was allowed to express and birth the vision. In the Guiding Light Assembly building the contractor actually persuaded the client to adopt an approach that he would find easier to build and I had to radically revise the design.

**You have referred to your approach to architecture as holistic. How would you describe it?**

When I design, I design holistically. From the parti, the concept, I'm thinking of the architecture but not as a static form. I am considering its transition in time and space: how the forms are viewed externally, by passers-by, at high speed from a car, how it is viewed in the day, at night, and how the building transitions diurnally to nocturnally. The interior vistas, the promenade through the building in time. The elements of awe, rest, and wonder. The interior architecture, the different forms of lighting, task lighting, display lighting, mood lighting, integral art work, the soft and hard finishes, etc. are integral to my design from inception, including the interior and exterior landscape and how the landscape is seen from within the building and from without as an appropriate setting for the building. I see the building as a total whole, as a living organism.

**Your professional and philanthropic activities make you a role model who inspires many. As if this were not enough, you also dedicate time to mentoring young girls and teenagers. Why do you think it is so important to support female creativity?**

The planet is facing so many challenges right now that will need innovative solutions. Africa's case is peculiar: it will need to leapfrog in its solutions to avoid the learning curve of the global north. It is therefore extremely important to support female creativity simply because women are 51.8% of the human race and trying to solve the challenges facing the human race without fully engaging women is like trying to fight with your hands tied behind your back.
I say "never underestimate the potential of a human who still has a pulse". Can we imagine where life on earth and the advances in medicine would be if Marie Curie had not carried out her work on radio activity? There are treasures in women and the youth who are often marginalised in the patriarchal gerontocracy that's so prevalent on the African continent and that's why my philanthropic organization, founded in 1999, is named Awesome Treasures and focuses on women and young people.

**CNN profiled you as "Africa's Starchitect". Would you dream of designing outside of Africa or do you plan to focus on further developing African architecture?**

The world is a global village so the moniker "Africa's Starchitect" points to my origin but not my sphere of operation. I would bring a fresh perspective to design globally and especially to the global north. I was appointed a visiting professor at the Technical University of Munich in 2019 and I find it laudable that the faculty understand that fresh perspectives besides that of the global north are sorely needed. The architectural discourse has been dominated by a western perspective; we have learned from Europe for centuries, from North America and relatively more recently from Asia, but learnings from Africa are markedly absent from the narrative. It's like trying to develop a cure for cancer without even looking at the vast Amazon forest for perhaps that rare flora or fauna which may hold the key to a cure. That is the strength I bring to the architectural discourse: since I was a toddler I have been acculturated to be global in perspective but I am rooted in my origins and bring the fresh perspectives of my roots.

GUIDING LIGHT ASSEMBLY
LAGOS, NIGERIA, 2002

"In the design of the church, we departed from
the traditional typology to create a contemporary
ecclesiastical but multi-functional space," Adenowo
comments about one of her first buildings. Striking
is the contrast between the compact outer shell and
the spacious, well-lit interiors. The embedded façade
is actually made of floor-to-ceiling windows, while a
gigantic skylight tops the assembly hall. A functional
plan of the latter consolidates the community and is
organized on two levels, separated by light galleries
and a terraced seating area. The building also
houses offices for the church staff, situated around
a small internal courtyard with a Baptismal font.

AD STUDIO
LEKKI, LAGOS, 2014

The architect's headquarters reflect her philosophy. The flexible, dynamic, and multifaceted building was conceived as "an organic harmony of spaces" to inspire creativity. The impressive entrance is dominated by the white nautilus stairs spiralling dynamically up to a skylight and vertically communicating all levels of the building. While offices were planned on the ground and first floors, the third floor offers a stunning roof garden, library, a lounge, and even a gym. The unorthodox shape of the studio is very light thanks to large window surfaces. To let even more light into the interiors, some of the walls are semi-transparent as they are made of luxfers.

REEVE ROAD
LAGOS, NIGERIA, 2018

Located on a long and narrow plot, the house is built according to a program and spatial relationship derived from traditional Yoruba architecture. Reflecting the hierarchy of spaces, the interiors were planned to comfortably divide private and public rooms. One contemporary touch is the way the architect filled the interiors with light, starting at the entrance with a three-floor reception area encompassing a helical staircase and topped with a skylight. Light streams in through extensive windows in numerous rooms on all levels, which adds lightness to the structure. A huge roof garden, also accessible through an external spiral case, creates an entertainment sphere with panoramic views of the neighbourhood.

# AMALE ANDRAOS

Amale Andraos' (b. 1973) adventure with architecture started when she watched her father, architect and artist Farid Andraos, at work. Born in Beirut, Lebanon, she received her Master's degree from the Graduate School of Design at Harvard University. The experience of living and working in various countries, including Saudi Arabia, France, Canada, and the Netherlands, has given her the ability to look at things from many different perspectives. Andraos is the co-founder of New York–based WORKac, which creates architecture and strategic planning "at the intersection of the urban, the rural and the natural," as stated on the firm's website. The main goal of the practice, established and run together with her partner Dan Wood, is to re-invent the relationship between urban and natural environments and to invent solutions for optimal integration between architecture, landscape, and ecological systems. Andraos and Wood work on all their projects very closely, supported by a dedicated team. Their creative process takes the form of an open and open-ended discussion and exchange, where the couple progresses only when they agree. "This means that projects never move forward based on one or the other's ideas but rather, that we debate them until we arrive at something neither of us imagined. Ideas get nested, layered but also harshly criticized and edited in and out," explains Andraos. The range of projects developed by WORKac is quite wide, however the portfolio that has earned them international acclaim is dominated by public buildings, like museums, schools, and libraries. Independently of the kind of commission, WORKac's inventive architecture result in fresh visions and unorthodox spaces.

The architect is also the dean of Columbia University's Graduate School of Architecture, Planning and Preservation (the first woman to hold that position), a role she has undertaken with a fresh and inspiring approach. Trying to redefine teaching architecture today, she has restructured courses and intersected disciplines, all to encourage cross-disciplinary exchanges and to enable programmes to meet current needs. At the core of her mission at the university is to revitalise conversations and to blur traditional definitions in favour of transdisciplinary thinking and practice.

Extensive research, criss-crossing disciplines and perspectives, and the constant exchange of ideas, are main focuses of both aspects of the architect's work – developing her practice's portfolio and teaching. Numerous publications also offer an insightful reflection on how climatic issues influence architecture. "We are living at a time of seismic change, a time when climate change, rapid global urbanization and the development of new technologies are altering the planet in ways we have yet to fully register and act upon, with urgency but also with care," Andraos remarks. She goes on to explain that "architecture and the built environment are central to those issues and concerns and cities in particular, still hold the promise of shaping a more sustainable, equitable and creative world. Yet this promise cannot be fulfilled without projecting into the future while simultaneously reflecting on the past, with a commitment to improve upon the foundations of our disciplines, alter our modes of practice, and reframe the scales of our engagement."

KEW GARDENS HILLS LIBRARY
QUEENS, NEW YORK CITY, USA 2017

The spaces of this social institution
were designed as a series of
reading rooms for different age
groups, defined by the expressive
articulations of the roof, "touching
the ground to provide privacy for
the teens and the librarians' offices,
lifting up to give the library a sense
of monumentality at its most public
corner, and lifting again at the kids'
corner to provide child-size views",
as described by the architects.
The massive yet dynamic curtain-
like façade is made of custom
glass fiber–reinforced concrete
panels with rippled folds. The roof's
slope, covered with grass, visually
connects the building with an
existing garden at the back.

# MIAMI MUSEUM GARAGE
## MIAMI, USA, 2018

How to transform a multi-level parking lot into a fanciful space for social interaction? WORKac's answer is to add an expressive façade with a series of vertical public spaces connected with staircases and original tunnels. The architects managed to carve within this outer skin: a gallery for graffiti art, a children's play area with a slide and climbing wall, a garden with a single palm tree, a DJ platform, a lending library, a listening lounge, a fountain, a bar, a car washer/charger, and a space for pets. Additionally, at the roof level, some parking spaces were replaced with a small auditorium and beach area.

RHODE ISLAND SCHOOL OF
DESIGN (RISD) STUDENT CENTER
PROVIDENCE, USA, 2019

The juxtaposition between the light
structure of new addition and RISD's
original brick building from 1948
is visually striking and reinvents
the connection between the street
level and the school's interiors. The
pavilion does not function merely as
the new entrance or a space where
students can interact. A floating
curved wall wrapping around the
main lobby, an acoustic curtain
creating a classroom/gallery space
and clad in perforated metal panels,
additionally houses a new lecture
hall also used for screenings and
the mail room. These playful forms,
as much as the use of colour and
materials, resonate perfectly with the
artistic character of the school.

# GAE AULENTI

Gae Aulenti (1927–2012) studied architecture at the Polytechnic University of Milan in 1954. At the beginning of her career she worked as a graphic designer and editor at 'Casabella Continuità' magazine. The beginning of the 1960s marked her first furniture design and lighting projects that quickly brought her recognition. Aulenti simultaneously started teaching, initially as a professor of the Venice School of Architecture and later at the Milan School of Architecture. At the time, neither running an individual practice nor being active in both architecture and design were common for a woman. "Women in architecture must not think of themselves as a minority, because the minute you do, you become paralysed," she famously said, adding that "it is most important to never create the problem".

Aulenti worked on a wide range of projects, from set design for La Scala to showrooms for Fiat and Olivetti, to product design in collaboration with leading brands. Many of the objects envisioned by the architect have become design icons, like her glass coffee tables on wheels. Some are still in production today. In the field of architecture Aulenti's focus was restorations of historical and typically monumental buildings. Her main goal for their revival process was to emphasise their original character and offer a special experience to anyone who visited them, while their functionality was as crucial as the aesthetics.

The most spectacular moment of the architect's career took place in Paris, where she was commissioned to create one of the world's most exceptional museums in the former Orsay railway station, designed by Victor Laloux and built on the occasion of the Universal Exhibition in 1900, on the Left Bank of the Seine. Its metal structure was concealed by an exterior limestone envelope to harmonise with the Louvre and the Tuileries nearby. Although it was the first station designed for electrically powered trains, it soon became obsolete, due to its short platforms, which could not be adjusted to the length of newer, longer electric train models. The building was used for various purposes from the 1940s to the 1970s, until the authorities decided to transform it into a museum. A.C.T. Architecture team won the competition for the reconversion in 1978. However, the second consultation two years later appointed Gae Aulenti to transform the interior of the former station into a museum. The realisation was criticised among professionals, mainly for retaining some of the rich decorations of the original station and its barrel-vaulted structure; the spacious open interior was considered to overpower the side galleries displaying artwork. Nevertheless, the newly renovated museum attracted record numbers of visitors and the project for Paris led to numerous other commissions to reconvert historical buildings into exhibition spaces.

In 1986 Aulenti adapted the interiors of Palazzo Grassi, built on the Grand Canal in Venice between 1748 and 1772. At the time, the palace had been purchased by Fiat with a mission to establish a space for art and archaeology exhibitions. More than two decades later, the building was purchased by art collector François Pinault and underwent a renovation by the Japanese architect Tadao Ando to re-open in 2006. Aulenti also designed spaces for the Asian Art Museum in San Francisco and the Museu Nacional d'Art de Catalunya in Barcelona. Another interesting project was the Torrecchia Vecchia in Lazio, Italy, in the early 1990s. Within a private estate, the architect transformed a barn from the 17th century into a villa. These are just some of the many examples which demonstrate that the architect favoured working on projects involving reconverting existing buildings with a long history.

pages 19-21
MUSÉE D'ORSAY
PARIS, FRANCE, 1986

Aulenti's visually powerful idea was to construct two towers at the ends of
the central aisle of the former train station. The immense volume of the nave
was transformed into a spacious exhibiting space. The project is considered
ground-breaking, as it marks the first time a purely industrial building was
restored to house a major art collection. The renovation included restoring rich
decorations to their former glory, like the ceiling rosettes in the arched bays.
In parallel, advanced solutions were implemented, including air-conditioning
vents and devices reducing sound reverberation. The converted building
opened in 1986, and quickly became of the capital's icons. It became home
to a representative collection of works from the period between 1848 and 1914,
exhibited on three main levels. The result was spectacular.

VAN GOGH
/ARTAUD
Le suicidé de la société

# SANDRA BARCLAY

Lima-born Sandra Barclay (b. 1967) received a degree in architecture first from the Universidad Ricardo Palma, in Lima, Peru, in 1990 and three years later from the École d'Architecture de Paris-Belleville. She also studied at the Universidad Diego Portales in Santiago, Chile for a master's degree in 2013. In 1994, still in Paris, she and Jean Pierre Crousse co-founded Barclay & Crousse Architecture. Since 2006 the practice has been based in Lima and through their innovative and award-winning projects the architects have put Peruvian architecture back on discipline's world map. Peru is a great source of inspiration for the architects. "We are very sensitive about how to work with the logic of that territory or landscape, as if the building can continue using this logic", reflects Barclay. One of the architects' most famous realizations is the Paracas Museum in the ancient Peruvian desert. Completed in 2012, it is an excellent example of how the practice draws from their native country's traditions while designing. While the arrangement of the interiors is partly informed by the labyrinthine spatiality used by ancient Peruvians, the geometry of the volume responds to the pre-existing demolished museum while the roof, treated as a fifth façade, is a reinterpretation of the motifs known from the traditional Paracas textiles. Last but not least, the patina of the outer shell created by polishing cement gives the structure a look similar to the pre-Columbian ceramics which are exhibited in the museum. These interesting heritage references translated into the materiality or aesthetic of their buildings are always very subtle. The duo's goal is to use local materials and resources and to work with skilled craftsmen. They are also committed to delivering solutions that can be adapted to local weather conditions, like natural ventilation and cooling.

Their massive constructions, each with an original take, employ geometry in a most unique way. The buildings designed by Barclay & Crousse are like bridges between the past and today, with their characteristic patina juxtaposed with a purely contemporary architectural language. Working across typologies, the architects focus on the discipline's essentials. By working with space and light, which are central in their approach, they wish to comfort people and provide well-being. Keen on low-budget projects offering numerous possibilities, Barclay & Crousse favour simplicity in their realizations. "We consider our projects as being part of a design laboratory that explores the bonds between landscape, climate and architecture, in order to challenge those notions of technology, usage, and quality of life that, from the specific conditions of developing countries, can inform and be pertinent in a global context", they explain.

Barclay lectures internationally and has also devoted herself to teaching since 2006 at the Pontificia Universidad Católica del Perú. In 2019 she was invited along with Crousse by the Norman R. Foster Foundation as a Visiting Professor at the Yale School of Architecture. In 2016 Barclay & Crousse curated the Peruvian Pavilion at the 15th Venice Biennale obtaining the Special Mention of the jury and participated in the main exhibition of the following edition of the prestigious event.

PARACAS MUSEUM
PARACAS, PERU, 2012

Located in Peru's most important coastal
desert, the archaeological site museum is
built on the ruins of the former building
destroyed in an earthquake in 2007. Defined
by a rhythmical arrangement of geometric
forms, it is split into two parts. The main
volume houses the museum as well as
conservation spaces, while a narrow volume
running along its length is dedicated
to interaction and learning spaces, like
workshops rooms. According to the architects,
a great challenge was to integrate the
volume into the landscape, which as it
happens was the cradle of the culture. They
hence designed it with exposed concrete
and reddish cement, which blends it into the
surrounding red dunes.

UNIVERSITY FACILITIES UDEP
PIUNA, PERU, 2016

The architects envisioned the university facilities as an extension of the arid forest of Algarrobo trees, typical of the northern Peruvian desert, which provides shade in a climate that is both hot and dry. From the exterior, the building appears as monolithic, while once "inside" one discovers a group of eleven independent buildings, under generous cantilevered roofs that emerge from each one, providing shadow over multiple gathering and circulation places. This solution creates a permeable building, which enhance the natural ventilation while offering protection from the sunshine creating a comfort zone for this particular climate.



SANDRA BARCLAY

# SANDRA BARCLAY

Lima-born Sandra Barclay (b. 1967) received a degree in architecture first from the Universidad Ricardo Palma, in Lima, Peru, in 1990 and three years later from the École d'Architecture de Paris-Belleville. She also studied at the Universidad Diego Portales in Santiago, Chile for a master's degree in 2013. In 1994, still in Paris, she and Jean Pierre Crousse co-founded Barclay & Crousse Architecture. Since 2006 the practice has been based in Lima and through their innovative and award-winning projects the architects have put Peruvian architecture back on discipline's world map. Peru is a great source of inspiration for the architects. "We are very sensitive about how to work with

the logic of that territory or landscape, as if the building can continue using this logic", reflects Barclay. One of the architects' most famous realizations is the Paracas Museum in the ancient Peruvian desert. Completed in 2012, it is an excellent example of how the practice draws from their native country's traditions while designing. While the arrangement of the interiors is partly informed by the labyrinthine spatiality used by ancient Peruvians, the geometry of the volume responds to the pre-existing demolished museum while the roof, treated as a fifth façade, is a reinterpretation of the motifs known from the traditional Paracas textiles. Last but not least, the patina of the outer shell created by polishing cement gives the structure a look similar to the pre-Columbian ceramics which are exhibited in the museum. These interesting heritage references translated into the materiality or aesthetic of their buildings are always very subtle. The duo's goal is to use local materials and resources and to work with skilled craftsmen. They are also committed to delivering solutions that can be adapted to local weather conditions, like natural ventilation and cooling.

Their massive constructions, each with an original take, employ geometry in a most unique way. The buildings designed by Barclay & Crousse are like bridges between the past and today, with their characteristic patina juxtaposed with a purely contemporary architectural language. Working across typologies, the architects focus on the discipline's essentials. By working with space and light, which are central in their approach, they wish to comfort people and provide well-being. Keen on low-budget projects offering numerous possibilities, Barclay & Crousse favour simplicity in their realizations. "We consider our projects as being part of a design laboratory that explores the bonds between landscape, climate and architecture, in order to challenge those notions of technology, usage, and quality of life that, from the specific conditions of developing countries, can inform and be pertinent in a global context", they explain.

Barclay lectures internationally and has also devoted herself to teaching since 2006 at the Pontificia Universidad Católica del Perú. In 2019 she was invited along with Crousse by the Norman R. Foster Foundation as a Visiting Professor at the Yale School of Architecture. In 2016 Barclay & Crousse curated the Peruvian Pavilion at the 15th Venice Biennale obtaining the Special Mention of the jury and participated in the main exhibition of the following edition of the prestigious event.

PARACAS MUSEUM
PARACAS, PERU, 2012

Located in Peru's most important coastal
desert, the archaeological site museum is
built on the ruins of the former building
destroyed in an earthquake in 2007. Defined
by a rhythmical arrangement of geometric
forms, it is split into two parts. The main
volume houses the museum as well as
conservation spaces, while a narrow volume
running along its length is dedicated
to interaction and learning spaces, like
workshops rooms. According to the architects,
a great challenge was to integrate the
volume into the landscape, which as it
happens was the cradle of the culture. They
hence designed it with exposed concrete
and reddish cement, which blends it into the
surrounding red dunes.

UNIVERSITY FACILITIES UDEP
PIUNA, PERU, 2016

The architects envisioned the university
facilities as an extension of the arid forest
of Algarrobo trees, typical of the northern
Peruvian desert, which provides shade in a
climate that is both hot and dry. From the
exterior, the building appears as monolithic,
while once "inside" one discovers a group of
eleven independent buildings, under generous
cantilevered roofs that emerge from each one,
providing shadow over multiple gathering
and circulation places. This solution creates
a permeable building, which enhance the
natural ventilation while offering protection
from the sunshine creating a comfort zone
for this particular climate.

REGIONAL GOVERNMENT HEADQUARTERS
MOQUEGUA, PERU, 2018

The main goal of this new civic centre, was to
enable an area destined for a large civic space
that was not envisaged in the competition
program. The architects envisioned a circular
compact solution, that refers to a unique
historical and geographical land mark, the Cero
Baúl mountain nearby.  While from the exterior
it appears  as a massif, opaque building,  it
has a complex spatial arrangement inside with
numerous ingenious solutions to provide access
for natural light and communicate between
different levels in unorthodox ways.

# DEBORAH BERKE

American architect Deborah Berke (b. 1954) is a graduate of the Rhode Island School of Design with degrees in Fine Arts and Architecture. Her professional career began at the Institute for Architecture and Urban Studies in New York. Berke continued her education at the City University of New York, where she gained an Urban Planning degree. "Those forces are so significant in influencing architecture – zoning codes, legal codes, real estate transactions, decisions so far beyond what the architect gets to do with their pencil – and architects don't know enough about them and should, so that they have control in shaping the environment", she remarks. She founded Deborah Berke

Partners in 1982 and built up a great team in her New York-based office. The architect's website bio explains that "Deborah sets the creative direction for the practice and brings her design vision to each project. Her approach to architecture, which is informed by her pursuit of authenticity, love for the visual arts, and intellectual rigor, pervades our design processes and our projects." The practice has realised numerous projects in New York City and in cities in the middle of the U.S., in large part due to family rules the architect set for herself after having her daughter, in pursuit of remaining a present mother. Her portfolio, embracing all kinds of projects, from academic to residential to cultural architecture, demonstrates Berke's commitment to sustainability and communities. The architect has also gained recognition for her remarkable adaptive reuse architectural designs and for restoring significant landmarks of New York.

Among her many other roles, Berke is a founding trustee of New York City's Design Trust for Public Space and a member of the Pritzker Prize jury. Passionate about teaching, Berke has been an adjunct professor of the Yale School of Architecture since 1987; she was the first woman to become Dean of the in July 2016. Maintaining the school's established reputation is equally important as expanding its profile by putting stress on issues like sustainable architecture, engagement of the architects, and cross-disciplinary collaborations to exchange ideas. "Architecture is often seen as an elite profession. One, that doesn't have to be the case, and two, that shouldn't be how it functions in the world. Architecture can be, and must be, good as architecture, and it also do good. Sometimes by program and sometimes by impact, by presence", reflects Berke.

Discussing the situation of women in the discipline, she stresses the fact that there are numerous reasons why female architects, engineers, and developers are underrepresented, even though their presence is steadily growing. As Berke remarks, "almost all the schools of architecture are now 50% female in terms of the student body, so the question looking forward is what should architects do to keep these women in the profession?". The architect suggests that schools should act as role models by employing women faculty members and holding lecture series with both male and female speakers to model the behaviour. "I believe that the profession of architecture needs to look like the public it serves," she contends, "and that's everyone".

Located just beside the High Line, this structure of a partly glazed white brick volume sitting on a metal base with a concrete block sidepiece is visually striking with its elegant simplicity. The brief for a new building for the esteemed New York gallerist Marianne Boesky was to create an architecturally distinct building, invitingly private and suited to its West Chelsea site. Arranged in a sequence, the interiors combine an extensive entry hall, project rooms, storage spaces, offices, a private viewing room, and exhibition spaces with the main significantly sized gallery, topped with three large skylights facing north to carefully filter daylight.

## 48 BOND STREET
## NEW YORK, USA, 2008

"We created a granite volume with angled 'bay windows' located irregularly within an otherwise strict grid, and floated that composition above a glass base", explains the architect. The concept was inspired by the historical architecture on this unusually short Manhattan street. The minimalistic façade allows the building to be immersed into the existing fabric, while the angles interrupting its smoothness give a contemporary look. Interestingly, the street level windows provide a sneak peek into the long swimming pool located in the basement. There are four different types of units in the building; all of the apartments' interiors were also designed by the studio.

CUMMINS INDY DISTRIBUTION HEADQUARTERS
INDIANAPOLIS, USA, 2017

The rhythmically articulated façade of
this elegant office building is visually
delightful with its subtle disruptions of
the shape's regularity, both horizontally
and vertically. The highly accessible
interiors are composed of a series of
double social hubs, each of which
has a signature staircase connecting
the floors that enhances encounters.
In addition to these spaces for
collaborative work, the architect's
studio also created a variety of office
spaces to foster more contemplative
or focused kinds of work. Thanks to the
thin profile, the interiors are entirely lit
by daylight, while the entirely glazed
façade minimises heat gain to offer
extensive views of the city.

# TATIANA BILBAO

could be adapted to work for any number of family members (and could expand as it grows) and also to varying climatic conditions across the country by using different materials. "Architecture is not about building a building; architecture is about building a community," Bilbao proposes.

A significant aspect of Bilbao's realizations is that she places architecture into an interesting dialogue with nature. In Bilbao's context-conscious architecture, there is no competition or even discord between the two. In some of her latest realizations, the architecture, although also expressive, becomes an integral part of the natural environment. At the same time, the architect's works are assemblages of interestingly juxtaposed, geometrical forms. This marriage – although one might expect it would be clashing – creates stunning visual effects but also very practical buildings that suit their requirements and more. Aiming at designing multifunctional spaces, Bilbao's principles are to easily communicate with the spaces' users, but to also give them the tools to adjust the architecture to their needs.

Asked about a key project in her studio's evolution, Bilbao points to her very first project, which was a collaboration with Mexican artist Gabriel Orozco on Observatory House, his beach house near Puerto Escondido. Bilbao, in charge of drawing up the detailed plans based on Orozco's concept and dealing with the local engineer, learned how to work with basic materials and geometry, and how to translate a complex vision into an actual building. Experiencing every stage of the construction process also taught Bilbao that constrained access to technologies in Mexico does not necessarily have to limit architecture. Interestingly, Bilbao doesn't use advanced computer programmes while working on new buildings; she only brings her concepts to life with the help of hand-made models, numerous sketches, and collages, which she believes make the creative process more genuine and thus easy to connect to. The lack of computer renderings enables ideas to evolve freely through the creative process, while collages reflect on the complex character of any context. "It allows a lot of voices to be in one place", the architect explains. Extremely responsible in using resources, Bilbao has an insightful approach to creating spaces, truly taking many perspectives into account.

Bilbao's impressive portfolio has earned her many prestigious honours, like the Global Award for Sustainable Architecture, which she received in 2014. She has taught as a visiting professor at the Yale School of Architecture and is one of the Mexican women regarded as a role model who has paved the way for female architects.

Mexican architect Tatiana Bilbao (b. 1972), born in a family of architects, studied architecture at the Universidad Ibero-americana. Her first professional role was being an advisor for the city minister of urban and housing development in Mexico City. After co-creating a firm with other partners, Bilbao founded her independent multidisciplinary practice, Tatiana Bilbao Estudio, in 2004.

Bilbao has received international recognition in large part for her socially conscious approach to architecture. At the Chicago Architecture Biennial in 2015 she presented a very flexible prototype for a low-cost house as a potential solution to Mexico's social housing shortage. The layout of the building

# "It would be ideal to create spaces that could become platforms for people to decide about their own needs and their own ways of living."

In one of your interviews you say: "Our studio is not about the form or shape of a building but what it does to people". Is matching architecture to people's needs the most important aspect in architecture?

Definitely, and more than that. For me it would be ideal to create spaces that could become platforms for people to decide about their own needs and their own ways of living. I'm not pretending that I could understand someone's need or that I could really response to that, because you would need to be this other person, which is not possible. I really would like to believe that our architecture could make it possible to incorporate people into the process. We have to create architecture that can be adopted by anyone to develop their own way of living and adapt it to their own culture and possibilities.

How would you describe the relation between nature and architecture in your work?

This is exactly the same way of thinking as I think of people. You are never going to understand nature. It is the force that drives us, and nature is going to be there always. The question is: how can we people be integrated into that power and not compete against it; how can we create more possibilities and not dominate it.

Just like in the Mazátlan Aquarium project in Mexico?

In this case we allow nature to dominate the building. I would like to create space where people can go and see nature as a dominating force. You cannot educate the population in an aquarium where you keep fish in tanks with purple light as a way to explain how important the fish is. It sounds like a joke. This is why I think, it is going to be a space protecting nature, where nature is allowed to be as it really is. For me this building is totally dominated by nature; this is how it is conceived.

Your studio is well known for building without advanced machines or materials. Instead of being high-technology dependent, you cherish simplicity in both material and the building process. How does this influence your architecture and the creative process?

I believe that to be able to translate an idea from the mind to a physical building, you need to have a physical process. For me architecture needs to be physical. I imagine it in my mind, then translate it with my hands. I see computers as a tool but not as a medium that translates the idea. I think something gets lost in cyberspace. This is why I can only see doing architecture with my hands. Also, I have understood that when you build models, which I love, using your hands plays a very important role. Apart from the fact that we don't have machines to build things, a building that has been built with hands, many many hands, obviously, really has a different expression and definition. Materiality plays a big role. I also think that architecture can become a platform for people to create their own spaces for living when it is easy to relate to. I think the relationship can only start when it's honest. This is why I like to promote the honesty of the use of material or labour.

You often mention that dealing with many constraints in Mexico, be it technological limitations or lack of materials, makes your studio's work very efficient. Does your approach differ when you design abroad?

I think that the culture I have lived in has taught us to think in terms of basic necessities. They need to be fulfilled before anything else. That is why you have to think very efficiently. If you don't have many resources, you work with the ones you have to make the best of it. You simply have to be creative to find solutions. I am very lucky to come from this context. It is human nature that when you have resources, you use them without responsibility. For me being responsible in architecture is not to use resources that could be used differently or in the future. It defines what I do.

What is the Mexican architectural scene like? Has it been challenging to run a practice as a women architect?

For me it was actually an opportunity, which I do not necessarily like. Fortunately, I was in the correct moment at the correct time. I started my office when women were needed in the profession. I immediately started receiving commissions because I was a woman. I had way more opportunities than my colleagues who were men and had to fight for projects. It has not always been great because I don't like the idea that being a woman would be a decisive factor.  But then I understood one of my male friends who told me one day: "I know, Tatiana, how much you hate it but you need to be there, because then the generation to come will be more equal." And this is true; maybe this is my fight to make the world more equal.

BIOINNOVA
TECNOLÓGICO DE MONTERREY CAMPUS CULIACÁN, MÉXICO, 2012

"The building was designed to consider academic and professional life as a growing tree", explains the architect. The visually stunning play of geometrical forms that seem to defy gravity is enhanced by the use of glass with rhythmically divided façades. Rectangular volumes with a replicated floor plan pile up as a reference to a constellation of branches. The floor housing the accelerator, incubator, and office space supporting students' start-ups, which is the most important part of this common space for academic and business environments, has been shifted 180 degrees. Flexibly planned open-space interiors emphasize the collaborative aspect of the building.

## ACUÑA SUSTAINABLE HOUSING
## ACUÑA, COAHUILA, MEXICO, 2015

Following extensive research, including social consultations, and a presentation at the 2015 Chicago Biennale, the Sustainable Housing project was realised as a complex of 16 houses experimentally built in Acuña with funds from Mexico's federal housing agency, which also commissioned the studio to work on public spaces completing the development. As the architect remarks, "the original prototype was modified to account for budgetary, climactic and cultural differences". To make it an affordable solution to the housing shortages, the simplest version of the house can be constructed for no more than $8,000. The layout can be freely modified depending on the current needs of inhabitants.

## LOS TERRENOS
### SAN PEDRO GARZA GARCÍA, MEXICO, 2016

The mirrored glass of Los Terrenos blends this unique vacation house into its hilly site covered with trees. The interplay between the size and geometry of the building and its invisibility is striking. While the reflective outer surfaces are camouflage-like, from the inside they allow a perfect view of the surroundings. The structure consists of two volumes, one larger and rectangular, housing the kitchen, dining, and living areas (a decorative lattice as a semi-open wall adapts the interior, controlling ventilation and sun access). The second is L-shaped and contains two bedrooms. Both are built with natural materials including wood, clay bricks, and rammed earth.

# LINA BO BARDI

Lina Bo Bardi, born Achillina Bo, (1914–1992) was a graduate of architecture at the University of Rome. Upon completing her studies, she moved to Milan, where she started her professional career collaborating with Carlo Pagani and Gio Ponti. In parallel, Bo Bardi began working as a design journalist. At the age of 28 she decided to establish her own practice. During the war she worked on illustrations for various magazines and eventually acted as deputy director of the renowned Domus magazine. In 1946 the architect married art historian and critic Pietro Maria Bardi and they moved permanently to Brazil, where he established and directed the country's first modern art museum and she developed her eponymous practice.

The couple founded and edited the architectural magazine Habitat between 1950 and 1953; the publication quickly became influential for its innovative graphic design and critical features on art and architecture in Brazil. The approach it represented – seeing architecture as spaces that must be lived in to be complete – offered a foretaste of Bo Bardi's design philosophy. In the 1950s, Bo Bardi also designed many pieces of furniture including her famous bowl-like chair.

The architect's distinctive style is expressed in radical forms, daring constructions, and playful compositions of volumes. It also celebrates two materials – glass for its transparency and lightness and the brutalist power of concrete, which the architect boldly used. In some of her projects, both are juxtaposed contrastingly. Her first major work in Brazil was Casa de Vidro (The Glass House), which Bo Bardi designed for herself and her husband. Echoing American modernist language, the house's main goal was to establish the perfect relationship between the interiors and the surrounding wooded area. Thus the structure, suspended over a steep hill and sitting on stilts, is practically transparent and fluid inside. Visitors may have the feeling of being in a tree house in the middle of tropical nature. Completed in 1951, the house is located on the outskirts of São Paulo and now serves as the headquarters of the Instituto Lina Bo e P. M. Bardi and the couple's archive.

Another curious construction was developed between 1957 and 1968 and was commissioned by her husband for a new home for the São Paulo Museum of Art (MASP). The colossus, supported by massive rectangular columns made of red-painted concrete, is elevated above the level of the street. This quite unusual solution creates a large outdoor yet covered space under the building. The main volume is mainly glazed, which also influenced the interior arrangement. Bo Bardi invented an innovative hanging system that displayed artwork on glass or freestanding and far from the walls to offer a new experience to museumgoers. Bo Bardi's last big project was the Teatro Oficina in 1991, the main concept of which aimed at reducing the distance between the audience and actors or the backstage and stage spaces. The architect passed away one year later, leaving projects already underway for the new headquarters of São Paulo's city hall and the Cultural Centre for Vera Cruz. Her buildings, as much as her numerous writings, have influenced many architects and left a strong mark on modern Brazilian architecture.

pages 37–39
SESC POMPÉIA
SÃO PAULO, BRAZIL, 1986

Originally known as Fábrica da Pompéia, the building is a former
barrel factory. Converted into a playfully designed complex, it houses
a theatre, numerous sports halls, and a swimming pool as well as
restaurants, spaces for workshops, leisure areas, and exhibition halls.
Due to the interdisciplinary mix of spaces and the scale, it has become
both a centre for the local community and a landmark of the district.
Bo Bardi not only preserved the industrial character of the original
architecture but emphasised its roughness by removing external plaster.
Two of the main design features are the numerous interventions marked
contrastingly in red, and the concrete towers connected by dynamically
composed aerial walkways.

# CAROLINE BOS

A graduate of History of Art at Birbeck College of the University of London and Urban and Regional Planning at the Faculty of Geosciences of the University of Utrecht, Caroline Bos (b. 1959) has taught internationally. In 1988 Bos decided to extent her theoretical and writing projects to the practice of architecture and, together with Ben van Berkel, she co-founded a studio, initially under their own names, which ten years later became UNStudio. From the outset the duo aspired to create a multidisciplinary environment. Inspired by Ricardo Bofill, famous for working with both artists and architects, they established a mixed studio that brings together people with diverse areas of expertise. Today,

with offices in Amsterdam, Shanghai, Hong Kong, and Frankfurt, and a team of over 200, they develop a wide range of projects from architecture, to interior and product design, from urban development to infrastructural projects. Bos, who is the studio's Principle Urban Planner, emphasises the meaning of digital technology, which is at the core of the practice. Their innovative means of expression and complex structures, thanks to which UNStudio has gained international recognition, would not be possible without techniques capable of re-working data. "The relevance of architecture is situated in the essence of what is so specific about our time," suggests Bos in one of her interviews. "So this is also why we follow technology", she continues, "we follow it and we try to understand it at different levels, not just for our own efficiencies, or just for design, but because of how it impacts architecture and society at large".

Two pillars of the studio are research and sustainability (although the architects prefer to refer to this latter concept using another term, a combination of affordability and sustainability, namely 'attainability'). Environmental issues shape each project from scratch, as the main challenge is avoid wasting valuable resources. Bos is convinced of the power of architecture and urbanism to make positive contributions to local conditions and to people's lives. As for research, dedicated groups, called knowledge platforms, study issues crucial for particular projects and gather unique information that they feed into the projects. The underlying idea is to understand the current needs of users, depending on the spaces the studio is currently designing, and the expanding role of architects in today's rapidly changing world, all leading UNStudio to fulfil its mission "of producing user-centric designs that are adaptive, resilient and future-proof, whatever the future may bring".

Asked in an interview for ArchitectureAU* about architects' impact on infrastructure, Bos contends that they contribute complex contextual ideas about how things relate to each other. "With a bridge, for example, you can look at how the landing relates to the different city parts and what identity it can give to the surroundings. I think architects can interpret the question in various ways and add different layers of significance to the project," she explains. All projects across UNStudio's work demonstrate this multi-perspective approach.

BRAINPORT SMART DISTRICT
HELMOND, BRANDEVOORT,
THE NETHERLANDS, ONGOING

UNStudio's statement describes this as "unlike anything we have designed before", explaining that their "urban vision for Brainport Smart District is a flexible grid that will develop around the demands of its inhabitants". The next decade will see the development of 1,500 new houses and business spaces built around a central park. The innovative spatial plan, designed and constructed in parallel, will adopt to new ways of living and working. The main goal is a sustainable, circular, and socially cohesive area with joint energy generation, water management, and food production. The future-focused 'living lab' meets the application of the latest technologies and establishes a new relationship between architecture and landscape.

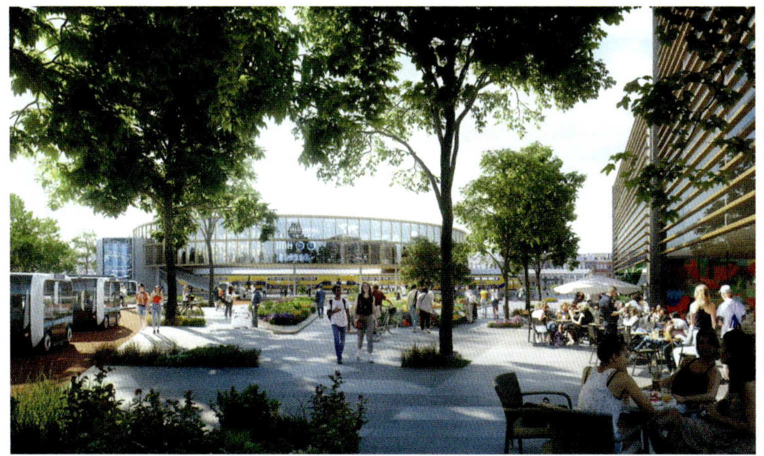

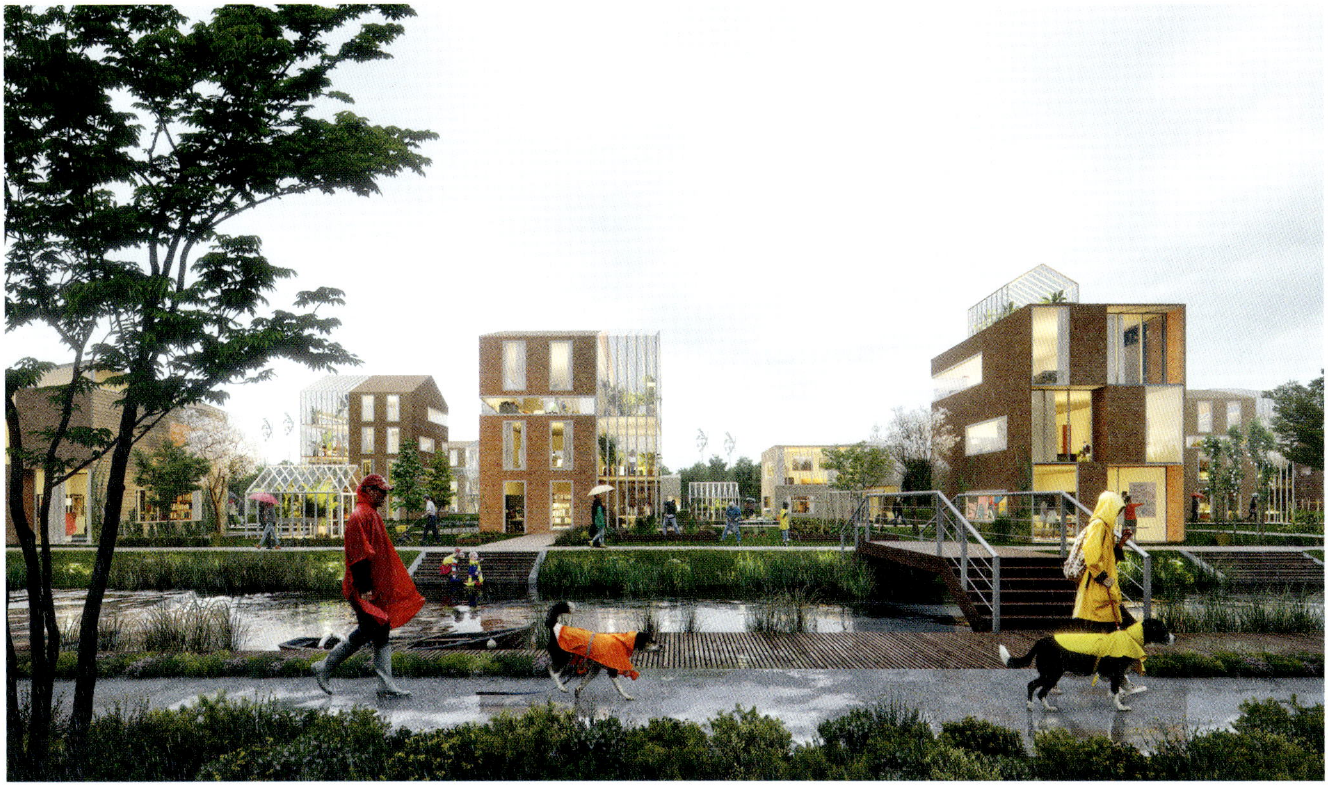

ARNHEM CENTRAL STATION
ARNHEM, THE NETHERLANDS, 2015

The development of the masterplan for Arnhem's complex
station took 20 years and involved extensive research on the
flow of passengers and transportation modes. The expressive
organic structure is covered by a dramatically twisted roof,
allowing column-free spans up to 60 metres in the central
transfer hall. The station is a masterpiece of structural
engineering, made of steel using boat-building techniques
on an unprecedented scale. As the flowing interiors enhance
circulation, the curves of the building elegantly blur the division
between the inside and outside of the terminal. This large urban
plan development, which also includes numerous commercial
and residential spaces, reinvented the whole area of the city.

# ALISON BROOKS

Born in Ontario, Canada, Alison Brooks (b. 1962) graduated with a BES and B.Arch. from the University of Waterloo in 1988, when she also moved to London. Her first years in the United Kingdom were dominated by collaboration with Ron Arad on a range of projects, such as Chalk Farm Studios and the interior architecture of the Tel Aviv Opera House. In 1996 she established her own practice, which initially gained recognition for experimental one off houses followed by urban housing, won through design competitions, that she describes as 'the social project of architecture'. Her successes in creating innovative housing across the UK combined with a highly identifiable formal and material language has resulted in an increasing number of commissions for cultural buildings. All of her realisations are visually powerful combinations of architecture and sculpture, with great attention to detail. Ingenious forms are enhanced by restraint, using a reduced amount of materials in order to, as Brooks says, give a sense of essentialness to everything. Her portfolio also illustrates her context-aware approach, which,

as the architect's statement reads, emerges from broad cultural research, so that each project is a specific response to place, community, and landscape. Her new project at Oxford University, the Cohen Quadrangle, exemplifies her inventive reinterpretation of the archetypal Collegiate quadrangle. The Quad integrates new social learning spaces, dramatic cloister and fluid roof forms and is the first Oxford College to be designed by a female architect. Creating a dialogue with history and with both current and future users of her buildings, many of her projects are transformational in the context of urban regeneration. Brooks is deeply involved in the conception of all her practice's work. "The moment I sit down, focus, and start to draw, the project's functional potential, cultural memory and instinct combine in wonderful and unpredictable ways. It's a process of discovery, of staying open. My team of architects are also brilliant designers; we compare and critique our collective work. I stay connected to all our projects and keep a constant open line of communication with my teams when I'm travelling," she explains. For the architect, the cultural research she carries out at the outset of a project is like a conduit into the spirit of the place. Throughout the project many ideas are tested. "At key moments I sit alongside my 3D designers at their workstations and make decisions as we move through and around the Rhino model," Brook says, describing their creative process. "We're hyper critical but at the same time there's room for instinct, for intuition, for good ideas from everyone," she emphasises.

To mark the 21st anniversary of establishing her studio, Brooks published a book titled "Ideals then Ideas", which offers insight into the practice's works within conceptual, formal, and material themes that have emerged over the past two decades. Asked about the biggest challenge for architecture today Brooks answers: "The climate crisis is our biggest challenge; I would categorise the correction of this global issue as a social, political, and cultural ideal. For millennia the western concept of 'civilisation' has represented human mastery over nature. We need to overturn this way of thinking so that the future of humanity and nature are both considered 'culture'. This implies a huge shift in our collective, societal mindset." Brooks lectures internationally on architecture and urban design and has held teaching positions at Harvard GSD, the AA and ETSAM. She is the only British architect who has won all of the UK's most prestigious awards for architecture: the RIBA Stirling Prize, Manser Medal, and Stephen Lawrence Prizes.

## QUARTERHOUSE
### FOLKESTONE, UNITED KINGDOM, 2009

A vital part of Folkestone's revitalisation, this new
cultural venue combines three main roles. With a
large multipurpose auditorium and exhibition space,
it is a home for the performing arts. It also houses a
business enterprise centre located on the top floor.
The first floor café/bar makes it a social hub for
the wider public. The fluted mesh cladding on the
rhythmical façade was inspired by scallop shells.
While the main idea was to create the illusion of
curvature, the flute spacing is a reference to stage
curtains. The complex modulated surface interacts
with sunlight during the day and illuminations at
night to create intriguing visual effects.

THE SMILE
LONDON, UNITED KINGDOM, 2016

Made of American tulipwood,
The Smile, a 34-metre-long tube in
the form of an arc, with its ends 3
metres above the ground, is a tour
de force of engineering (developed
in collaboration with Arup). Built for
the London Design Festival in 2016 to
demonstrate the structural potential
of cross-laminated hardwood, this
public pavilion offered visitors a truly
sensational spatial experience. From
the entrance, which is exactly in the
middle, where the arc sits on the
ground, visitors can move up towards
either of the ends, designed as viewing
platforms. Perforations in the walls
close to the top on both sides enhance
the play of light within the sculpturous
and dynamic structure.

pages 47–49
EXETER COLLEGE COHEN QUAD
OXFORD, UNITED KINGDOM, 2017

Brooks' new Cohen Quad building is an impressive expansion of the 700-year-old Exeter College campus located in the very heart of Oxford. It houses rooms for 90 students, an auditorium, and seminar rooms, as well as social learning spaces, a café, an archive space, and offices. This dynamic S-shaped volume embraces two courtyards that the architects connected with a three-dimensional ambulatory. The multi-level common space at the centre of the building opens onto both courtyards, and is thus perfect for both social gatherings and scholarly exchange. The curved roof made of patterned stainless steel runs down the side walls, creating a visually intriguing envelope that contrasts with the historical context.

# SARAH CALBURN

South African architect Sarah Calburn (b. 1964) graduated from the University of the Witwatersrand and worked in Paris, Hong Kong, Sydney, and Melbourne. After completing a Master of Architecture at the Royal Melbourne Institute of Technology, she returned home and decided to establish her own Johannesburg-based practice in 1996. Working on a wide range of projects, from residential to office architecture, from school buildings to retail spaces, she is engaged in teaching and in activities aimed at developing discussion about South African architecture. Calburn is particularly known for initiating the dialogue of

analysing and re-imagining the country's capital. In 2010 she was programme director of the first Architectural Biennale organised in Johannesburg, where numerous interdisciplinary practices, both local and international, participated in a critical conversation about the urban features of Johannesburg.

"If I were to define Architecture, I would say this: Architecture is not the 'containment of space', it always involves the making of a conscious and critical 'opening of space'", Calburn says. She has gained recognition for designing architecture that is in a unique relationship with the landscape. The architect actually integrates the landscape into the structure, where the boundary between both becomes fluid. Thanks to numerous transparent volumes, Calburn succeeds at offering views both in and out of her buildings, which often become invisible in their surroundings. One of the architect's mission focal points is spatial intelligence, which stands for a "critical awareness of what space is, what are its effects, its affects. It's knowing how to manipulate it to various ends, being dextrous with your materials". Each of Calburn's projects demonstrates her deep understanding of space in the way she envisions buildings that create a harmonic fusion and intermingle with the landscapes. The architect stresses the fact that she always starts her creative process from the site, be it urban or rural. "A 'naked' landscape contains the possibility of architecture, the possibility is in large part concerned with framing – both ways. In and out", reflects Calburn. "As we frame the landscape, so it frames us. We are always in an active and mutually deforming relationship...", she adds. Landscape, according to the architect, is wrongly regarded as 'passive' – a site available to be built upon or conquered, or in other cases merely playing the role of a beautiful backdrop. A building and the landscape should be considered simultaneously to design creatively richer and environmentally responsible spaces.

Calburn's landscape-based design approach also results in particularly striking visual effects due to local weather conditions. "In the gorgeous South African climate", the architect's statement explains, "our buildings are intimately involved with light effects, the heady experience of space and place, and the fluidity of the perceptual boundary between interior and exterior". From yet another perspective this philosophy is Calburn's way of influencing attitudes and consequently action, as she is interested in how her buildings might change the mental frames of their users towards a heightened awareness of the environment.

This house, designed for a well-known artist and his family, is set on a rocky mini-cliff. Made of two concrete rectangular boxes hovering over the ground and connected with a glass bridge, the structure is supported by steel columns. The main living area is located above, in between the tree tops outside. "In actual fact, the experience of the cliff side and the trees from the interior living space is one of looking into a large aquarium. The interior seems to contain the exterior, the architecture seems to be between the landscape", reflects the architect.

ROEDEAN SCHOOL. CENTRE FOR MATHEMATICS EXCELLENCE
HOUGHTON, SOUTH AFRICA

The architect is a second-generation student of the
school. When commissioned to design an addition to the
historical building, Calburn used her intimate relationship
with the complex; growing up among these buildings
helped form her spatial imagination. To integrate old and
new, she envisioned a geometric glass structure acting
as a link between the buildings. The fully glazed walls
minimalise the visual dominance of the modern structure,
which acts as a frame for vistas of various elements of
the complex, or, as the architect's statement reads, "to
create views of the famously beautiful gardens and draw
attention to aspects of the original architecture".

COCOON HOUSE
ILLOVO, JOHANNESBURG, SOUTH AFRICA, 2011

Calburn planned a courtyard house with all rooms
communicated through an egg-shaped atrium.
The elliptical shape of this light-bringing heart of
the house articulates the division between living
spaces on the ground floor and the private area
above. One of the inspirations for this house,
designed for a single woman, is the female
courtyard space of an Indian Haveli, where all
everyday activities are performed. "All doors around
the courtyard slide back into walls, so that at
night, although the exterior may be closed down
for safety – shutters pulled – the egg-garden is
still available for fresh evening air, the moon, and
stars...", muses the architect.

# FERNANDA CANALES

Mexican architect Fernanda Canales (b. 1974) received a BA from the Universidad Iberoamericana in Mexico City, an MA from the Universidad Politécnica de Cataluña, Barcelona, and a PhD in Architecture at the Escuela Técnica Superior de Arquitectura in Madrid. Her career began in Japan, where she worked at Toyo Ito's office and became interested in his explorations of flexibility, fluid space, and the concept of immaterial architecture or the relation between body and space. In Spain, Canales gained experience at the studio of the legendary Ignasi de Solà-Morales. In 2002, back in Mexico, she opened her own studio, focusing on architecture, urban design, and research.

An acclaimed critic, the architect also devotes her time to writing about architecture; she has published more than 100 essays in the professional press to date.

Characteristic for her thoughtful practice is rethinking traditional approaches to architecture, especially to planning houses. Canales is always in search of atypical solutions with a sensitive approach to the context, whether it is a landscape or urban environment. Independently of the type or scale of the project, the architect's first task is always to immerse herself into research on the climatic conditions and history, or simply the views from on site. These explorations and her understanding of the reality of the location in person are essential to her creative process. Measuring architecture with her body, as she describes it, is the most important part. The design must always be a relevant response to the site, starting from the point of the selected materials as well. Canales likes working with materials that reflect local conditions or traditions. An important source of inspiration for Canales is Mexican architecture, in particular residential architecture. Her extensive research on its history through social, political, and artistic prisms resulted in an in-depth study, a two-volume publication "Architecture in Mexico, 1900–2010", which accompanied an exhibition curated by the architect in 2014. On the one hand, the broad studies have allowed her to make sense of enormous contrasts in the Mexican landscape. "Understanding different eras gives me a better sense of problems that we think are new, but that have actually been around for decades", remarks Canales in one of her interviews. However, she also believes that preserving history happens not only through buildings but also through a deeper understanding of particular places. Her pursuit of inventive housing solutions and interest in Mexican architectural features meet in the architect's contribution to the Housing Research and Practical Experimentation Laboratory project, a community development for innovative, low-cost housing designs to improve workers' quality of life.

Canales remarks that there is a tradition of strong, creative women in Mexico but only over the last decade or so has their work been recognised and celebrated. Asked about the challenges of being a female architect, she says: "It opens the possibility of imagining buildings and cities with perspectives and priorities that have still not been taken into account". Based on the great responses to her projects, the well-thought-out ways they initiate dialogue with their natural or historical surroundings, and her truly original structures, it seems that Canales' voice is getting stronger.

pages 55-57
ELENA GARRO CULTURAL CENTRE
MEXICO CITY, MEXICO, 2012

To build a new cultural centre, Canales had to preserve a listed building from the early 20th century on the site. This adaptation included creating a massive entrance, which became a new interconnection between the street and the old house. The geometrical triple-high foyer with a gigantic glazed façade is striking thanks to the view of floor-to-ceiling bookstore shelves and has become a contemporary frame for the historical part of the building, which now houses a library. The latter is enveloped at the back by a rectangular three-level-high addition with an auditorium, storage, and parking spaces. The architect also planned a series of courtyards and gardens on the plot.

LIBROS
MÚSICA
PELÍCULAS
REVISTAS
CAFÉ

The architect's departure point was the question of how to create a new house for twelve families that share the same site but different services. Additionally, the size of the rectangular plot is no bigger than 400 square metres. Aiming at the redefinition of private domestic spaces within a collective residential building, Canales planned the three-storey building with four apartments on each level, plus a subterranean parking level and a rooftop with terraces. The floor-to-ceiling windows and extensive balconies provide spectacular views. The interiors are also lit by an aesthetically pleasing patio (a solution supporting cross ventilation) finished with concrete lattices in geometrical patterns and turquoise-hued surfaces.

CASA BRUMA
VALLE DE BRAVO, MEXICO, 2017

Two main conditions of this project were to preserve all trees on the site and to provide as much light in the interiors as possible. Canales, together with Claudia Rodríguez, developed an original concept of a house made of different spaces, located in nine individual, yet interconnected blocks around a linking central patio. The main living spaces have been linked by roofed corridors, while the garage and the guest part are accessible from the courtyard. While each volume of this fragmented house has a different height relating to the topography, their orientation depends on the sun's passage. All spaces open richly to the surrounding landscapes of the steep site.

# LUCÍA CANO

Madrid-born architect Lucía Cano (b. 1965) studied architecture at ETSA (Escuela Técnica Superior de Arquitectura) in her home city. At the beginning of her career Cano worked with her father, Julio Cano Lasso, a renowned Spanish architect, together with her three brothers, who also chose this professional path. In 1998 Cano established a common practice with her husband José Selgas. Their Madrid-based studio, SelgasCano, realises projects in Spain and internationally. The studio has gained recognition for buildings that are in harmonious relationships with their surroundings, often literally submerged into the site. They humorously say that some clients complain about their projects' lack of visibility but architecture as a single gesture is not interesting to them. They even go as far as understanding

architecture not as creating buildings but rather as making sensible decisions within the surroundings. Their main belief is that nature should take precedence over architecture and so they design structures that fuse with the context instead of dominating it. Cano recalls in one of her interviews: "My father's office was part of the home, and a part of our lives when we were young. Everything he did, designed, and the way he gradually adapted the home to the way we changed was done in constant harmony with nature. This is an important element that is now in what we do. It's a lifestyle that actually shapes you culturally". With this approach, the architects enjoy investigating unexplored places as much as ideas.

Aiming at rejecting clichés, they are known for bold experiments with materials, colours, and shapes. Inspired by the psychology of colours, each project generates numerous renderings to test various colour palettes before the final decision, which is also dependent on the choice of materials. As the duo is particularly keen on experimenting with materials, and especially their properties in filtering light, the process of finding the most intriguing and satisfying solutions is as exciting as it is technically challenging. As a result, they envision striking buildings where dazzling hues are equally important components as the volumes themselves. Their choice of colours, however, is not merely an aesthetic or psychologic consideration – they also have to be practical. Their sophisticated use of hues becomes even more visually striking as SelgasCano play with the notion of transparency and translucent surfaces, which enhances the sculpturous qualities of their works.

The playful nature of their concepts is particularly visible in their temporary architecture, which allows for an interaction with a wider audience, like the annual Serpentine Gallery Pavilion at Kensington Gardens, which they realised in 2015 as the first Spanish architects to do so. Although SelgasCano use various architectural languages and wish to escape definitions, there is a thread running through all their realizations. They offer highly sensory experiences for the users, carefully choreographed by the architects, mainly through the use of light. "We think of light as being 'energy'; colour as an effect on it; and translucency as a way for the light to pass through", they remark, suggesting that "light is an inescapable and important part of the building, maybe the only important thing".

## SELGASCANO OFFICE
## MADRID, SPAIN, 2007

Hidden in the woods, and partly submerged in the ground, is the office of the SelgasCano practice. The architects' idea was to work under the trees, so they planned a light structure with a partly transparent roof (one side of the long and narrow building, with the desks, is protected from direct sunlight) opening to the surrounding nature. The concrete and steel structure is supported by fibreglass, polyester, Plexiglas, and polycarbonate elements and was a challenge to build, given the small scale of the building. The roof with curved edges proved to be technically demanding despite its simple-looking form.

MÉRIDA FACTORY YOUTH MOVEMENT
MÉRIDA, SPAIN, 2011

The architects have explained that this building is "designed as a large canopy that is open to the entire city and available to anyone who would like to come". The structure encompasses a series of sculptural volumes, each with an independent access. Covered with a one-metre-thick thermal covering, protecting the building's visitors from both rain and sun, the cloud-like orange roof is translucent to allow light to pass through. As a fanciful playground for young adults, the space offers a wide variety of activities, from skateboarding to acrobatics and street theatre, and houses concert and tightrope walking areas and a ballroom.

## PLASENCIA AUDITORIUM AND CONGRESS CENTER
CARTAGENA, SPAIN, 2017

Planned to sit on the border between the town and the country, this auditorium was placed significantly below the street level to emphasise the differences between these two worlds. Interestingly, the main entrance is located at street level, and connected with the building through an orange gangway and a 12-metre-deep vertical canyon. The architects' main goal was to take up as little area as possible to have a minimal impact on the land. This determined the programme of the biomorphic translucent volume – the ground part with the stage area and the tiers in the main hall forms the base, which supports the rest of the spaces on top of it: the entrance lobby, a secondary hall, exhibition spaces, and a restaurant.

# ODILE DECQ

French architect and urban planner Odile Decq (b. 1955) is known for her engagement in debates on architecture as well as for being an advocate of equality in the discipline. She decided to establish an individual practice immediately after graduating in the 1980s, without having worked for any other architects. The first commission that gained her Paris-based studio attention was the Banque Populaire de l'Ouest in Rennes, France in 1990. This realization marks the dynamic evolution of her very expressive and highly original portfolio, where all projects are realised under Decq's direction. While the architect's creative work embraces architecture, urban planning, design, and art, her conceptual process is based on experimentation. The philosophy of her studio is to design something particular, which is achieved by employing the most advanced contemporary technologies. Decq's buildings share a complexity of forms, creating curious compositions; bold shapes with an unexpected twist and dynamic, often organic, structures house interior arrangements that are far from obvious. Her visually powerful concepts always engage in an in-depth conversation with the context. Her eccentric aesthetic decisions enhance the sensual experience  of those using the space and articulate buildings' functions. Decq is a maverick, rebelling against traditional ways of approaching architecture, always in pursuit of imaginative solutions.

Teaching architecture has been a very important part of Decq's work. She was a professor in France and also served as the director of the École Spéciale d'Architecture in Paris between 2007 and 2012. She has also been a guest professor at a number of universities around the world, including the Bartlett in London and Columbia University in New York. This multifaceted experience resulted in Decq creating her own school in Lyon in 2014 – the Confluence Institute of Innovation and Creative Strategies in Architecture. The mission of this significant project is the reinvention of architecture education. Interestingly, neuroscience and sociology, among other unconventional subjects, are also part of the course. Decq claims that it is essential for architects to be able to answer complex questions concerning various disciplines to find specific solutions. "I want to challenge the way students can help the world in the future," she says. The architect also stresses the fact that education has a crucial role to play in elevating the status of women in architecture, which she describes as a tough profession.

In 1996 Decq received the Golden Lion Award at the Venice Biennale for the early years of her extraordinary career and noticeably unique work. She was also awarded the prestigious Jane Drew Prize in 2016, to mention only some of her most important honours. "For me, architecture is an adventure", she has mused in an interview, "it has to be a place where people can move, live in good conditions, and forget the hardness of the life outside, so it has to have a kind of humanistic approach, whatever the project is – a museum, housing, offices, whatever – so it always has to have something in addition to the functional programme to provide people with something which is better and more comfortable".

pages 65-67
FRAC BRETAGNE
RENNES, FRANCE, 2012

The minimalistic façade of this design contrasts with complexity of the interiors. The solid and quiet outer volume turns into a dynamic and ethereal space, with a vertical void running over the entire building's height. This vertical space offers an upward promenade through the building, but also connects numerous functions that the museum combines – from conservation, exhibition, and educational spaces to a library and an auditorium. A visit to the museum becomes a sensory experience with no centralised space, only continually changing perspectives. Within one building, the architect innovatively demonstrates, through structure as much as through materials, how ambiguous architecture can be in a forceful dialogue between density and transparency.

SAINT-ANGE RESIDENCY
SEYSSINS, FRANCE, 2015

The architect approached
the challenging site, which is
very steep and narrow, in the
most visually original way.
Her main objective became
allowing for an unobstructed
view of the city of Grenoble
in the valley and the French
Alps beyond. To achieve this,
Decq envisioned a slightly
twisted tower rising up to the
height of three levels from
a one-level horizontal base
used as an art studio. The
result looks like a sculpture
embedded in the hillside.
Windows that face three
different directions contribute
to a greater amount of light
inside during the daytime.
The structure, made of timber
over poured concrete, has an
asphalt finish for waterproof
protection, which makes it
disappear against its wood
surroundings.

LE CARGO
PARIS, FRANCE, 2016

Le Cargo is part of a large-scale urban refurbishment
in the northeast 19th district of Paris coordinated by
OMA and realised by 15 other architects. In addition
to housing and commercial and public spaces, the
transformation programme also included offices. Decq
converted the former Macdonald warehouse from the
1960s into the biggest start-up incubator in Europe.
The building, dedicated to supporting start-ups in
the tech and creative industries, offers an innovative
take on working space: it is organised around a
central patio, with outdoor terraces and a mix of
co-working and meeting rooms. The aesthetic reflects
the dynamic character of Le Cargo, like the circular
windows in various sizes crowning the façade.

# ELIZABETH DILLER

Elizabeth Diller (b. 1954) is one of the founding partners of Diller Scofidio + Renfro, a studio active not only in architecture and urban design but also in fields like installation art, multi-media performance, and digital art. The New York–based practice was established in 1981 together with Ricardo Scofidio (Ben Gilmartin joined the studio in 2004 and became the fourth partner in 2015). They have completed several major architecture and planning projects in New York City, such as the High Line development and the transformation of Lincoln Center for the Performing Arts. Diller Scofidio + Renfro have gained recognition for spectacular museum realizations, like The Broad in Los Angeles, built for

philanthropist and art collector Eli Broad, and the renovation and expansion of the Museum of Modern Art in Manhattan. Imaginative irregular shapes, visually light structures, play with transparency, and ingenious solutions are among the practice's trademarks, which are expressively present yet skilfully woven into the existing fabric.

Diller is known for her constant sketching, never short of stunning new ideas. Inspired by art, her cross-genre projects demonstrate an interdisciplinary way of thinking. One of the first projects that brought wide international attention was the poetic Blur Building on Lake Neuchatel in Switzerland, created for the Swiss Expo in 2002. This installation, a temporary pavilion made of fog, took the shape of a cloud-like structure cantilevered above the water. Ever since, Diller continues to generate surprising and innovative concepts. As a result of her multi-perspective approach to creating architecture, and public spaces in particular, Diller's numerous significant realizations have a lasting effect on the urban fabric, which we can best observe in New York City. Projects like the High Line and, more recently, The Shed, an impressive multi-arts centre, reinvent the city, showing the power of architecture bringing people together. Another captivating aspect of Diller's work is that her projects reach far beyond the current situation. Given the pace of changes and the unpredictable nature of the future, the architect aims at buildings with inventive solutions today that could offer variable and flexible space to support any use in the future. This is particularly important while envisioning buildings to house art institutions, which is Diller's domain. In one of the interviews she argues that "we have to think about how to make today's spaces, which are adequate, not feel too small tomorrow".

Diller, a Professor of Architecture at Princeton University and an International Fellow of the Royal Institute of British Architects, graduated in Architecture from the Cooper Union, although she wanted to make movies at the time. This is where she met Ricardo Scofidio, a tutor who became her future partner at work and in life. Their extremely successful and creative partnership (developed further with Renfro and then Gilmartin), has taken on some of the most exciting architectural challenges today around the globe. The Financial Times called Diller "one of architecture's most articulate voices", while her clients claim she can do the impossible. The architect's concepts, which blur the boundaries of various media are indeed visionary.

# "It's really important for architects to advocate the democratization of space for its health, recreational, and social value."

As a student you were not so much interested in architecture, but you instead wanted to make movies, and art was the main source of inspiration for you. The idea was crossover work with space and media. How has this interdisciplinary way of thinking influenced your architectural projects?

I went to school at Cooper Union to study art. I was interested in film and multimedia installations. On a whim, I saw a class called "Architectonics" in the course catalogue and I was curious about what it meant. I slowly became interested in the discourse around architecture, and got more broadly interested in the discipline but not in the profession. Previously, I was interested in photography and time-based media, but I started to think in three dimensions. So I decided to get an architecture degree, but not with the intent of joining the profession. My only intent was to make a career in plastic arts and work with sculpture and media in a spatial way. I became keenly interested in working in space and time.

When Ric and I started working together, we imagined an alternative practice: not an architecture practice, but a practice where we could teach, write, and make installations. We wanted to create agendas that followed our curiosity, independent of the profession, which we felt was intellectually bankrupt at the time. We had little interest in making buildings. Later, things started to open up for us, and I saw the light. We've

come into the field slowly, but on our own terms, progressing form experimental work to new institutions that foster experimentation, like The Shed, rather than building up a practice from apartment renovations and shops. However, we balance the permanent building projects with independent projects like art installations, curatorial projects, theatre works, and dance productions. We collaborate with an array of experts in different disciplines: from robotics engineers to composers and choreographers, to climatologists and material scientists. We follow a vision and do all the research necessary to get there.

From the beginning you've run a common practice with your partner Ricardo Scofidio. Today the studio is led by 4 partners, together with Charles Renfro and Benjamin Gilmartin. Could you tell us about your creative process?

We have a collaborative design process, which I think is unique relative to other design firms. Ideas are generated collectively at our studio; it is not the endeavour of a sole practitioner. The four partners work together on each project. We include staff at all levels in the design process with the expectation that everyone puts ideas on the table. The many points of view interrogate different solutions. Multiple ideas are generated to test the limits of a problem. Although we all have different opinions, we recognize that the best idea wins – even if it comes from the janitor. Not many ideas survive the challenge, and the process is brutal.

Your architectural works are changing the city of New York, which is a great starting point for a discussion about public spaces, including museums or interdisciplinary cultural spaces, which have become community meeting points. What direction, in your opinion, should rethinking public spaces take?

At a time when our cities are being rapidly privatized, it's important to protect the decreasing publicness of our cities and defend the importance of parks and public spaces. It's really important for architects to advocate the democratization of space for its health, recreational, and

social value. That drove our work on the High Line and at
Lincoln Center, where we felt it was important to extend
the openness and accessibility of the public realm into
institutional space just beyond the walls and to infuse
both with cultural offerings. There should be spaces you
can enjoy with or without a ticket.

With MoMA, we put special emphasis on the museum's
public spaces and the interface with the City. The new
design is rid of the transactional feeling the museum had
when you stepped through its front door. We improved the
interface with the street and dropped the store one level
to become a double height space; the street provides
clearstory natural light into the store. The lobby sequence
is no longer a tunnel connecting 53rd and 54th Streets but
an open network in which one can see block to block, the
Sculpture Garden, the expansion to the West and access
from the East. This open lobby level can host installations
anywhere as well as the street gallery and the Projects
Space, which are all before admissions.

Even though more and more women are active and
successful as architects, it is still a big challenge. In your
practice you do many things to encourage young women
to come back to professional life, e.g., after a maternity
leave, and to support them further. How do you perceive
the evolution in the situation of women in the discipline
between the beginning of your career and today?

As a practitioner, I must say I haven't been subjected to
negative discrimination. Architecture has been male-
dominated forever and I am a grateful beneficiary of the
women's movement. No longer are we seeing the singular
heroic voice – that genius person that gets a lightning
bolt from God. Instead we're seeing collaborations of
different sorts, like the collective of my own partners at
DS+R.

However, I'm also struck by what I see as an educator
and professor at Princeton. Fifty percent of my students
are female and somehow only 20 percent make it to the
workplace. This is something that is difficult to decode.
How does this happen? Where is the attrition?

ELIZABETH DILLER

## THE HIGH LINE
### NEW YORK CITY, USA, 2014

Through its opening, the High Line
development has proved to be a great
success. The architects transformed an
abandoned elevated railroad between the
Meatpacking District and the Hudson Rail
Yards in Manhattan (1.5 miles long!) into
a public park. Realized in collaboration
with James Corner Field Operations and
Piet Oudolf, it has become an oasis of
green suspended over one of the busiest
metropolises in the world. Special types of
pavement allow vegetation to grow in a
natural yet controlled way. An original system
of seating offers numerous benches for
resting along the path. The architects observe
that "the park accommodates the wild, the
cultivated, the intimate, and the social".

## THE SHED
### NEW YORK CITY, USA, 2019

This ambitious building in the heart of New York, on nearly 20,000 square metres, houses a gallery space, a theatre, a rehearsal space, and a creative lab. The most amazing element, however, is a gigantic, telescoping outer shell, which opens up over the base of the building to spread over an adjoining plaza. When deployed, it nearly doubles the space to host truly large-scale events. The shell nested over the base allows the plaza to function as an open public space for outdoor programming. The flexibility of this beautiful building seems to be a brilliant solution for the arts, which are constantly evolving just as much as technology.

    ELIZABETH DILLER

## THE MUSEUM OF MODERN ART
## NEW YORK CITY, USA, 2019

The latest chapter of MoMA's reinvention process includes re-shaping existing buildings on various levels, designing a new multi-storey addition, and combining all into a seamlessly connected whole. All to create better communication, both vertically and horizontally, but also between the inside and outside. The expansion, which increases the exhibition space, is a combination of interlocking galleries of various heights. It will also include a customized studio space and a lounge with an outdoor terrace to offer the public more inviting spaces that enhance reflection. "This work has required the curiosity of an archaeologist and the skill of a surgeon", remarks Elizabeth Diller.

# JANE DREW

British modernist architect Jane Drew (1911–1996) was a role model for many generations to come. After her studies at the Architectural Association School of Architecture she established her initial practice with her first husband, James Alliston. Before World War II she took part in the Congrès International d'Architecture Moderne (CIAM), where she met Swiss architect Le Corbusier. Drew became an advocate for the modern movement in London. In 1942 she married her second husband, renowned architect Maxwell Fry. Four years later the couple established a common London-based firm, Fry, Drew and Partners, and focused on large-scale planning projects in tropical regions of the world. With their innovative concepts and distinctive aesthetic, the architects gained international recognition for their architecture for hot climates. They worked on numerous realizations in West Africa, including building new schools in Ghana (1947–1955) and creating a campus for the newly founded University of Ibadan in Nigeria (1949–1960). Crucial for them in these realizations were the natural and cultural contexts. In addition to responding

to sites' topography and local weather conditions, as well as incorporating traditional motifs, they also introduced advanced solutions, which significantly contributed to the development of architecture in tropical countries.

After World War II, Indian Prime Minister Pandit Nehru commissioned Drew and Fry to design the new capital city of Indian Punjab, Chandigarh. As Drew was working on a number of realizations at the time, she involved Le Corbusier and Pierre Jeanneret to participate in this ambitious and experimental project. While Swiss architects contributed with large-scale public spaces, Drew and Fry were mainly responsible for the hospitals and school buildings as well as housing. Their master-planning and urban design are considered a successful combination of visually impressive monumental architecture and modernisation that has led to a prosperous city. After completing Chandigarh, Drew and Fry also worked in Iran and Sri Lanka to further develop their innovative ideas for tropical architecture. Upon returning to London, Drew and Fry continued to work on hospital and educational buildings. Some of Drew's most impressive projects include the Torbay Hospital complex in Devon and buildings for the new campus of the Open University at Milton Keynes. The latter, realised in the 1970s, was envisioned as a complex of discrete buildings arranged harmonically in the landscape. Drew is also known for the reconversion of the historical headquarters of the Institute of Contemporary Arts in London, which she skilfully adapted to the institution's multidisciplinary activities. Drew was the first woman to serve on the Council of the Royal Institute of British Architects and the first woman to become full Professor at Harvard University.

To celebrate the architect as a role model, the RIBA Women Architects Group and the Arts Council of England launched a new award named after the architect in 1998. As initially formulated, the goal the award was to recognise the promotion of innovation, diversity, and inclusiveness in architecture. The prize is now given annually by the Architects' Journal (the winners are selected by the AJ Women in Architecture Judging Panel) to architectural designers who have raised the profile of women in architecture through their work and commitment to design excellence.

pages 77-79
THE UNIVERSITY OF IBADAN
IBADAN, NIGERIA, 1949–60

Established in 1948, the University of Ibadan was the first
university in Nigeria. Drew and Fry were responsible for
the first phase of development and took up the challenge
of creating the campus on an undeveloped site. The
architects, who specialised in creating architecture for
tropical climates, adjusted all buildings to the local weather
conditions. As volumes are located on an east-west axis,
the breeze is used for ventilation. Reinforced concrete
was chosen as the dominating material for its durability.
The new complex included a landmark tower, which has
become a symbol of the university, as well as a library, an
assembly hall, a theatre, and numerous residential buildings
combining private and common spaces. All of these
buildings remain at the heart of the campus and they are
still serving their original functions today.

# FRIDA ESCOBEDO

One of the brightest stars of the young generation, Mexican architect Frida Escobedo (b. 1979) started working on her own directly after graduating in architecture and urbanism from the Universidad Iberoamericana in 2003. Initially, she teamed up with Alejandro Alarcon to create Perro Rojo studio, starting an individual practice three years later. From the outset Escobedo taught and took many different commissions for both designing and restoring spaces, which quickly gained her international recognition and many prestigious prizes. In 2011 the architect decided to make a small break to continue her education and completed the "Art, Design, and the Public Domain" programme at Harvard, which highly influenced her further work. "The experience was an opening to a completely different world – we had industrial designers, visual artists, film producers –

there was only one other architect, and also a marine biologist. We were all trying to see how our expertise all fit into a spatial practice," she says. The knowledge she gained at Harvard shifted Escobedo's focus to more public projects, experimenting, and more research. An important moment in her career was the Serpentine Pavilion in Kensington Gardens in London 2018 (she was the youngest architect to be commissioned for the Pavilion project to date), which was well received and gained her significant attention. Today, working between Mexico and the U.S., Escobedo designs both large-scale and temporary architecture, teaches, curates exhibitions, and publishes books. Always attracted to the arts, as an architect she often blurs the boundaries between both domains.

In her projects, Escobedo achieves an elegant simplicity in form and materials. Asked about the inspirations for her structures, she speaks about striking a good balance between having a studio in Mexico City and being able to be in conversation with her team. At the same time, she explores numerous ideas outside of the studio, especially while teaching at various universities. Meeting students and fellow teachers has become an opportunity for her to see perspectives other than those of her Mexican background. "It is important not to repeat references all over again, but just to keep expanding, and your curiosity helps you to grow," she emphasizes. The buildings designed by Escobedo demonstrate her incredible sense of materials, of her feeling for patterns; their outer surfaces, either semi-transparent or richly textured, employ immersing plays of light and shadows. The architect continues to challenge perception and our senses. Her geometrical and minimalistic architecture implies motion, whether the passage of light or users' movement across buildings. The "aesthetic aspect is really important and one of the reasons that I'm interested in playing so much with the idea of light and shadow, mass and void, interior and exterior, is because I usually work with simple materials, to elevate the space," explains the architect. One of the themes that particularly interests Escobedo is rethinking ruined and abandoned spaces in a contemporary way. She asserts that "this is a very important thing to think about right now. We, architects, increasingly consider adapting buildings rather than creating new ones. We need to start thinking about designing with less. Adapting spaces is a very effective strategy of doing that".

## LA TALLERA
### CUERNAVACA, MEXICO, 2012

The stunning La Tallera is a transformation of the former house and studio of Mexican artist David Alfaro Siqueiros. Escobedo created a new cultural centre including an art gallery, artists' residence, café, and library. What visually dominates the structure are two gigantic murals, rotated on both sides of the entrance, on the façade. As a result, a smooth spatial relation with the surrounding plaza opens the building to the public. Another intervention was using perforated concrete blocks to create a semi-transparent wall around all elements. This envelope with a triangulated pattern allows a play of light and shadow but also consolidates the complex.

This installation is located at one of the façades of the Highland Halls of Stanford University, a newly added residential building for the Graduate School of Business, designed by Legorreta. Named "A very short space of time through very short times of space", it is made of russet-hued steel lamellas that are movable and can create various sounds. The title is a quote from a passage of "Ulysses" by James Joyce, when Stephen is on the beach and experiences the nature around him and its rhythmical music in a very sensual way. Another reference is the sound children make when trailing sticks across a fence.

MAR TIRRENO
MEXICO CITY, MEXICO, 2019

Thanks to a private alley and numerous
patios belonging to individual
apartments, this residential block in
the heart of busy Mexico City creates
a serene and private atmosphere.
Inspired by typical working-class
neighbourhoods from the early 20th
century, the building is divided into
two parts, connected with an internal
corridor, which leads in from the
entrance and forms a meeting area for
the inhabitants. Mar Tirreno strikes a
balance between the visual opposition
of solid and void. Once again the
architect enhances the volume by using
rhythmically textured concrete walls
with perforated parts to filter the light in
a most spectacular way.

# YVONNE FARRELL & SHELLEY McNAMARA

Upon graduating from University College Dublin in 1976, Irish architects Yvonne Farrell (b. 1951) and Shelley McNamara (b. 1952) were invited to teach at their alma mater. Their mission lasted until 2006, and in 2015 they were appointed adjunct professors. As much as educating future architects was important for the duo, Farrell and McNamara decided to also be active in the discipline and to open their own practice with three other architects (none of whom remained part of the firm). Their studio, Dublin-based Grafton Architects (named after the street of their first office), established in 1978, has gained international recognition over the decades. A particular focus was put on higher education buildings such as the impressive Universita Luigi Bocconi in Milan (2008), the UTEC university campus in

Lima, Peru (2015), and the Toulouse School of Economics in France (2019). However, the studio's designs include a much wider scope of typologies. They are responsible for civic buildings like the Department of Finance in Dublin, completed in 2009, and the Solstice Arts Centre in Navan from 2007; they also design commercial and residential architecture.

The buildings of their practice Grafton Architects, independent of the scale and function, offer a very consistent vision of magnificent architecture that is made for people to meet and interact with each other. Their monumental structures feature sculpturous façades with a visually intriguing play of solid versus transparent, and spacious interiors made of intersecting volumes. Their open-space plans, communicating the interior vertically as much as horizontally, are always skilfully and subtly zoned. While fostering social exchange and bringing people together, the buildings are nevertheless not devoid of more quiet or contemplative spaces adjusted to the function's needs. The complexity of Farrell and McNamara's spatial arrangements is enhanced by the use of natural light. Glazed façades, inventive skylights, and large windows filter significant amounts of light. This not only creates a subtle visual emphasis of the rhythmical geometry of the volumes, it also softens roughness of robust materials, like the stone or concrete that they often use. The light access points also contribute to, on the one hand, defining the zones within buildings, and establishing the inside-outside relation, on the other. Although monumental, the studio's architecture never loses sight of the users. Each building offers well-thought-out structural solutions that counterbalance the large scale and play a crucial inviting role.

In addition to being professors at the Accademia di Architettura in Swiss Mendrisio, Farrell and McNamara regularly lecture in European and American schools of architecture. In 2018, Farrell and McNamara curated the Venice Architecture Biennale with the theme 'Freespace' and focused on the generosity of architecture. In 2020 they were awarded the prestigious Pritzker Architecture Prize. In a statement the jury praised one of the most remarkable aspects of the duo's work: "A constant in their approach, the architects have an understanding of how to design complex sections of buildings in such a way that views connect deep interior spaces with the larger exterior realm and allow natural light to penetrate and animate spaces deep inside a building".

SOLSTICE ARTS CENTRE
NAVAN, CO. MEATH, IRELAND, 2007

This multifaceted volume sits on the sloping plot of the historical market centre of Navan. As the architects have emphasised, it was a challenging spot, due to the road infrastructure dominating over the architecture. Interestingly, the brief changed during construction and so the initial plan for a courthouse on top of a theatre was transformed into a combination of a theatre and a gallery. These two functions are clearly visible in the intriguing structure – the glass walls of the serpentine foyer, envisioned as a curtain wrapping the building, are topped by a black top volume housing the exhibition space. The latter looks as if it were floating above the ground.

pages 86–88

## UNIVERSITY LUIGI BOCCONI – SCHOOL OF ECONOMICS
## MILAN, ITALY, 2008

This massive building occupies a corner plot outlined by two busy streets. Its curved and complex structure echoes the city's hustle and bustle. The sculpturous form offers various perspectives depending on the angle and the passage of light. The architects envisioned a building consisting of five conference halls, lecture theatres, and courtyards, all of which are accessible to the public, as well as offices for the professors in the upper part. The most impressive features are the intersections both vertical and horizontal within the building. The dynamic spatial arrangement is visible even from the street level with the auditorium undercroft emerging from the underground level and filled with light filtered through the glazed façade.

YVONNE FARRELL & SHELLEY McNAMARA

The main objective in this project was to create a work of inviting architecture that would foster social interaction. The Town House is open to the public and brings together the university's main library and archive, dance studios, a theatre, and adaptable learning rooms, as well as two cafés. It was envisioned as an open space, the arrangement of which is quite complex, given its multipurpose character. Various functional areas interlock and overlap, with an open staircase woven into the interior, which links all levels and encourages internal circulation. It is also possible to move through the building using external colonnades, which define the distinctive façade and express the openness of the building.

# DORIANA FUKSAS

Doriana Mandrelli Fuksas (b. 1955) graduated with a degree in History of Modern and Contemporary Architecture from the University of Rome "La Sapienza" and continued her studies at the École Spéciale d'Architecture in Paris, where she earned a degree in Architecture. The architect joined Massimiliano Fuksas in 1985 to co-create one of the most fascinating studios of our time. They work in both Rome and Paris, running an international architecture company that also has offices in Shenzhen, Dubai, and New York and has created numerous realizations all over the world. Their wide variety of projects, from museums to cultural centres and offices, is complemented by the Fuksas Design studio, which Doriana Fuksas has headed since 1997. Creating furniture and design objects for their architectural projects is not the only goal. Their collaborations with the world's best manufacturers result in many innovative and aesthetically pleasing industrial design pieces. Between 2014 and 2015 the couple also contributed as authors of the design column in the Italian journal "La Repubblica".

As much as they frequently point to the fact that they do not have one signature particular style, their buildings speak with a recognisable and very expressive architectural language, which has clearly evolved over their decades of common work. Each of their projects is different and adjusted to its specific context. Working with classic materials has led to discoveries of novel shapes. These forms, whether organic or geometric, are always a kind of surprise in their realizations. "Our work aims at understanding facts, context culture and identifying problems. Through a negotiation with these challenges emerge simple forms and varying scales. Lack of a distinct style and the ability to create an entire building out of a quick sketch is what we aim to do at Studio Fuksas", they explain. Combining various styles and elements without restricting themselves to one defined method is their way of coming up with such unique design concepts. Doriana Fuksas remarks: "Ideas never come out of the blue; you need to look around and pay attention to how people live. Architecture should accommodate people, their environments and their desires. Architecture is for people; otherwise, it is a mistake".

Speaking about her inspiration, Doriana Fuksas reflects that she prefers to draw from creators of other disciplines, suggesting that "it's better to observe things that are not strictly connected with your world". Since she first studied art history, her fascination with visual artists has remained strong. She also favours Japanese literature to, as she says, read about something she does not know about, experience different emotions, and understand other cultures. In addition to all her activities in the fields of design, Doriana Fuksas has taught at the Institute of History of Art at the Faculty of Letters and Arts and at the ITACA Department of Industrial Design at her alma mater in Rome. During the 7th Venice Biennale of Architecture in 2000, titled "Less Aesthetics More Ethics", Fuksas curated four "Special Projects" – Jean Prouvé, Jean Maneval, the Peace Pavilion and Architecture of Spaces, and the Contemporary Art section.

## ARMANI 5TH AVENUE
## NEW YORK, USA, 2009

With the highly sculpturous effect of a curvaceous staircase, the architects turned the four-level showroom (including the basement) into a dynamic and fluid space. The swirling whirlwind, made of steel coated in plastic, is an entirely free-standing structure that fluidly connects the building vertically. To enhance this visual continuity, the spaces and walls on all floors are also curved. Special lighting emphasises this sensual geometry. "The movement of the staircase is evident in every aspect of the interior design, from floor and wall display units to desks and armchairs, which mirrors, enhances, and becomes part of the same vortex", reflect the architects.

## SHENZHEN BAO'AN INTERNATIONAL AIRPORT – TERMINAL 3
### SHENZHEN, CHINA, 2013

"The concept of the plan evokes the image of a manta ray, a fish that breathes and changes its own shape, undergoes variations, and turns into a bird, to celebrate the emotion and fantasy of a flight", explain the architects. The sculpturous volume in the form of a 1.5-kilometre-long tunnel indeed appears to be an organic creature more than an architectural building. The shape, including the roof's profile, refers to the irregular lines of the landscape. This impression is enhanced by a honeycomb wrapping made of glass and metal panels, which also creates light effects. The alveolus-shaped motif has also been employed inside the building.

NEW ROME – EUR CONVENTION
CENTRE AND HOTEL 'THE CLOUD'
ROME, ITALY, 2016

The result of 18 years of planning and
construction, the complex is a fully
earthquake-proof structure and offers
a new meeting area in a busy part of
the city. Constructed from 37,000 tonnes
of steel (the equivalent of four and a half
Eiffel Towers), it consists of a new public
space, the New Rome/EUR Convention
Centre, housing conference and
exhibition spaces, as well as a 17-storey
hotel. The 'Cloud' is an independent
cocoon-like structure in the heart of
the complex. Eco-friendly features of
the project include integrated air-
conditioning carried out by a reversible
heat pump, photovoltaic roof panels,
and rain water harvesting, as well as
natural ventilation systems.

# JEANNE GANG

In 2019 American architect Jeanne Gang (b. 1964) was named by TIME magazine as one of the 100 most influential people of the year. A graduate of Architecture from the University of Illinois and the Harvard Graduate School of Design, Gang also studied in Switzerland. "I was initially thinking of becoming a painter or an artist, but I was also always interested in math and science. Architecture combined these two for me, the analytical side and the more, let's say, sensitive or observant side", Gang recalls. Her professional career began in Europe, where she worked for Rem Koolhaas at the Rotterdam-based OMA. Upon returning to the U.S., Gang established her studio in 1997.

With the Studio Gang headquarters in Chicago, the practice also has offices in New York, San Francisco, and Paris and projects throughout the Americas and Europe. While architecture and urbanism are the main focuses of their activity, the office also realises interiors and exhibition projects. The studio is responsible for several truly innovative and visually stunning projects starting with the 82-storey Aqua Tower in Chicago, known as the highest skyscraper ever designed by a female architect (now the title now of the architect's Vista Tower in Chicago to be completed in 2020). Its unique façade, with a rhythmical yet irregular sequence of undulating terraces, was inspired by terrestrial topography.

A Professor in Practice of Architecture the architect is active on various civic and design-focused committees and advisory groups. Gang has also authored several books. "Reveal" features the studio's work and process. "Reverse Effect: Renewing Chicago's Waterways" offers a bold vision of a radically greener future for the Chicago River.

Even if Gang's projects vary in scales and typologies, they nevertheless demonstrate common threads. On the one hand, the architect pushes the boundaries of the discipline to foster stronger communities and enhance people's interactions within architecture. Another focal point is the ingenious way she juxtaposes technology and nature in designing new buildings. With an amazing sense of shape and texture, particularly visible outside, Gang employs solutions that transform architecture into an environmentally friendly discipline. Like with the roof of the studio's Chicago. Gang leads a 21st century dialogue with nature on various levels, be it technological or aesthetic. She also uses her distinctive voice to advocate for more activism among architects. "Architects have special skills. They are able to connect the dots between different disciplines, and they're able to communicate ideas to the broader public", she muses, adding that "we are able to project what something could look like in the future, and we're all about making plans. And that is very useful. I think architects should use these skills more to push issues that they care about for the greater good". Gang's work ingeniously demonstrates how to move crucial issues forward and envisions the architecture of tomorrow.

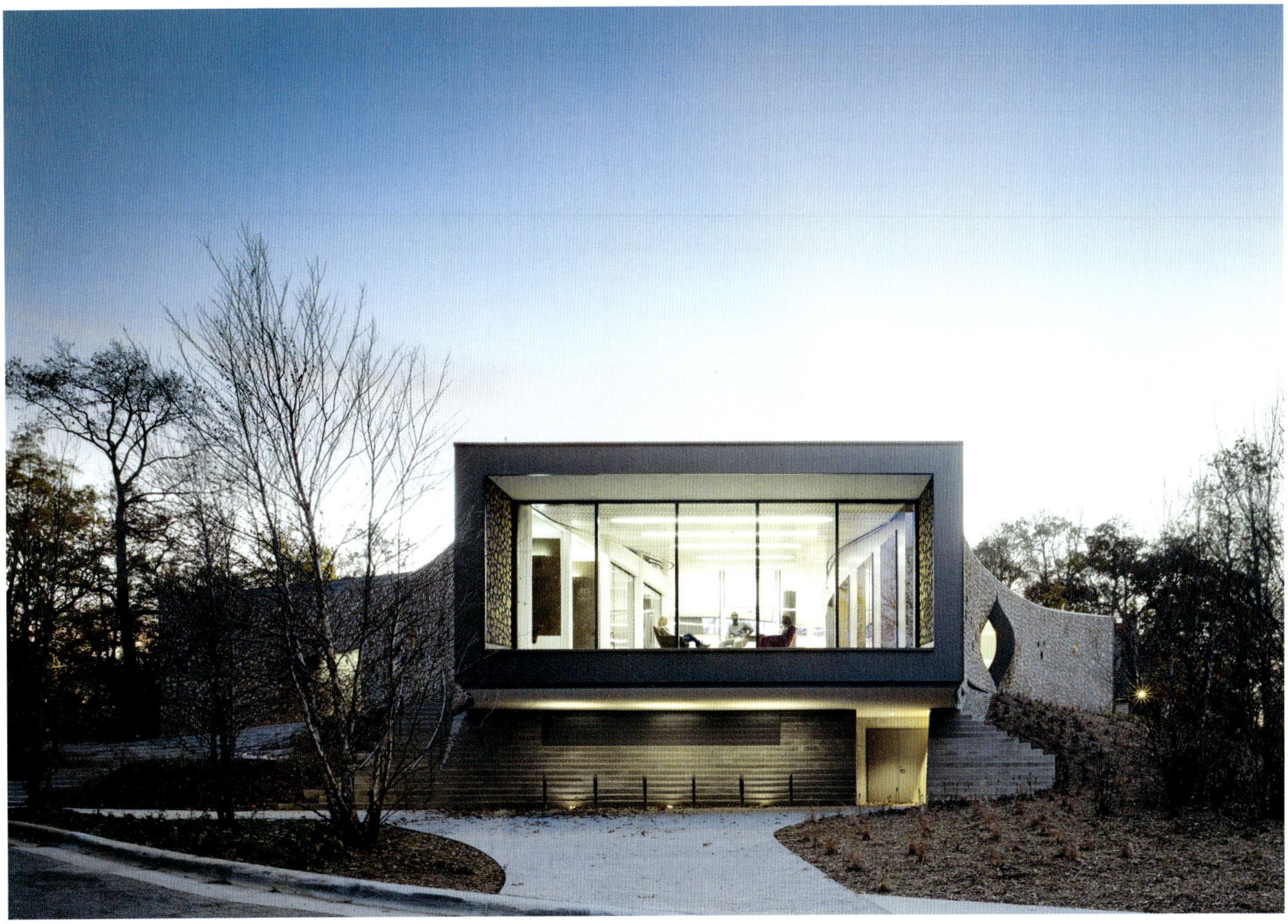

ARCUS CENTER FOR SOCIAL JUSTICE LEADERSHIP
KALAMAZOO, MI, USA, 2014

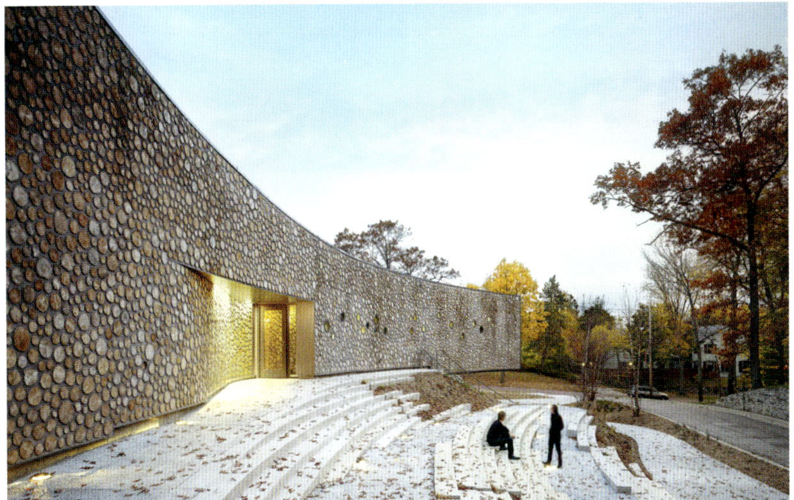

The Arcus Center, focused on activities in the fields of human rights and social justice, is an inviting meeting place bringing together students, scholars, social justice leaders, and members of the public to encourage discussion and learning. The architect envisioned an open building, filled with daylight, organised along three axes with a living area and kitchen in the middle for more informal encounters. "The plan encourages convening in configurations that begin to break down psychological and cultural barriers between people", explains the studio. The wood masonry creates another original visual effect while also reducing carbon pollution.

WRITERS THEATRE
GLENCOE, ILLINOIS, USA, 2016

Designed to resonate with the character of the village's downtown, the building is an intriguing contrast between two intimate performance spaces opening onto the a central gathering space. This light and transparent lobby, which can open to the adjacent park, is an elegant combination of glass and timber construction. It accommodates multiple uses, from informal performances to various community events. The focus for the theatre's two performance spaces, a main stage and a smaller black box venue, was to employ innovative staging and seating configurations to enhance the audience's experience.

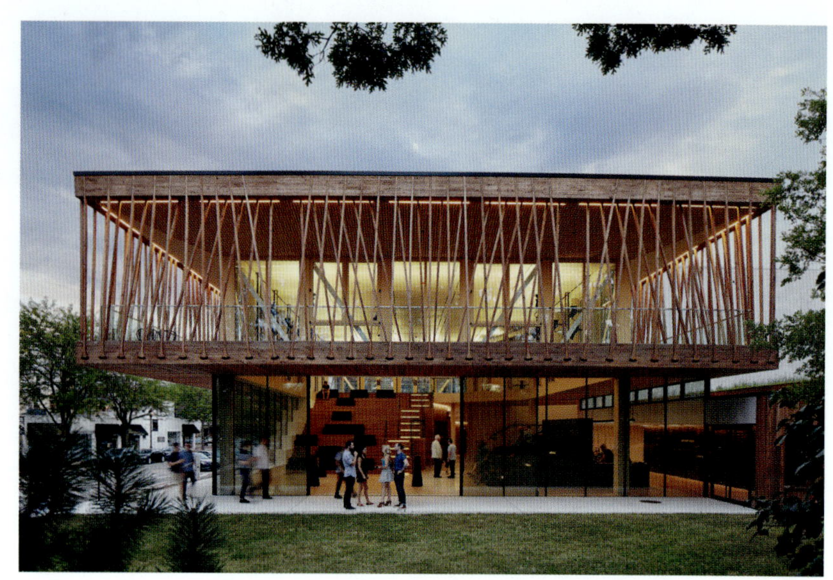

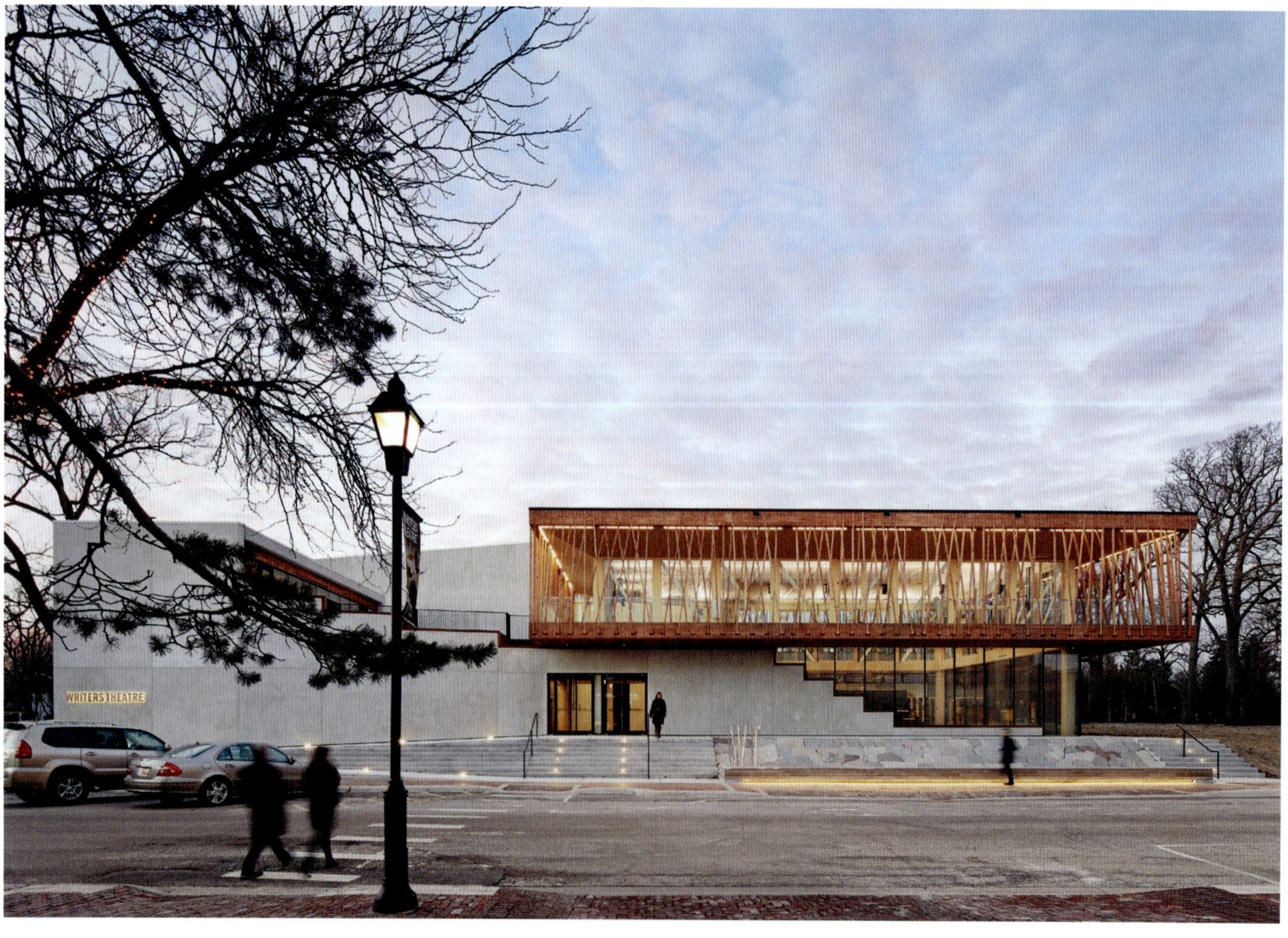

SOLAR CARVE
NEW YORK, USA, 2019

Employing advanced technologies, this high-rise building is located
between the High Line park and the Hudson River, allowing views onto
green spaces in bustling Manhattan. At the core of this innovative concept
was exploring how to shape architecture in response to solar access, but the
project also considered other site-specific criteria that could have a positive
impact on the environment. The angles of the sun's path have sculpted
inside and outside of this unusual office building. It employs a geometrically
optimised glazing system in a pattern of three-dimensional facets.

# EILEEN GRAY

One of the pioneers of modern architecture as well as design, Irish-born architect Eileen Gray (1878–1976) spent her childhood in London. She was one of the first women admitted to one of the most prestigious schools in the capital – the Slade School of Art, where she took up painting. After an apprenticeship in a London lacquer workshop, she decided to move to Paris. It was 1902 and Gray continued her training in lacquer technique and cabinet-making. Successful in creating lacquered screens and decorative panels, she opened her own gallery in 1922. Gray designed interiors and pieces of furniture In 1925 she began to use chrome, steel tubes, and glass in her projects. Over two decades she created innovative designs and collaborated with leading modernists including Le Corbusier, who was among those encouraging her to pursue an architectural career.

Before designing her most famous villa, E-1027 in Roquebrune-Cap-Martin on the French coast, Gray spent a couple of years in the south of France to study the terrain, path of the sun, and wind. The project was challenging and the plot on the rocky shore was remote, without an access road. The white volume of the house is skilfully harmonised with the natural surroundings, as it was the architect's wish not to alter the topography. The interiors were organised on two extensive floors connected by a central staircase, which also provided access to the roof. The spatial arrangement created a flexible space, with rooms that were divided with light partition walls, some of which were even movable. In addition, the terraces were equipped with special screens which could easily transform them into indoor spaces. The living area, taking up most of the interior, was spacious and filled with natural light; it opened to spectacular sea views through the full-height glass façade. Jean Badovici, French architect and critic and the architect's partner at the time, took part in the planning of E-1027. One of his main ideas was to add the sculpturous spiral staircase to the minimalistic volume. He also advised on the structural issues. Therefore, Gray shared the authorship of this spectacular project. The name of the house is a reference to both designers' initials, using the numbers of their positions in the alphabet (10, 2, and 7). Gray, however, was the one who designed the furniture for the interiors. Shortly after the house was completed, Gray and Badovici separated. She then left to build her new home, Tempe à Pailla, in Menton near Castellar. Built on the rocks, it was a single-floor space with a living room that extended onto a garden through a terrace and staircase.

Lou Pérou in Saint-Tropez was another challenging realization and her last residence. Gray designed it in her seventies, when she bought a vineyard near Saint-Tropez. She decided to convert a small stone building into a house, naturally with a terrace to enjoy beautiful views of the natural surroundings. The structure was an interesting mélange of old and new elements and it looked different from various perspectives. After the war Gray focused on furniture design. Near the end of her life, the architect teamed up with London-based design specialist and gallerist Zeev Aram, who introduced her designs onto the world market. Shortly before her death in 1976, the architect gained well-deserved international recognition.

pages 99–101
E-1027
ROQUEBRUNE-CAP-MARTIN, FRANCE, 1929

An icon of 20th-century architecture, this modernist villa
sits on the rocky shore of the Mediterranean Sea. The
minimalistic white cube with a flat roof is a reinforced
concrete construction based on pilotis. The L-shaped
volume has floor-to-glass windows, letting plenty of light
inside and most importantly opening it to a picturesque
view of the sea. To maintain fluidity between the inside
and the surrounding context, each room in the house
had a designated outside space. For the interiors, Gray
envisioned a flexible system of partly movable light
partitions, which provided a spacious and adjustable
space. Two levels of the villa were centrally linked by
an original spiral staircase, which also led to the roof.
All furnishing was also designed by the architect.

# ZAHA HADID

Born in Baghdad, Iraq, Zaha Hadid (1950–2016) initially studied architecture at the American University of Beirut. In 1972 she decided to move to London, where she graduated from the Architectural Association (AA). After working with Rem Koolhas at OMA, in 1979 she established her London-based practice, Zaha Hadid Architects. Working successfully across the globe, she received numerous prestigious prizes and titles, including the highest honours: in 2004 Hadid was awarded the Pritzker Architecture Prize, as the first woman recipient in its history; in 2012 she was made a Dame Commander of the Order of the British Empire by Queen Elizabeth II.

The architect's spectacular and imaginative visions had a great impact on contemporary architecture. Employing the power of advanced design as much as materials, she continually pushed the boundaries of architecture. Each subsequent project brought surprising new innovative solutions and bold shapes, as if the architect were steadily challenging the discipline, and herself, to prove that one could continue to achieve more. Beyond this, her goal was also to invent a new way of designing buildings, far from the classic typology. Hadid believed that most typical buildings like museums or libraries did not have to follow the same ordinary pattern and be built according to particular principles. Stretching the limits, she developed designed many realizations that were ahead of their time and each concept was as unorthodox as it was innovative. With her fearless and charismatic personality, she was a virtuoso in designing outstanding buildings that seemed impossible, but only until the very moment she made them real.

Over the decades Hadid developed a recognisable visual language characterized by curved, organic, and somewhat futuristic shapes. Her concepts were usually very complex and far from anything designed before. Hadid, known for developing them through a process of expressive sketching, got the most out of the evolution of advanced computer technologies for model-making. Her radically new ideas for architecture resulted in numerous multi-layered environments, which had a prodigious impact on the urban landscapes of many cities around the world. A significant part of Hadid's enormous portfolio were public spaces, but she found each commission interesting, as they offered a new perspective and opportunity for a different way of getting closer to people. The architect's focus was always on initiating an intriguing dialogue between new creations and the existing fabric, based on various considerations. Gravity-defying geometrical volumes, a contemporary take on traditions, surprising vistas that change depending on the perspective, both indoors and outdoors, and unexpected spatial arrangements were only some of the aspects of her visionary constructions. Compared by many to sculptures, Hadid's inventive spaces were made to be explored. In her practice, designing meant creating experiences both through forms and selected materials.

Her unconventional approach to architecture and consequent realizations ensured that all of her buildings gained the status of landmarks. Hadid's avant-garde achievements inspired and were widely admired, even if some caused controversies. Zaha Hadid Architects, with a team of several hundred people, continues the architect's legacy, completing some of the architect's last designs and developing new projects all around the globe.

LOIS & RICHARD
ROSENTHAL CENTER FOR
CONTEMPORARY ART
CINCINNATI, USA, 2003

The Rosenthal Center
was the first U.S. museum
designed by a woman. This
first freestanding building
for The Contemporary
Arts Center in Cincinnati,
which dates back to
1939, is striking with its
play of massive concrete
blocks contrasted with
transparent glass sections
in the façade. This
sculpturous shape stands
out expressively from the
surrounding architecture
and leverages its corner
location. The interiors
are equally surprising: a
zig-zagging staircase in
a narrow slit at the back
of the building leads to
exhibition spaces that
vary in size and shape.
"Together, these varying
galleries interlock like a
three-dimensional jigsaw
puzzle, made up of solids
and voids," explained the
architect.

## MAXXI: MUSEUM OF XXI CENTURY ARTS
## ROME, ITALY, 2009

This geometrically complex building of significant volume, envisioned together with Patrik Schumacher, is defined by its urban context. The walls in "a confluence of line", as architects call it, intersect to separate indoor from outdoor and integrate the building into its surroundings. The massive interiors, shaped by flowing walls, seem to be in constant movement. Visitors are invited to explore these organic spaces by navigating curved corridors and following meandering passages or interconnections, starting in an extensive and high-reaching lobby which provides access to all parts of the building. Continuously changing vistas also create flexibility for a variety of displays.

HEYDAR ALIYEV CENTRE
BAKU, AZERBAIJAN, 2012

The main goal of the architects was to establish a fluid relationship
between the volume and its surrounding plaza. The curvaceous shape
blurs into the terrain through numerous folds and undulations, enabling
seamless access from all perspectives. The idea to employ fluidity
draws from the regional heritage, as a reference to historical Islamic
architecture elements, just as to continuous calligraphic and ornamental
patterns. As the architects describe the process, their "ambition to
achieve a surface so continuous that it appears homogenous, required
a broad range of different functions, construction logics and technical
systems". Co-designed with Patrik Schumacher, the Heydar Aliyev Centre
was a key realization for the post-soviet modernisation of Baku.

# ITSUKO HASEGAWA

for her acquaintances, who respected her philosophy and approach to architecture. In the male-dominated field at that time, though, it was difficult for her to get significant commissions for public buildings, the designs of which, as she stresses, were limited only to authorised senior architects. The competition for the Shonandai Cultural Centre in Fujisawa in 1984 – which Hasegawa considers the first genuinely open competition, and which she spectacularly on and was thus able to realise one of her most playful designs – was a game-changer. The project created many places where people can meet each other, something that makes a successful public space in the eyes of the architect. Since this realization Hasegawa has received many commissions for many other public buildings – especially museums – through competitions, and consequently has been able to realise her first-prize proposals without major changes. School and housing, whether single or multi-family, projects remain important elements of her multi-faceted portfolio.

Asked about her source of inspiration, Hasegawa explains: "I was born in the suburbs where I was surrounded by beautiful nature. My life was in nature until my primary school time. I grew up with a fascination for wildflowers, green mountains, and the glitter of the sea. Probably from these experiences, I continue to think about nature, tradition, and sustainability. I get ideas from these, together with the conditions of the site". The architectural language Hasegawa has developed through her career frequently draws on the natural world, yet her designs are quintessentially Japanese in expression. The combination of the simplicity of her materials and the lightness of her structures with their subtle forms all resonate with the surroundings. It is important for the architect to fill the interiors with light. Last but not least, from the beginning of Hasegawa's professional path, she has been interested in sustainable solutions that make her projects environmentally conscious. Her complex designs often become landscapes or mini-universes, which are informed and which engage with the context of the site. Her interesting mélange of light constructions, modern materials, and futuristic shapes produces quite a unique style.

Hasegawa, an Honorary Fellow of the RIBA and the AIA, is a recipient of many prizes in Japan and internationally, from the Design Prize of the Architectural Institute of Japan in 1986 for her Bizan Hall design and the Japan Cultural Design Award for residential projects, to the Royal Academy's Architecture Prize for lifetime achievement, awarded in 2018.

Regarded as one of the most important Japanese architects, Itsuko Hasegawa (b. 1941) graduated from the Department of Architecture at Kanto Gakuin University and was also a research student at Tokyo Institute of Technology. Before opening her Tokyo-based atelier in 1979, she first worked with Kiyonori Kikutake and afterwards Kazuo Shinohara. Kikutake was one of the founders of the Japanese Metabolism movement, interested in megastructures and organic forms. Shinohara was an influential architect, teacher, and theorist, with a focus on traditional Japanese architecture heritage. Interested in tradition, Hasegawa also launched her own research and travelled around Japan to study traditional Japanese housing. At the outset of her career, Hasegawa designed houses and clinics

## SHONANDAI CULTURAL CENTRE
## FUJISAWA, KANAGAWA, JAPAN, 1990

The first big competition won by Hasegawa was
part of the revitalization of the whole general
area. A combination of reinforced concrete and
steel, the complex speaks with a language of
forms inspired by nature. At the core of this
playful design was the idea to locate most of the
spaces underground, which initially caused quite
a controversy. Visible on the surface is an open
plaza, accessible to all, surrounded by a series of
pavilions, arcades, and forest-like parasols with
mesh tops, as well as futuristically sphere-shaped
buildings housing a civic theatre, planetarium,
and observatory. Elements of sunken gardens on
all four sides surround this original architecture
with nature.

YAMANASHI FRUITS MUSEUM
YAMANASHI, JAPAN, 1995

Commissioned by an agricultural
association, the museum is located in
an extensive park. Several connected
volumes are dominated by three main
buildings, designed with the help of CAD
(Computer-Aided Design). Taking the
shape of spheres, they are inspired by
different stages of fruit growth. The first
one (the Fruit Plaza) reflects the seed in
the tree, the second imitates the new
seed germinating in the sun (the Tropical
Greenhouse), and the seed in full growth
is represented by the third inflated
sphere (the Fruit Workshop). Varying in
their structural complexity, they all have
similar transparent outer shells in glass
and steel.

ITSUKO HASEGAWA

FUJINOKUNI SENBONMATSU FORUM / PLAZA VERDE
NUMAZU, SHIZUOKA, JAPAN, 2013

With spectacular views of Mount Fuji and
Suruga Bay, "Plaza Verde" is one of few
all-in-one convention complexes in Japan;
it includes conference and exhibition
spaces, as well as a hotel and a municipal
facility. With a practical and spacious
interior layout, this multiple-use building
is visually striking. Its façade, covered with
a mesh-type green wall system, unifies all
parts of the complex, and represents the
architect's dialogue with the surrounding
landscapes. Together with the green
roof, this wall system makes the building
environmentally friendly. The development
of the design involved consultations with
the local community, whose wishes helped
to make the forum open to the public.

# ANNA HERINGER

German architect Anna Heringer (b. 1977) is one of the biggest advocates of natural building materials internationally. Throughout her inspiring career, she has successfully demonstrated the truth of her main belief that "architecture is a tool to improve lives". The year she spent volunteering in Bangladesh at the age of 19 inspired this innovative approach to architecture. What she learned from her Bangladeshi host organization, the Dipshikha NGO, was that the most effective strategy for sustainable development is to look at existing resources, not to depend on external factors. And this is exactly what Heringer does in her architectural practice. While focusing on using exclusively natural building materials that are sourced locally, her designs are 100% sustainable and handmade. Realised together with local communities and craftsmen, the

designs are informed by techniques and traditions typical for each particular region. Her projects are culturally sensitive as well as humanitarian and envisioned with the users' needs in mind. For the architect, sustainability is "a synonym for beauty". She considers a truly sustainable building to be one "that is harmonious in its design, structure, technique and use of materials, as well as with the location, the environment, the user, the socio-cultural context". The motivation in her practice is to use architecture as a medium to support local economies and enhance cultural and individual confidence, as much as to foster ecological balance. "The use of natural building materials is vital in order to enable a sustainable and fair development," stresses Heringer.

Many of her ground-breaking projects have been realised in Bangladesh, like her diploma work, the innovative METI School in Rudrapur from 2005 (a collaboration with Eike Roswag), which earned her the prestigious Aga Khan Award for Architecture in 2007. Heringer's goal is not only to preserve the environment but also to influence the lives of people living in less privileged regions of the world, by implementing lasting, affordable, and eco-friendly solutions that could revolutionise housing and public buildings in poor and overpopulated areas. She and Martin Rauch have co-developed the method of Clay Storming, which she teaches at various universities, including the Harvard Graduate School of Design.

Interestingly, although three billion people across the globe live in buildings made of mud, Heringer is one of the few architects interested in working with mud. Moreover, she also effectively uses bamboo or straw. She points at the fact that there are two issues working against the more widespread use of mud – first, it has long been branded a poor material, and thus generally has had a bad image, and second, there is no lobby behind it. "From climate-neutral production to socially just implementation, earthen structures help mitigate the biggest problems of our times: climate change and poverty", she says, explaining why she favours the advantages of the material, which could efficiently replace typically used concrete. Heringer is an honorary professor of the UNESCO Chair of Earthen Architecture, Building Cultures, and Sustainable Development. During her powerful TED talk in 2017 Heringer said that her dream would be to build a rammed-earth skyscraper in Manhattan and she strongly believes that constantly advancing technologies will eventually make it happen.

## METI SCHOOL
### DIPSHIKHA, BANGLADESH, 2005

Heringer teamed up with the local NGO Dipshikha, which manages a development programme in the impoverished and overpopulated area, to design a new school for the community. Together with Eike Roswag, who was responsible for technical planning, they created a light and sustainable structure made of mud and bamboo. Handmade by local craftsmen (even future students helped with small details), the school houses several spacious classrooms on two levels, some with playful cave-like spaces for children to play and learn in. Perfectly adjusted to local weather conditions, the building is easy to ventilate and well lit, keeping it independent from electricity.

## DESI TRAININGCENTER
## RUDRAPUR, BANGLADESH

DESI is a vocational school for electrical training. Its headquarters include classrooms, offices, and instructors' residences. In contrast to the traditional way of organising households in rural Bangladesh into separate structures around a central courtyard, Heringer incorporates all functions into one volume. The ground floor with a veranda for practical training is made of cob walls, which are a mix of earth, straw, and water, while the top level made in bamboo has a lattice façade. The building is supported entirely by solar installations (both electric power and hot water), which were all done by the DESI students.

ANNA HERINGER

## THREE HOSTELS
## BAOXI, CHINA 2016

The first edition of the International
Bamboo Architecture Biennale in the
region of Longquan demonstrated
the potential of bamboo in concrete-
dominated Chinese architecture.
Heringer designed three gigantic
hostels for the event, using this
locally sourced material and proving
its structural quality as much as its
high aesthetic value. The Dragon,
the Nightingale, and the Peacock
represent the state-of-the-art
handiwork of local craftsmen and
draw from weaving traditions in
the area. The round core is made
of stone and rammed earth, for the
staircase and sanitary facilities, while
the woven, cocoon-like external shell
contains platforms covered with mini
tents for the guests.

# FRANCINE HOUBEN

Dutch architect Francine Houben (b. 1955) is the creative director and founding partner of Mecanoo, established in 1984. Combining the disciplines of architecture, urban planning, and landscape, the practice has realised an impressive number of significant buildings, from single houses to skyscrapers, libraries to museums, and even a chapel. The architect is preoccupied by a focus on process, context, and sustainable solutions, rather than on form. Inspired by her university teacher Max Risselada, but also by Charles and Ray Eames and Japan, Houben has gained recognition for her sensitivity regarding light and her use of materials. Her goal from the outset has been to engage with the human, technical, and aesthetic aspects of the discipline in an unorthodox way.

Houben's multidisciplinary practice, with headquarters in Delft, is composed of architects, interior architects, engineers, urbanists, landscape architects, technicians, model makers, and film journalists. The team, which she calls a symphony orchestra, is very diverse; around 40% are women and members come from all over the world, from China to Spain, and from the UK to Korea, which makes it easier to understand both clients and context. Each of Mecanoo's buildings is very different, which the founder attributes to the studio's lack of a form-based approach. Style, according to the studio's statement, is an outdated phenomenon. The fundamental principles of Houben's architectural vision are: "designing primarily for People, constructing spaces that are relevant to Place, and forging connections that give a building Purpose." This attitude is the thread which ties together all of their realizations. Another essential aspect is contextualisation. Houben pays close attention to the local needs, and observes people in different cities, in different climates, and from different cultures. "We are searching to create identity in a world of globalisation, especially when designing public buildings and public space," she remarks. Her inspiration for structural solutions and material choices also comes from specific sites and locations. As Houben summarised in one of her interviews, architecture is about the future, shaping the world and creating spaces open to inevitable yet unpredictable changes. Her designs are thus flexible and universal in terms of forms, use of light, and their contextual relations. Houben feels that "architecture must appeal to all the senses. Architecture is never a purely intellectual, conceptual, or visual game alone. Architecture is about combining all the individual elements into a single concept. What counts in the end is the arrangement of form and emotion."

In 2001 the architect published her architectural manifesto under the title "Composition, Contrast, Complexity" (Houben has published several other books exploring the practice's work). Despite the fact that when she studied at Delft University of Technology, only 4% of all students were women, gender has never been an issue for her. "As a child, I lived in many different places and my mother always arranged the renovations and relocations. In my eyes she could do anything," Houben recalls. "She has been my source of inspiration in many ways. From her I learned to be independent and self-reliant as a self-evident force with which I approach the world. I am grateful to her for that," she emphasises.

MONTEVIDEO RESIDENTIAL TOWER
ROTTERDAM, NETHERLANDS, 2005

As part of the revitalisation of the
Wilhelmina Pier at a former dock,
aiming at building residential and office
towers, Houben designed a dramatic
structure made of intersecting volumes,
part of which cantilevers over the
quayside. Referring to the past of the
place, which was a departure point for
ocean liners heading to the U.S., the
windows, loggias, and balconies on the
façades create a rhythmic pattern that
resembles the sectioning of an ocean
liner. The structure is vertically split into
three parts – the inviting lower two-
storey base made of steel is the base
for a ninety-metre-tall concrete structure
in the middle, and both are crowned
by a steel top inspired by that of an
American skyscraper from the 1930s.

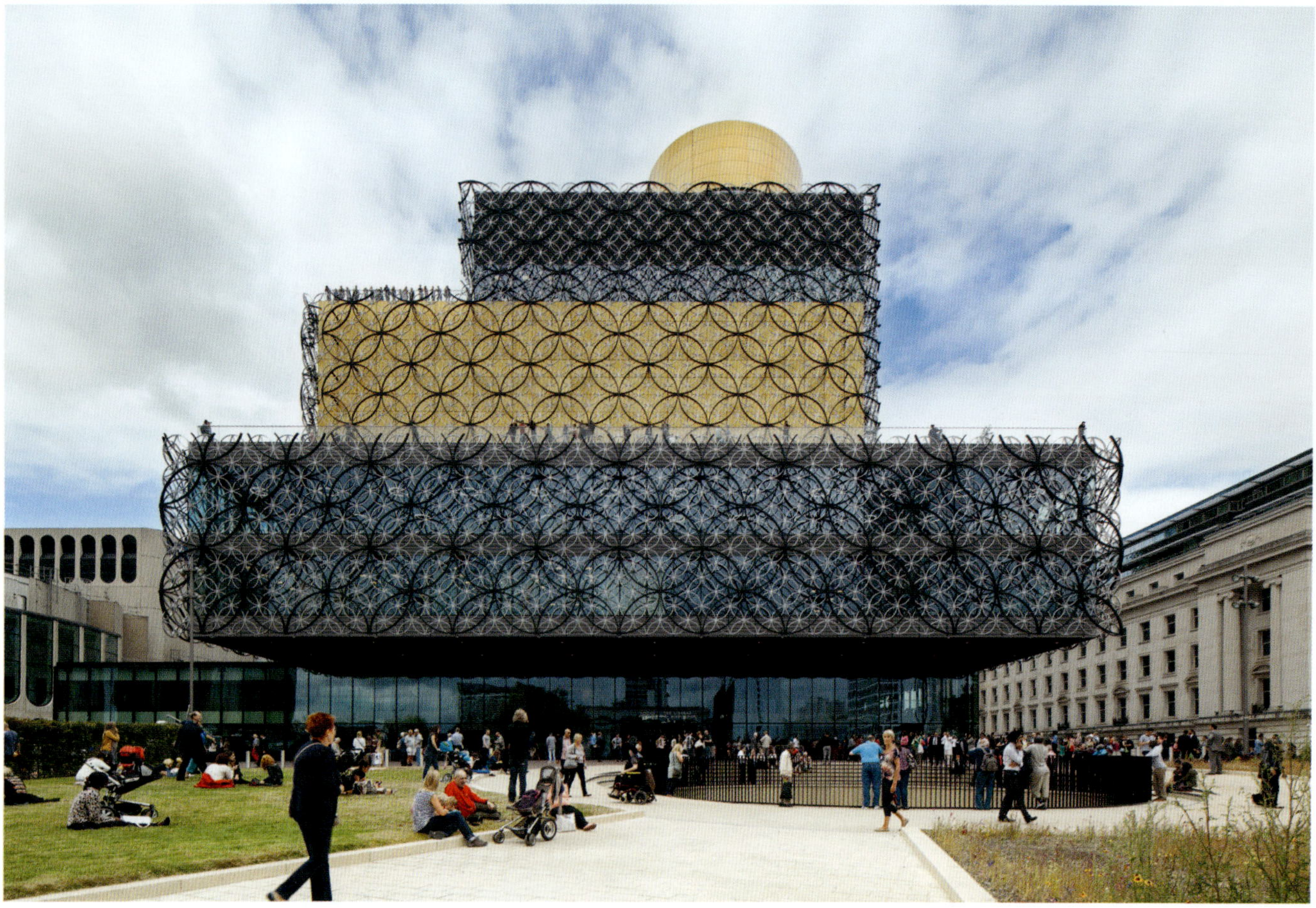

LIBRARY OF BIRMINGHAM
BIRMINGHAM, UNITED KINGDOM, 2013

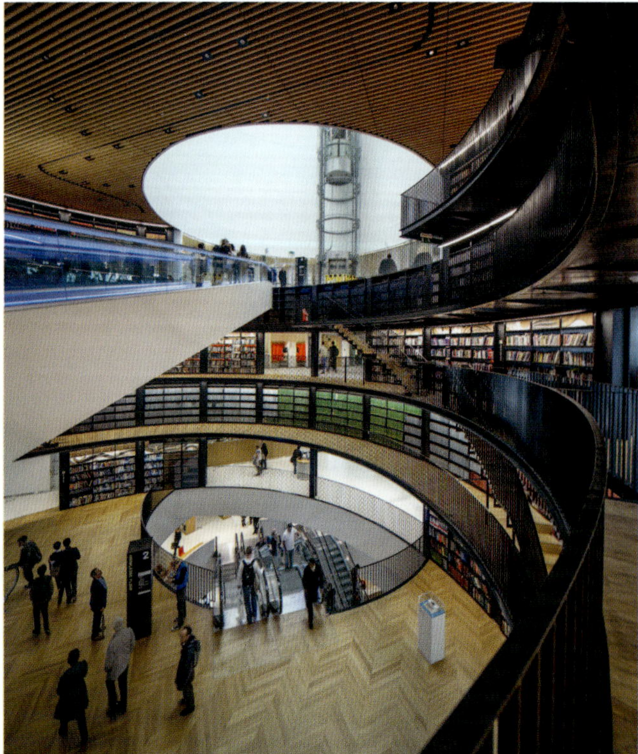

The complexity of shifting volumes reflects the numerous facilities housed by the library, with rotundas connecting the floors. "The building is an ode to the circle: an archetypical form that embodies universality, infinity, unity, and timelessness", suggests Mecanoo's statement. The structure also refers to the traditions of heavy industrial metalwork and the fine gold and silver smiths of the Jewellery Quarter. The decorative pattern of overlapping circles on the façade translates into beautiful play of reflections inside. While three garden-like roof terraces and the golden rotunda designed for the Shakespeare Memorial Room originally from 1882 crown this sensational building, the sunken circular courtyard in front of it functions as a public performance space.

pages 117–119
## NATIONAL KAOHSIUNG CENTRE FOR THE ARTS
## KAOHSIUNG, TAIWAN, 2018

Houben celebrated the transformation of Kaohsiung – which used to be a major international harbour – into a modern and diverse city by creating a spectacular arts centre. Built on former military terrain within a subtropical park, it takes the form of a gigantic horizontal structure with a curvaceous roof. It was developed in collaboration with shipbuilders and inspired by the shape of local banyan trees with their characteristic vast and undulating crowns acting as a shelter from both rain and sun. Underneath the roof, Houben planned an expansive and well-ventilated public space called Banyan Plaza. On the top, the architect nestled an open-air theatre, smoothly connecting the architecture with the surrounding landscape.

# ROSSANA HU

Rossana Hu (b. 1968) received her Master of Architecture and Urban Planning from Princeton University, and a Bachelor of Arts in Architecture and Music from the University of California at Berkeley. After her studies she worked at Michael Graves & Associates; Ralph Lerner Architect in Princeton; Skidmore, Owings and Merrill in New York City; and The Architects Collaborative (TAC) in San Francisco. In 2004 she and her partner Lyndon Neri co-founded their own studio: Neri&Hu Design and Research Office. Their multi-cultural team realises projects across disciplines and around the world. This interdisciplinary architectural design practice is based in Shanghai, a city that is one of the architect's inspirations. The core vision for the practice is, as they state, "to respond to a global worldview incorporating overlapping design disciplines for a new paradigm in architecture". All their projects are characterised by their contextual approach. They emphasise that critical probing into the specificities of programme, site, and function, as well as the history of the site, is essential to their creative process. The elements that matter most in their creations are their intriguing forms, special attention to details, careful selection of materials, sense of textures, and subtle play with light. The studio has gained recognition for their conversions and adaptive reuse concepts, as they often combine old with new in a most surprising and visually stunning way. The buildings they design, each very different, should thus be experienced slowly and meticulously. Their portfolio escapes generalisations, as each realization is an act of finding original touches rather than following one ultimately defined style. Their fresh take on both materials and forms, fuelled by their multi-cultural experiences and sophisticated aesthetics inspired by various – often contrasting – influences, turns their projects into extraordinary and fresh designs. It is perhaps because, as Hu describes in one of her interviews, they "believe in the subtext over the obvious and the poetic over the utilitarian". Even if the practical aspects are less interesting for them, all their projects are perfectly practical.

Architecture is the foundation of what they do, but Neri&Hu's creation of new buildings is counterbalanced by design, the second and equally interesting side of their practice. Apart from interiors, Hu and her partner design a range of industrial products for numerous European brands. In addition to this activity, the duo develops their own award-winning product line under the 'neri&hu' label. Since 2015 Hu and her partner have also been the Creative Directors of Stellar Works, a brand aiming at inspiring a renaissance in Asian aesthetics. Hu is also a Founding Partner and Creative Executive for Design Republic, a Founding Panel Member of 100% Design Shanghai.

In parallel to her creative work, Hu has been actively involved in teaching and research. Lecturing internationally at various universities and teaching at the Harvard Graduate School of Design and Yale School of Architecture has also been an important aspect of her work. Her professional expertise was valuable in her role for the Princeton University President's Advisory Committee on Architecture, where she advised the President on architectural design and campus planning issues of her alma mater.

"I am particularly drawn to poetry, literature, and music. The abstraction found in them is useful for expanding our thought process in the creation of architecture and space-making."

You established, and have run your practice together with your partner Lyndon Neri. What does your creative process look like? Do you always work together on new projects or is each of you responsible for particular aspects of design?

We work together almost like we are one person. Of course there are different strengths we carry into the design process, but we feed off of each other and make up for one another's deficiencies quite well. We hardly have to make any formal division of labor, as we know who is good at what, so we naturally jump onto the tasks at hand without having to negotiate or discuss.

Generally, most projects are shared efforts, and we work very organically depending on time, availability, and interest. Lyndon is better at the conceptual stage, and his creative process is mostly through drawing and form creation. I tend to do better at the development stage, and think through words and reasons more than drawings. We are both strong with visual language, and are critical with each project at different stages. There's a fundamental trust that allows a fluid working relationship, which is so important in our work, given the high speed and workload we often have to juggle. Comparatively, I am more of the editor who likes to delete elements... I also serve more as the critic in the office. Both of our aesthetic sensibilities are quite similar, and we share in the same vision for most projects.

Projects by Neri&Hu range from architecture and interior design to product design. How do all of these parts of your practice co-exist? Do you see them as complementing or rather as entirely separate? Is it helpful to take on so many and such diverse projects? Can small-scale projects be inspiring for large realizations and vice versa?

Interdisciplinary research is part of our design process. It is intrinsically intertwined with every project from the start. Architecture is still the foundation from which we do everything, so it is the most important for us. We see design as a holistic discipline, taking it from the renaissance notion of seeing design as a multidisciplinary approach.

These different parts often co-exist in one project; we could be working on a hotel building, designing the architecture, considering the site planning, then into the interior... finish with custom furniture and lighting design (product team) for special rooms, then top off with signage and way-finding design from our graphics team. Often we are brought into the naming process; then corporate identity creation is involved, which includes logo design and collaterals. (i.e., Da-An Kimpton Hotel in Taipei & Pernod Ricard Whisky Project).

It is helpful for us to have the "total design" (the term as referenced by Wagner/Gropius/Sibyl Moholy-Nagy/Wigley) vision for a project, then carry it through in these various scales and disciplines. By virtue of working with the varying disciplines, we are forced to confront design from different perspectives, and as a result create a more coherent project.

Buildings designed by Neri&Hu demonstrate your amazing sense of materials and textures but also ingenious ideas for spatial solutions. Where do you draw your inspiration from?

We are very much inspired by the everyday, the mundane, and the ordinary. The very fabric of Shanghai as a city and the everyday activities in and around the city are very much an inspiration. Of course, other creative fields also inspire us. I am particularly drawn to poetry, literature, and music. The abstraction found in them is useful for expanding our thought process in the creation of architecture and space-making.

Your projects are, on the one hand, a fusion of
international influences, while often playing creatively
with various traditions. On the other, you like being
challenged by buildings with a past, and inevitably
numerous memories. Why is refurbishing and creating
a hybrid of the old fabric with the new important to you?

This question is central to our attitude towards
architecture; we are interested in issues of cultural
identity as exhibited in the built environment and how
our memories shape our future. We use architecture
and design as a means to explore their intertwining
relationships, and establish ties between various
disconnects – so that pieces of fragmented pasts could
be linked to the future; so that detached memories
could be tied together to shape our living space; so that
distinct cultures could co-exist in a hybrid typology. We
are inspired by Svetlana Boym's term "reflective nostalgia",
wherein longings for the past could usher in the future.
As we exist in this juncture of super-speed technological
explosion, we find it even more relevant to place our work
within an understanding of tradition and history. Not so
that we repeat or replicate them, but we learn from them
to move forward and create anew.

What in your opinion are the biggest challenges of
architecture today?

In China, having enough time to create seems to be
the biggest problem. All projects need to be finished
yesterday, which leaves little room or time to think about
design in a critical and comprehensive way.
On the world stage, I feel that the relevance of
architecture ought to be re-appropriated. Formal gestures
are no longer enough, nor are mere aesthetic statements
sufficient. Architecture ought to engage more closely
with technology and society, and be more accessible to
creating values that benefit the public.

You have studied and worked across the world;
is it easy to be a female architect today?

It's always relative, isn't it... It's easier than ever before,
compared to any other time in history. However, it's not
easier than being a male architect, if that's what you
mean... :)



The Waterhouse is a five-star
boutique hotel, built on the base of
an existing three-story Japanese Army
Headquarters from the 1930s, which
occupies a corner plot. The idea of the
renovation, which included topping
the existing building with the new
fourth floor, was to emphasise the
stark contrast between old and new,
through the outer structure as much
as inside. The contemporary part, built
into the historical fabric, dominates
both structurally and colouristically. The
choice of materials for the new part is
a reflection of the industrial past of the
dock by the Huangpu River that the
hotel faces.

EXPERIMENTA
HEILBRONN, GERMANY, 2019

The location of the building on an island in the River Neckar in the centre of the city makes it possible to experience its complex volume from various angles. A spiral route shapes the basic structure of the architecture, enabling the visitor to glide diagonally through successive panoramas of the unfolding urban landscape. Each floor holds a thematic exhibition, while a chain of studios suspended in the heart of the building invites engagement in practical work. At either end of the route domed spaces provide points of arrival and departure: the rooftop observatory allows views into outer space, while the Science Dome on the lower ground floor offers insights into the virtual world of science.

# KRISTIN JARMUND

One of the leading architects in Norway, Kristin Jarmund (b. 1954) is particularly known for numerous realizations in her home city of Oslo. A graduate of the Norwegian Institute of Technology and the Architectural Association in London, she first gained professional experience in the firm of Telje-Torp-Aasen Arkitektkontor. In 1985, she started her own office, focusing on architecture and planning, as well as interior design. "The practice's design philosophy aims at solutions that reduce complex problems to simplicity in form and function, while at the same time allowing for a sensitive awareness to context and the human dimension", reads her firm's mission statement.

A wide array of projects allows her to explore different issues, like the importance of appropriate scale and proportions when designing architecture for children and youth (the architect's portfolio includes numerous schools and kindergartens).

Jarmund's realizations, varying in scale and purpose, demonstrate a great awareness of the context, be it urban fabric or natural landscape. The architect is interested in a dialogue between the present and past, landscape and building, a site and its surroundings. Whether by contrast or in relation to one another, architecture has to be consciously connected with its surroundings. Clearly the function of a building, and the client's wishes and budget create a frame, yet the creative process starts with the careful consideration of a number of aspects concerning the site, like analysing the topography and the structure's orientation towards both views or natural light and the neighbourhood. The architect suggests that "the typology of the other buildings around" is crucial, "for example whether the place is urban, suburban, or with single structures." She explains that "the scale and proportions of the surrounding built fabric is of importance for understanding how to work, and whether the scheme deserves to present itself as a contrast or as part of the context", emphasising that, "if it is a contrast, there should always be a reason for it".

Her practice pays special attention to environmental issues, which has earned Jarmund much praise. Her careful detailing and thorough choice of materials play a main role in her sustainable architecture designs. Climate challenges, as she notes, are particularly crucial in Norway, where extreme contrasts in temperature, heavy loads of snow on roofs, and limited sunlight require solutions that optimally adapt buildings to these contrasting conditions.

Interestingly, Jarmund considers architecture to be a litmus test. "Society as it stands is always reflected in architecture", she observes. "This is why built architecture – in my view – is one of the most interesting interpretations of where we are as a society, what knowledge we have, how we feel, what are our needs and demands – and what our dreams are." The architect continues, "I always ask myself how my architecture can be of future interest – how it can represent the present and at the same time hopefully add to and carry further the tradition of built culture that is already there – as part of the 'big novel' that consists of many chapters of history, linked together, shoulder to shoulder". In 2011 Jarmund received the Honorary Fellowship of the American Institute of Architects for her outstanding work in architecture and society.

## RAHOLT SECONDARY SCHOOL
## EIDSVOLL, NORWAY, 2004

The single-floor square pavilion is
located in a rural landscape. The
fact that it is made of glass and
based on a half-metre platform
makes it look as if it is floating
above the surface of the site.
At the heart of the building is
an open-air atrium; however, the
architect also planned another four
courtyards which are cut into the
structure to let natural light fill the
building. The interiors were playfully
envisioned as a village: instead
of corridors there are main streets,
narrow paths or squares, and
gardens with circular auditoriums in
three corners as orientation points.
The vivid colours additionally
enhance the architecture.

NORWEGIAN EMBASSY
KATHMANDU, NEPAL, 2008

Integrated into its slope site with extensive outdoor plateaus, the embassy building faces the Himalayan mountain range. The horizontal plan of a long, single-floor structure is broken up by a volume rising above the main entrance. Visually striking thanks to a zig-zag panoramic window, this volume houses the Ambassador's office. The building was constructed using local materials (and by employing local labourers) in order to integrate the building with the existing fabric. Four years after it was completed, the project saw an extension of a new residence for the Ambassador.

Located in the heart of the capital of Henan province, the former home of many emperors as well as the ancient political, economic, and cultural centre of China, this hotel was conceived as an "archive" of new and old. "Externally the archives are expressed as cantilevered stacked boxes, each carefully composed with subtle ins and outs to break down the bulky proportions of the original structure", explain the architects. To make the structure even more dynamic, the green-tinted glass in each volume has a slightly different hue. The main entrance is welcoming, with two floating canopies supported by a forest of bronze poles.

ROSSANA HU

ARANYA ART CENTER
QINHUANGDAO, CHINA, 2019

Aranya is a seaside resort community that pays special attention to the spiritual nature of everyday life, emphasising a "oneness with the environment", as described by the architects. Built of various textured concretes which break up the massive volume, the Art Center was inspired by the seasonal qualities of the ocean – calm in the summer and frozen in the winter. At its heart, an internal courtyard planned as a communal space for the residents can be used in numerous ways. The spiral interior arrangement leads from a café through an outdoor amphitheatre through gallery spaces, up to the rooftop, which offers panoramic vistas.

# LOUISA HUTTON

Following her studies at the University of Bristol and the Architectural Association in London, Louisa Hutton (b. 1957) worked for four years with Alison and Peter Smithson. In 1989 she and her husband, Matthias Sauerbruch, co-founded their own practice. The studio was initially based in London, where they both taught at the time. Four years later, on account of their having won a substantial commission in the form of a high-rise for the GSW Headquarters, they relocated to Berlin.

While designing numerous buildings in various European cities – such as Paris, Stockholm, Milan, Mestre-Venice, Helsinki, Geneva, Berlin, London, Frankfurt, Munich and Hamburg – the practice has explored various typologies and scales. The main focus throughout, however, has been the pursuit of

sustainable solutions in the post-industrial city. Over the years the practice has developed a close working relationship with a wide team of consultants and collaborators, so that they can employ technical and innovational thinking to deliver architecture that is just as sustainable as it is practical and aesthetically pleasing.

Speaking about her interest in architecture, Hutton recalls that her father "was an architect manqué, an engineer who had an excellent eye and who loved to design things and get them built. From him I probably inherited my sense of proportion as well as a love of detail". Sauerbruch Hutton find it crucial to envision buildings that are both welcoming and accessible, holding that they should offer an emotional bond to both passers-by and their users - connecting even through their smallest details, like thoughtful and nice-to-touch door handles.

Many of the studio's projects are public buildings and cultural spaces of various kinds, including the Brandhorst Museum in Munich and the M9 Museum Quarter in Venice that transforms an entire district, incorporating a contemporary architectural language into an historical context. Whether interwoven with the existing environment or freestanding in focal areas, the practice's realizations always respond to their surroundings. Their buildings often take the form of curious and seemingly complex shapes, yet have the rare qualities of being noticeable and surprising without "shouting" or dominating the landscape. It is the combination of the opportunities offered by the site taken together with the programme that usually form the genesis of the projects.

Quite early on Sauerbruch and Hutton gained particular recognition for their exceptional use of colour in architecture, treating it as an integral part of space-making - they even refer to it as a building material, just like concrete or brick. Colour and material concepts are explored iteratively through hand sketches, computer drawings and many physical models. All decisions are taken by eye.

Parallel to her architectural practice, Hutton taught at the Architectural Association and for five years was a visiting professor at the Harvard Graduate School of Design. In 2014 she was elected a Royal Academician of the Royal Academy of Arts in London.

Most recently the office has turned into an extended partnership with 19 partners and nine associates, thereby putting into legal form what it has been practicing for decades: an open, dialogigal process.

## IMMANUEL CHURCH AND PARISH CENTRE
## COLOGNE, GERMANY, 2013

This cluster of buildings
designed for the Protestant
Immanuel parish includes
a small chapel for private
prayer, a bell tower, and the
church. Grouped around a
raised lawn encircled by tall
trees, the collection of volumes is
smoothly immersed into the site.
The clear geometries of the three
structures are enhanced by their
simple, diagonally laid timber
cladding. By contrast, the interior
spaces of the church, made of a
system of prefabricated timber
frames, are left unclad. There
are two sources of light: behind
the altar top-light washes down
over a filtering screen, while
high above the gallery opposite
a tracery of leaves animates
a luminous, matte glass panel.

## M9 MUSEUM DISTRICT
## VENICE, ITALY, 2018

Mestre, that historically formed the mainland gateway to Venice, has recently gained a small museum quarter. Conceived as an agent of renewal to address the disparity of cultural wealth between the two cities, the proposal reinstates small-scale urban tissue. A new pedestrian route connects through the courtyard of a renovated former convent to a small piazza and two new buildings for M9, the museum of the cultural inheritance of the 20th century. While the smaller of these houses shops and the museum's offices, the larger holds the foyer, bookshop, auditorium, and a café on the ground floor. A dramatic staircase leads to the permanent exhibition on two floors and a large, daylit space for temporary displays above.

## TORGBYGGET
## OSLO, NORWAY, 2018

Torgbygget (or "The Building on the Square")
is located along the banks of the Akerselva
river in a former industrial district of Oslo,
which is nowadays undergoing urban
revitalisation. Jarmund refurbished an
original building by creating new façades
and interior finishes, and by improving
communication with the metro station
entrance. The new dynamic outer shell,
with rhythmically alternating windows,
echoes the multi-purpose character of
the complex, which consists of offices,
commercial spaces, and a health clinic.
The most interesting façade faces the
river to the west, with a series of extruded
boxes, marked with orange glass and
partly cantilevered over the water.

# AMANDA LEVETE

Welsh-born Amanda Levete CBE (b. 1955) is the RIBA Stirling Prize-winning architect and founder and principle of AL_A (run together with directors Ho-Yin Ng, Alice Dietsch, and Maximiliano Arrocet). Since 2009 the London-based architectural studio has been taking on ambitious challenges, designing bold architecture and developing urban projects. In recent years Levete has received well-deserved international recognition and numerous awards, in large part due to her extremely successful museum projects in London and Lisbon. In 2018 the architect was awarded the Jane Drew Prize by the Architects' Journal, which is known as the most prestigious architecture award for women.

Levete graduated from the Architectural Association. After her studies she worked as an architect at the Richard Rogers Partnership. In 1989 Levete joined Jan Kaplický, her husband at the time, in Future Systems, a design practice famous for bold experiments with the shapes of buildings. Together they created one of the icons of "blob architecture" (favouring wavy buildings devoid of edges or symmetry and made with the help of CAD software) – the visually stunning Birmingham's branch of Selfridges Department Store. This large, curvaceous structure covered with a dense pattern of discs earned the duo the RIBA Award for Architecture in 2004.

After establishing her own firm in 2009, Levete has continued to play with organic shapes. Her concepts are far from obvious, and her imaginative visions, translated into spectacular shapes, always add a truly unique element to the existing landscape. These realizations express the power of today's technology and architectural possibilities. An essential aspect of her creative process is the consideration of the relationship between spaces inside the buildings and the way they are connected with the outside environment. "Most fundamentally, architecture is the enclosure of space, the distinction between what is inside and outside," she suggests. "The threshold is the moment at which that changes; the edge of what is building and what is something else." Thresholds, as she writes in her feature for CNN style, are metaphors for the creation of new beginnings, connectivity, and transitions. And the architect's goal is to "create narratives within architecture". Another fascinating aspect of Levete's realizations is that the urban context – including from a historical viewpoint – defines the final design. Her breath-taking structures, often large-scale and complex, neither dominate the landscape, nor are they inaccessible. On the contrary, as much as her architecture inscribes itself on its surroundings, it is also inviting for people. The issue seems crucial for consistent urban planning and delivering buildings that will work for both their potential users and the current fabric. The architect highlights the fact that the issue of invitingness is even more important in the layouts of public architecture, which tend to be grandiose and overwhelming: "Most of the time, we cross thresholds unconsciously. Crossing the road and into the front door of our home is unremarkable, but the decision to cross the threshold and enter into an unfamiliar, institutional building is not always so instinctive," she suggests. Levete's solutions delight with forms and enhance people's experience of architecture.

"The message I want to project is that there is no limit to achievement in our discipline for anyone."

Your buildings are often a mélange of old and new, whether they are located in a historical district, like MAAT in Lisbon, or juxtaposed with old urban fabric, like your addition to the V&A Museum in London. Why is this dialogue between the history and modern elements so interesting for you?

For me, the dialogue between history and modernity is interesting when it highlights unexpected connections. Sometimes the decision to create a dialogue is very conscious and sometimes it's only when you start to put things side by side that you can see a resonance.

In projects like the V&A, we use modernity as a lens to give people a new reading of history: new experiences and new forms of revelation. Elements of modernity are intended to help tell untold stories, with contemporary interventions that are a reinterpretation of the spirit and the history of a place.

The resistance of history can be the fuel of the design process. We've often done our best work when we've come up against what might be seen as the resistance of history and we've responded by developing bolder ideas because that resistance has forced us to think harder.

Heritage is the only thing in life you can't design and it's our responsibility to preserve it. But it's also our responsibility to look to the future, and to do that we must also breathe new life and renewed purpose into our historic places.

**While stressing the fact that the era of building as icon is now over, you wish for your buildings not to shout but to push the boundaries of what's possible. This sounds particularly important when we think of spaces that bring people together. What is the recipe for a perfect public space?**

Yes, absolutely – public spaces are more crucial than ever before. In a world of huge economic and political uncertainty, people want places where they can come together and connect with each other. We think that with the internet and social media we're all more connected than ever before, but we're not – in fact, we're becoming more and more isolated from each other.

Public spaces create natural opportunities to connect people from different cultures and from different walks of life.

The perfect public space for me is free, open, unprogrammed, and allows appropriation by the public of the ground plane.

In Lisbon, the roof of MAAT was designed to be a new public square in the city, one that people can pass through or just be in; a place that visitors can use in whatever way they want. It's become a place for people to bring their kids, jog, or even cycle across it, and a place to watch the sunset. It's given people a new perspective on Lisbon as they look back towards the old city or out across the Tagus.

The V&A courtyard creates an exceptional place for London – an outdoor room of the Museum, a destination in its own right and a place for installations and events. But above all, it is a place for appropriation by the public, by day and by night.

**You identify three aspects that you find essential in architecture: place making, craftsmanship, and innovation. Which elements of the creative process are crucial to allow them to all come together?**

I would suggest that it's a fourth aspect – collaboration – that is the single most crucial element.

At AL_A, we're now four directors from three continents and we share a strong belief in the value of collaboration – collaboration not just between ourselves and the AL_A team but collaboration with clients and engineers and makers and contractors and people from other disciplines. Collaboration doesn't necessarily mean sharing views but it does mean sharing a common sense of purpose. It's collaboration, along with a desire to be both technically and conceptually inventive, which can make our buildings special.

Research also underpins everything we do. We love to explore the history, context, circumstance, sustainability, and conceptual potential of each project and to research technical possibilities, materials, structures, and techniques. We have a longstanding interest in and respect for craftsmanship. We seek out opportunities for exploiting the expertise of those singularly dedicated to materials and techniques. Working with craftspeople from concept to completion brings richness and depth to our designs, sometimes challenging them to translate their knowledge of, say, aeronautical engineering or boatbuilding materials, and applying it to architecture for the very first time.

**In 2018 you received the Jane Drew Prize. In your speech on this occasion you said that "there's never been a better time to be a woman than now". Do you think that the situation of women in architecture has changed profoundly over last decade?**

My experience of being a woman in architecture today is a positive one. I've been in practice now for over thirty years and I've seen huge changes for the better during that time.

Personally, I've not encountered any barriers to practice and the women starting their careers at AL_A will never be prevented from fulfilling their potential. The message I want to project is that there is no limit to achievement in our discipline for anyone.

However, I know that women often take enormous personal risks in order to pursue careers, particularly in risk-averse architecture firms who work for risk-averse clients. There are so many stories of women architects postponing having a family in order to move up the corporate ladder, only to find their path blocked. There is still work to be done on this, as well as supporting both women and men equally in maternity and paternity benefits.

**You are one of the strong voices today suggesting that architects should be more entrepreneurial and generate their own projects, including the funding, to be self-sufficient. What are, in your opinion, some of the greatest challenges for architects today?**

Architects are becoming more and more marginalised. We're obliged to drive down fees to unfair levels in order to win work. And the increasing demands made of us in competitions is out of hand. If this is hard for us as an established office, it must be much harder for those just starting out.

One response to all this, in a way that is positive for our discipline, is to be more entrepreneurial – be more self-sufficient, generate our own projects, identify unmet needs, find the site, write the brief, put together the funding... If we do this, we can start to move outside of a system that is eroding respect.

It's also time to reclaim and celebrate risk in architecture as a positive force. I think we can do this by taking on less predictable risks, working in less predictable ways, finding different ways to collaborate, and exploring fresh ideas in the field.

In fact, I think it's the architect's responsibility to be radical, to shake things up a bit, and to have the courage to take and manage risks. For me risk is exciting because it's about progress and exploration.

We also need to find more imaginative ways to re-purpose and re-imagine what we have. It's an expression of what I call the "new sobriety", an attitude that prioritises making the right decisions and using resources responsibly over form-making. Sometimes, the most radical thing is not to build.

**In one of your interviews you compare architecture and cinema, can you explain more about the parallels you see in both mediums?**

Both disciplines are immensely and inescapably collaborative. Both need a cast of hundreds, if not thousands, to generate and then turn an idea into a reality through a huge collective endeavour.

Architects and filmmakers require a huge range of specialists at the top of their game to submit to the ideal of the finished project. A feature film and a building operate on similar timescales, and similar budgets, and trace a similar journey.

Film can teach us a lot about how people experience cities. Vittoria De Sica's Bicycle Thieves made me first think about the importance of public space – it's left an impression that has stayed with me until today. The drama, the pathos, the friendships, the sense of community and solidarity, they are all played out in the bleak but powerful post-war landscape of Rome.

It's an essential piece of work for any architect – I still think it's one of the most evocative and best explorations in any field of the potency of public space in our cities.

MAAT (MUSEUM OF ART, ARCHITECTURE AND TECHNOLOGY)
LISBON, PORTUGAL, 2016

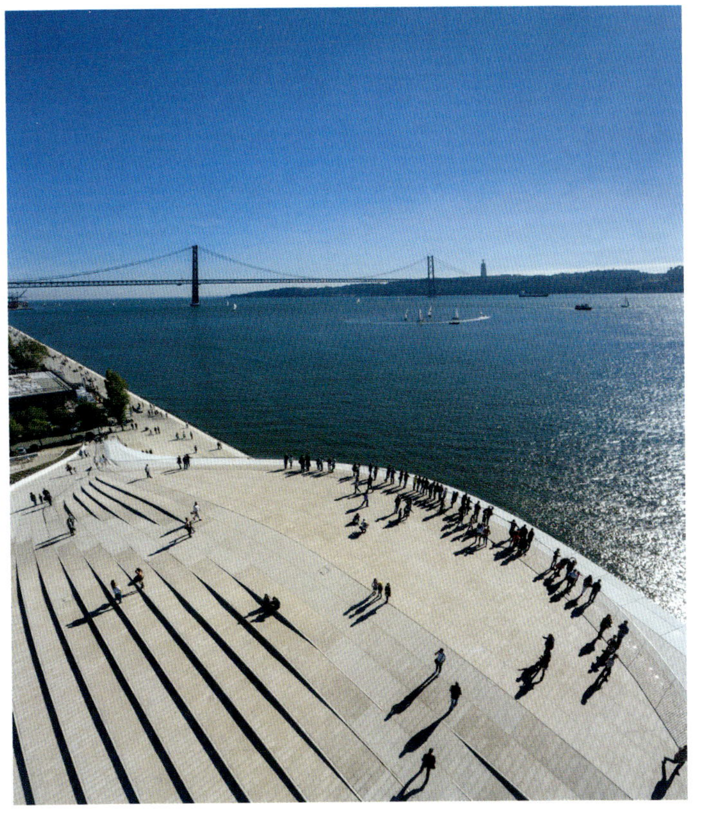

Stretching along the banks of the Tagus River in the cultural district Belém at the historical heart of Lisbon, MAAT's shape is inspired by the rippling of the water. This new venue takes the form of a low (for a smooth visual connection with the river) curved dome topped with an undulating roof covered in 15,000 white, three-dimensional ceramic tiles, creating a complex 'skin'. This stunning texture interacts with light and changes colour depending on the time of day. Visitors experience the building from various perspectives – on a grand rooftop terrace, from the waterside promenade, or in the galleries located below ground level.

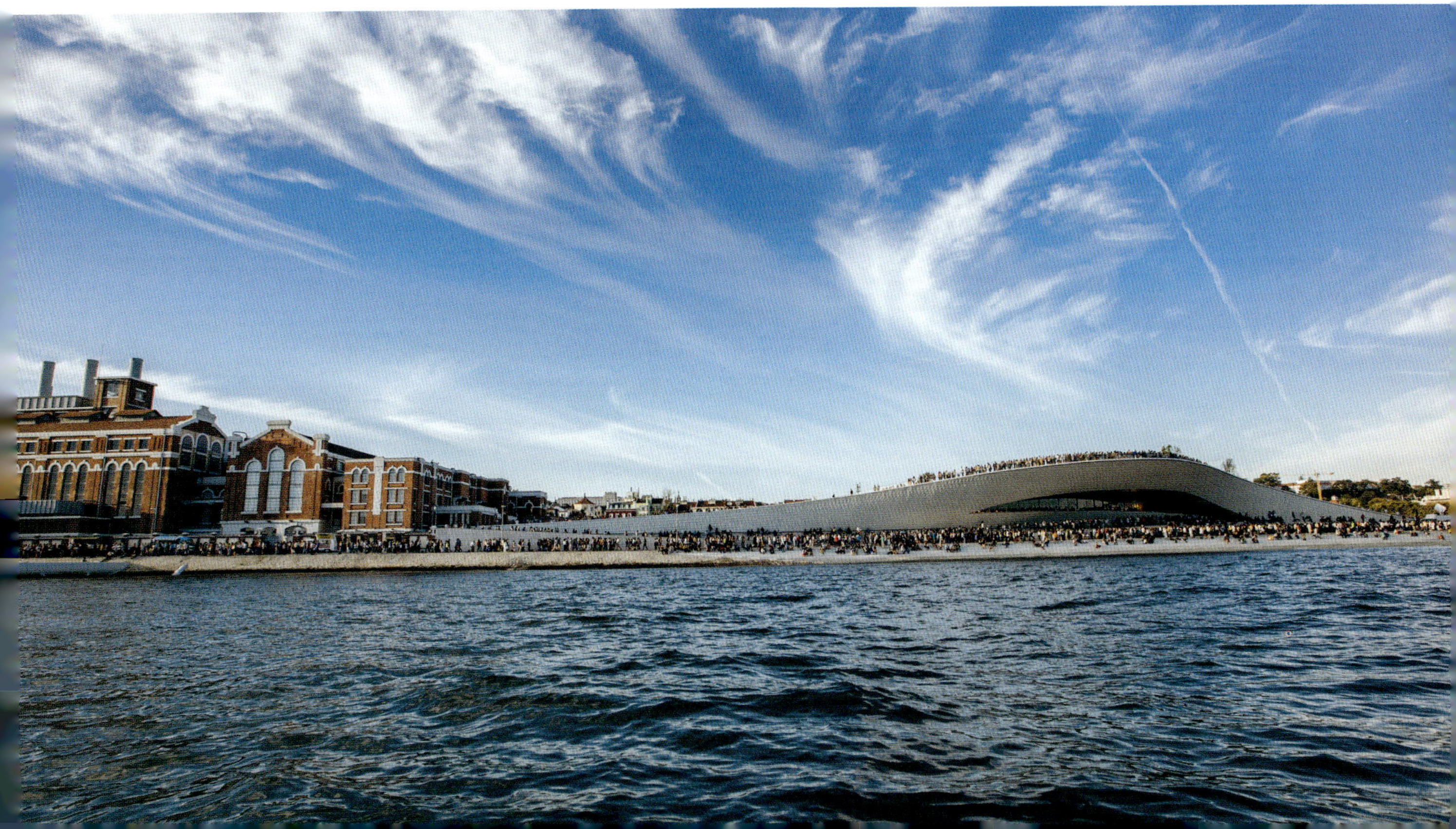

CENTRAL EMBASSY
BANGKOK, THAILAND, 2017

Located on the site of the former gardens of the
British Embassy along Ploenchit Road, the Central
Embassy complex combines the roles of luxury retail,
entertainment, and hotel complex. This mix of uses
is embraced within an elegant and highly original
silhouette. The complex's shape is cohesive, particularly
through the outer organic shell that envelops its two
parts – a vertical 27-storey hotel tower and a horizontal
7-storey shopping mall. Bound through this notion of a
continual looped form creating the visual fluidity, the
shell is covered with a system of aluminium shingles,
each with two surfaces, "to reflect both the chaos of the
city and the sky itself", as the studio states.

VICTORIA & ALBERT MUSEUM EXHIBITION ROAD QUARTER
LONDON, UK, 2017

This commission included creating a new gallery for the museum's headline exhibitions (the result – one of the largest and most flexible spaces in the UK, 18 metres below ground), a public courtyard (never previously seen by the public with historical façades), and, last but not least, a new entrance leading through the former boilerhouse yard. The Sackler Courtyard is covered by 11,000 handmade porcelain tiles drawn from the V&A's ceramics collection and houses a café meandering between historical parts. Typically for Levete's realizations, this one, too, aims at breaking down the separation between inside and outside, making the trespass between the street and the museum building accessible and welcoming.

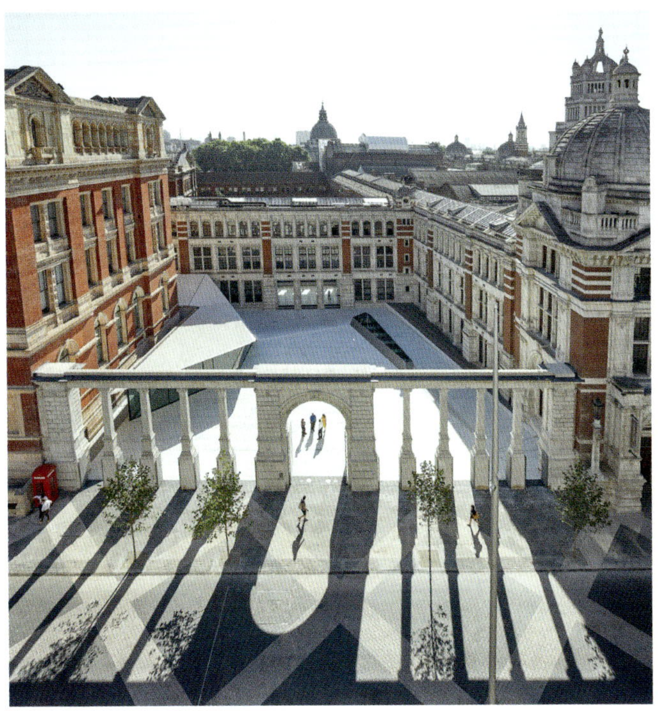

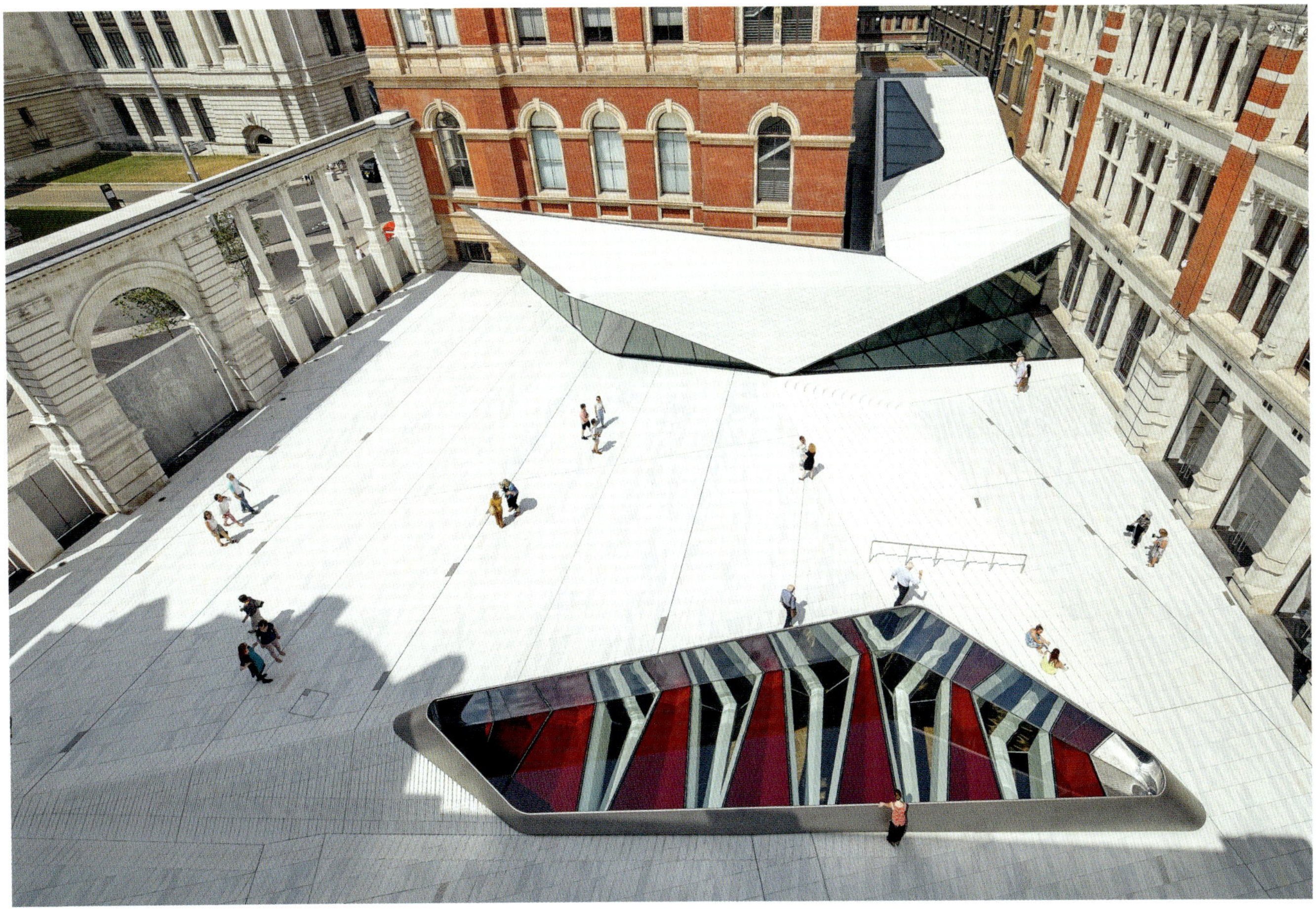

# INÊS LOBO

Inês Lobo (b. 1966) never considered any other profession since childhood but becoming an architect. She studied architecture at the Escola Superior da Belas Artes in Lisbon. Lobo started her professional career in 1989. Since then she has also been a teacher of architectural design. In 2002, she established her own Lisbon-based studio, which focuses on a wide range of projects, from education to housing to cultural institutions. The practice's approach is based on a careful understanding of contexts and on thê conviction that architecture directly influences the quality of life. "We believe architecture should provide a unique experience of use, of each space or a sequence of them. The light, materials, colour or the furniture are coordinated as part of a whole, converging to create a coherent image and that provides qualified experiences", reads her studio's statement. Another important field of the practice's expertise is urban design, with the transformative power to improve the fabric of cities, which is approached as a holistic process. Lobo often lectures in Portugal and internationally, and also curates exhibitions of architecture. Creating courses and educating architecture students remain an important part of her work.

Lobo's portfolio is dominated by large-scale projects for public spaces, within which her numerous school buildings illustrate how architecture should be adapted to today's needs. This is particularly visible in projects involving the reconversions of existing buildings. Reutilising constructions and improving them leads to innovative solutions that suit architecture's new roles. Whether it is an old industrial space, or a building constructed half a century ago, Lobo's thoughtful interventions preserve the original character and skilfully redefine the original structures with a contemporary language. The new creations are somehow inspired by their predecessors and at the same time forward-thinking. Independently of the scale, the architect's realizations – spacious, well-lit, geometric, and striking a balance between solid and translucent – escape simple definitions. Lobo experiments with form and materials offering architecture that is designed to be experienced. A common thread of all her projects is the thoughtful and detailed way the building are incorporated into their context, whether a natural site or urban fabric.

In a past interview, Lobo took up the subject of the status of architects today, pointing at the dangers of the separation of knowledge. According to Lobo, the profession should be reinvented to re-establish the role of architects and architecture in our life. Parallel to designing, architects should specialise in various areas. The ability to draw knowledge from numerous disciplines and to synthesise this as part of the design process seems crucial. Lobo additionally organises the educational programmes at the Universidade Autonóma de Lisboa (UAL), and invites teachers with various backgrounds. "It has always been Autónoma's major goal to say that an architecture course cannot be only done by architects", she emphasises, adding that "we always wanted for other subject areas to have a certain weight".

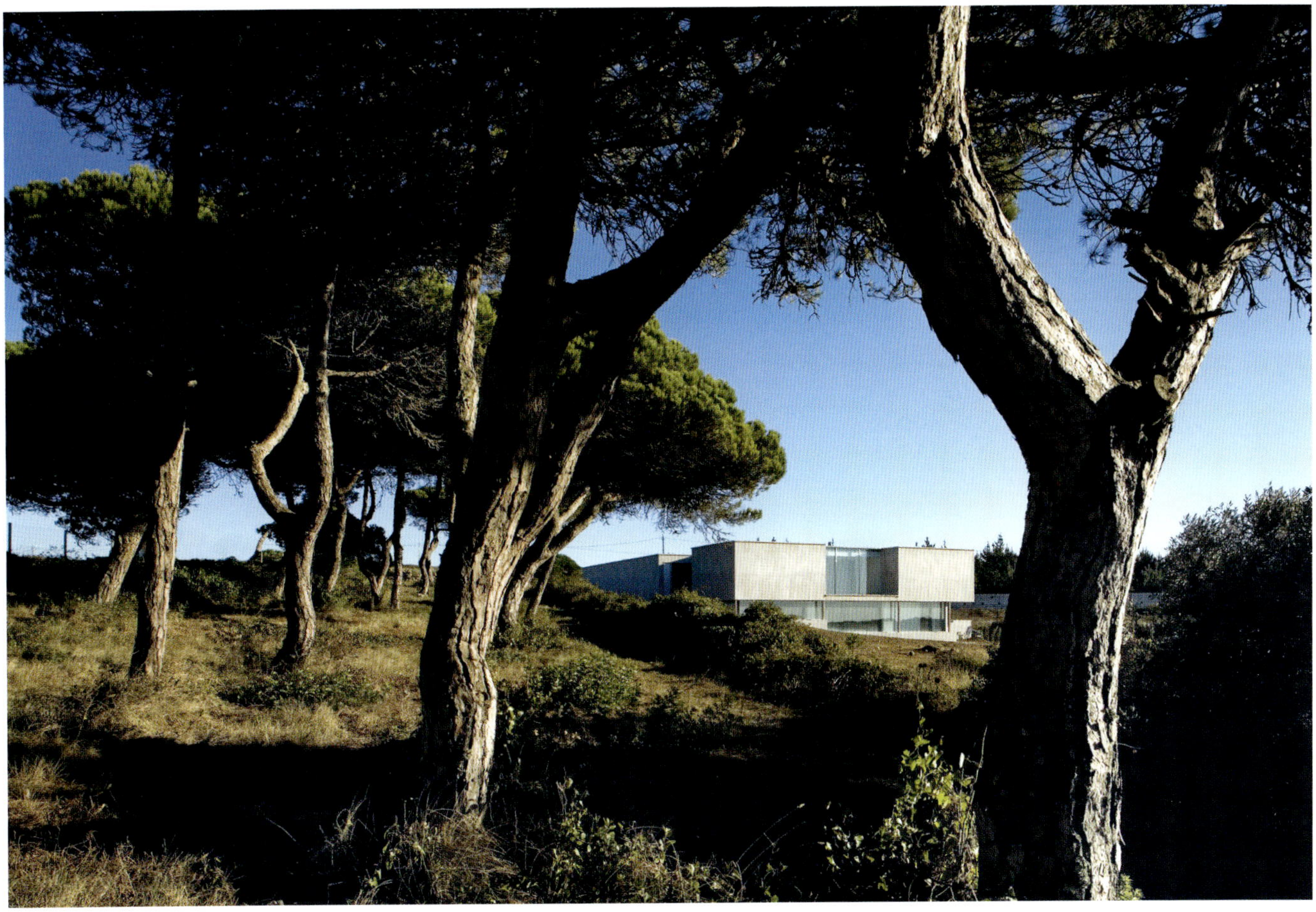

HOUSE IN MAGOITO, AZENHAS DO MAR
SÃO JOÃO DAS LAMPAS, SINTRA, PORTUGAL, 2009

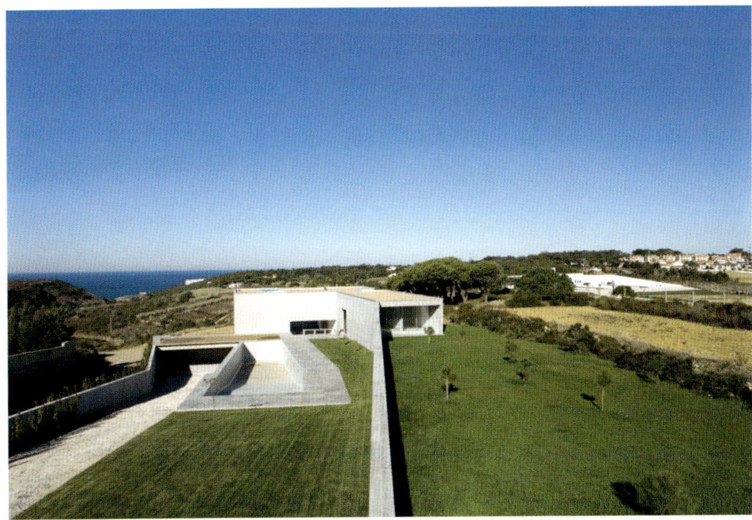

The geometrical volume of this villa is set among the beautiful scenery of the Sintra-Cascais Natural Park. Expanding along the plot, the building responds to the topography of the slope. The entrance is marked by two long walls, which smoothly become parts of the walls of the building itself. The solid structure is broken up by numerous glazed surfaces, in particular on the façade facing the sea. The inside-outside relation was crucial for the architect, who envisioned courtyards unexposed to the wind. Together with the garden, they are intended to act as open air living rooms. The courtyard facing south gathers around the main living area.

## ART AND ARCHITECTURE FACULTY
### ÉVORA, PORTUGAL, 2010

Lobo's reconversions demonstrate a great sense of balancing historical and contemporary forms. Always maintaining a visually stimulating dialogue between them, the architect draws the best from the original buildings and adds purely modern structures that enhance them. The Art and Architecture Faculty is not different. Realised in collaboration with Ventura Trindade Arquitectos, it is based in a former Milling Society building that later became a pasta factory. The large group of buildings was transformed into spacious and comfortable facilities with a new addition at the heart of it. The significantly large elongated volume is clearly marked by its metallic outer shell and links various parts of the complex.

## PUBLIC LIBRARY AND ARCHIVE LUÍS DA SILVA RIBEIRO
## ANGRA DO HEROÍSMO, AZORES, PORTUGAL, 2016

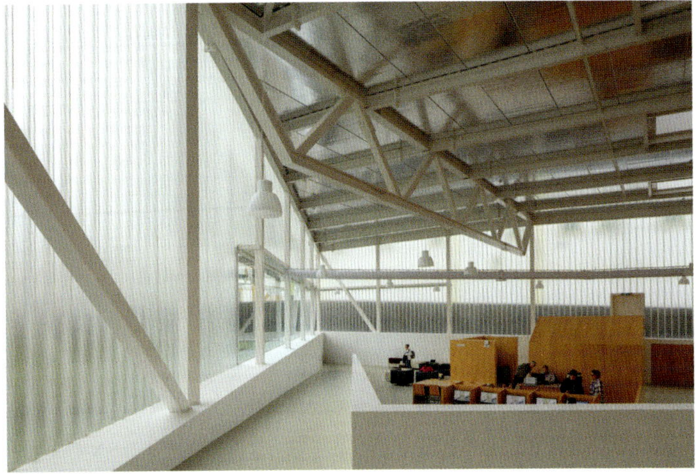

This light, horizontal structure is made of two superimposed bodies. Located in an annex of a palazzo in the heart of an Azorean city and incorporated into the historical urban fabric, it creates a public space both inside and outside. Although the modern forms starkly stand out from the surrounding architecture, they are well suited to the context. This relation is developed through the diverse heights of the extensive volumes as well as the building's bright and largely translucent walls. The inviting and well-lit interiors are designed in a uniform manner, as a fluent space with a continuous floor. The architects used distinctive furniture made of materials that contrast with those used in the structure to define the functional roles of spaces.

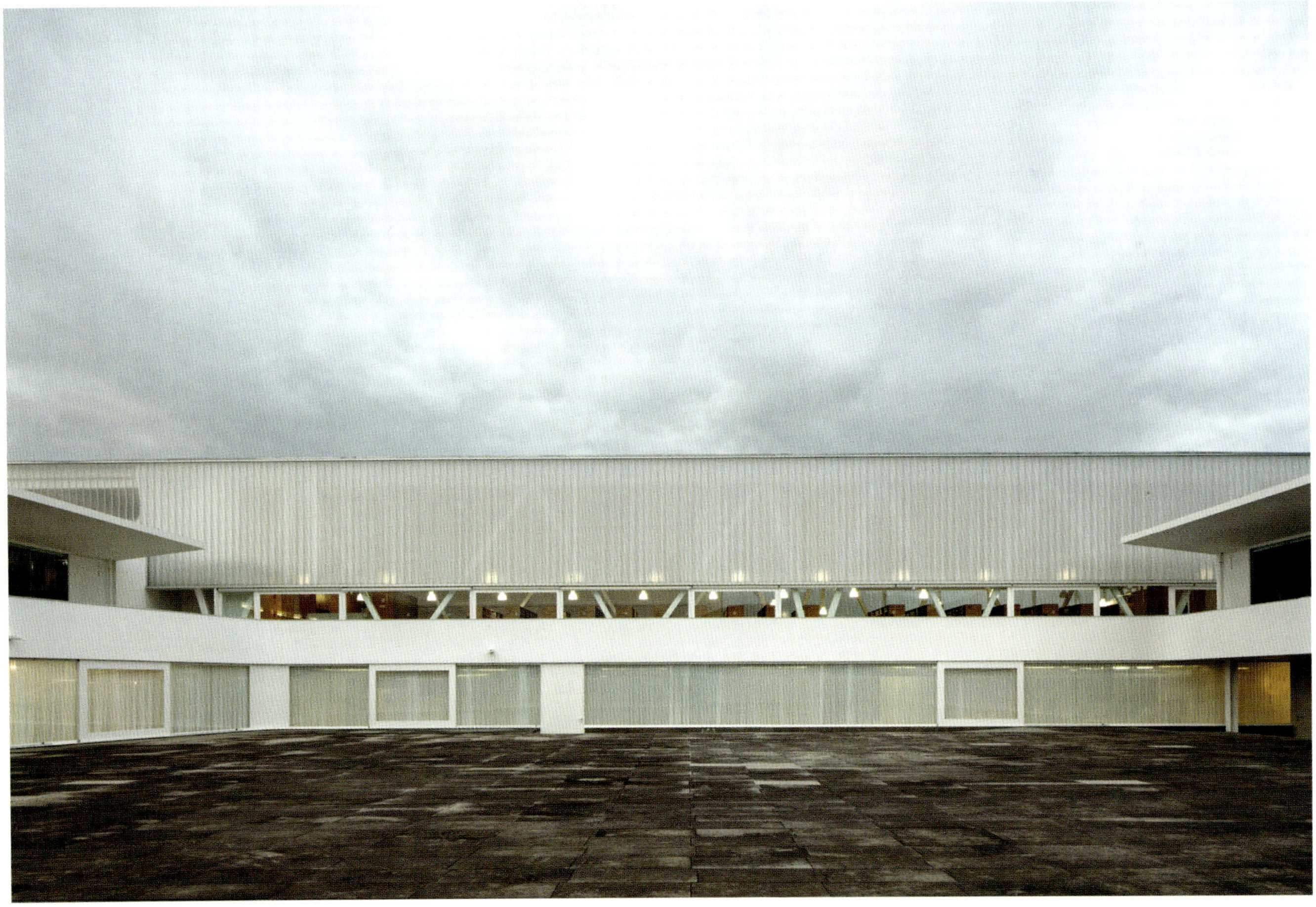

# ELLEN VAN LOON

In 1991 Ellen van Loon (b. 1963) graduated from Delft University of Technology and decided to move to Berlin in order to gain professional experience and space for experimentation. At the time, after the Wall had come down, the city was a dream location for architects in Europe. After working on smaller projects, she joined Foster + Partners and spent six years on the Reichstag renovation. Upon her return to the Netherlands, van Loon joined OMA (the Office for Metropolitan Architecture), the world-renowned practice focusing on both architecture and

urbanism, back in 1998, to become one of the partners four years later. Drawn by the conceptual approach of the studio's founder, Rem Koolhaas, which she also shared, van Loon has worked on numerous spectacular projects starting with the headquarters of Universal Studios in Los Angeles. "This was a moment when OMA was gaining a lot of momentum; we got many commissions for new projects and international work," she recalls. "It was a perfect moment to start." The first building van Loon realised on her own with OMA, Casa da Música in Porto in 2005, was a great success and visual masterpiece that brought her a lot of attention.

Her work has been continually praised for its mélange of sophisticated design and precision in execution. The architect plays with the senses of the users, trying to please but also surprise them. Her complex structures, often reflecting the mixed-use character of her buildings, is the thread running through all of her realizations, which are mainly public buildings, museums, and theatres. "I like complexity," she explains. "Not as a main goal, but I like complex interactions between programme parts, or certain elements in a design. It's like solving a puzzle, but also creating new relationships". An important aspect of her creative process is teamwork, especially because she works on four to five projects at a time. Her conversations about projects typically begin with a couple of people, growing larger together with the development. Van Loon likes managing the process when all issues and viewpoints come together to result in the best possible solution. The architect also places much importance on the materials, which she carefully selects. Enhancing her vision and adjusted to her far-from-obvious structural concepts, the materials are often juxtaposed in intriguing contrasts.

How people will use the spaces she authors and whether they will like them are essential issues for the architect. In one interview, she humorously quipped that the reason she includes a café in every building she designs is because it can be a good place to sit and observe people's first reactions, which are critical for van Loon. It took more than a decade for her to design probably her most celebrated and discussed project to date – the BLOX / DAC in Copenhagen. The building perfectly demonstrates van Loon's approach to architecture – turning challenging sites into assets, using formal complexity to solve problems in an innovative way, envisioning original structures, planning buildings to be sustainable, and designing dynamic and thus interesting environments.

## DE ROTTERDAM
## ROTTERDAM,
## THE NETHERLANDS, 2013

Three 150-metre-high towers, envisioned as a vertical city, dominate over the old harbour of the Wilhelminapier. Growing from a plinth-like base that communicates various functions, the buildings are interconnected and stacked irregularly. The massive, fractionated volume offers different views from different perspectives. Forming a significant part of the redevelopment of the district, the design offers a vibrant urban complex of apartments, offices, and a hotel, as well as a mix of conference, commercial, and leisure spaces. Named after a ship departing from the pier with passengers emigrating to the U.S. in the past, it is a project van Loon developed together with Rem Koolhaas and Reinier de Graaf.

pages 146-148
BLOX / DAC (DANISH ARCHITECTURE CENTRE)
GEN, DENMARK, 2017

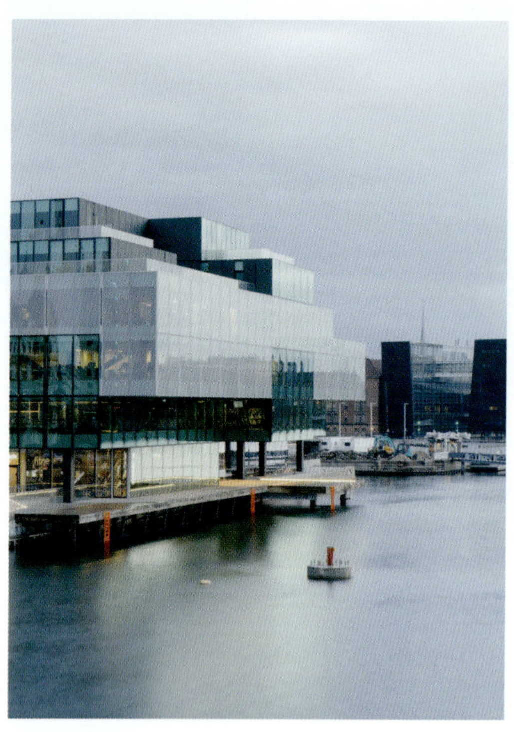

Located on a challenging site, with one of Copenhagen's ring roads passing right through it (!), the geometric BLOX structure activates the area between the parliament district and the inner harbour. Its numerous box-like volumes, each quite different, are stacked in a dynamic arrangement. The complexity of this innovative hub reflects its varied use. It is the home of the Danish Architecture Centre (DAC), the exhibition spaces and offices of which are placed in the heart of the building, and also houses co-working spaces, a café and a restaurant, a bookstore, a fitness centre, over twenty apartments, and an underground public carpark. The former playground incorporated into the plan transforms into an open-air cinema in the evenings.

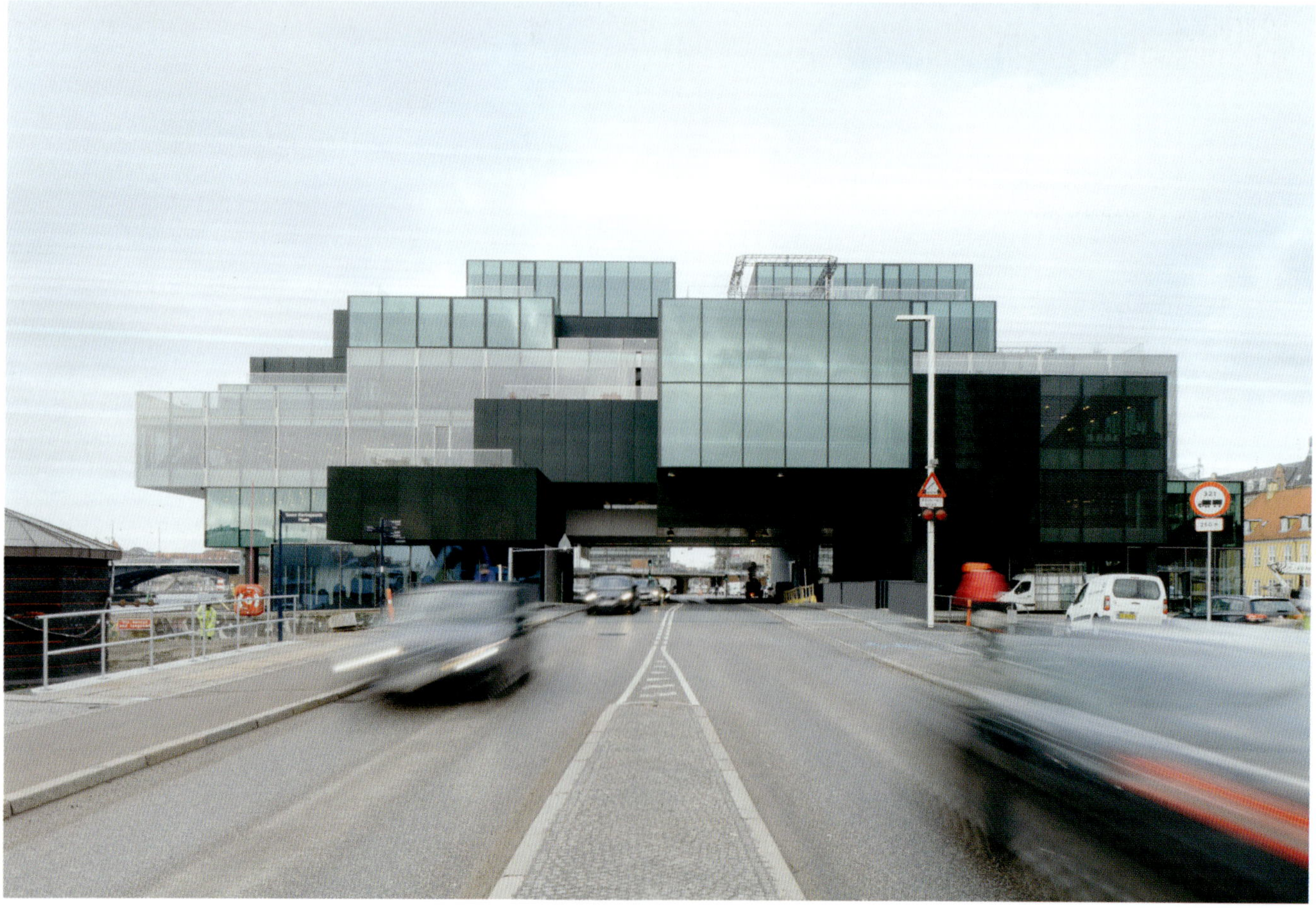

AXEL SPRINGER CAMPUS
BERLIN, GERMANY, 2019

The new building symbolising
the media giant's transition from
print to digital media, is located
in front of the company's previous
headquarters. Its façades are
torn by a visually spectacular
diagonal atrium. The contrast
between the dynamic multifaceted
shape and its otherwise regular
structure is enhanced by the use
of black and white. The interior
design was developed around a
series of terraced floors, creating
a central common space for
sharing ideas. Each floor, though,
also has traditional office spaces.
Visitors can access the lobby on
the ground floor, a meeting bridge
that functions as a platform for
viewing the daily operations, and
a roof-top bar.

# DORTE MANDRUP

Interestingly, Danish architect Dorte Mandrup (b. 1961) studied sculpture and ceramics, before eventually graduating from the Aarhus School of Architecture following a family tradition (her grandfather and great-grandfather were both architects). Mandrup's first work was with Henning Larsen Architects, and then between 1995 and 1999 she co-founded a firm with Niels Fuglsang. 1999 marked the beginning of a new professional era for Mandrup with a Copenhagen-based studio. Today, her international team who she cherishes numbers 70 and Mandrup remains the Creative Director, responsible for design in all projects.

"Our forte is designing for complex and challenging sites – and doing so with an insightfulness that addresses environmental and societal issues", explains Mandrup. One of the strong points of her practice is embracing the complexity of mix-use projects to accommodate various specific needs in one building. Transformations are another type of challenge the architect enjoys taking on; these require extensive research and deep analysis of existing structures to discover the potential. The numerous cultural and landmark or educational and workspace projects in her portfolio are characterized by her innovative approaches to form and material driven by experimental curiosity. Her skilful play with shapes and effortless poetry of forms are based on a deep understanding of each site, which is striking particularly in projects realised in landscape contexts demonstrating a purely Nordic attitude to nature with an observant, regardful, and harmonic approach. When the architect builds in urban environment, the design process is executed in an equally considerable way, only influenced by factors specific for a cityscape. Contextual analyses, as well as explorative prototyping, and extensive research on materials are at the core of Mandrup's work on new concepts. She explains that she tends to choose her projects and clients carefully because "only if clients and partners alike share the highest level of architectural ambition, are we successful in creating extraordinary architecture. Only when we share courage and patience to explore and experiment". Aesthetically original, complex, and reflective, Mandrup's realizations are a new fascinating chapter in Scandinavian architectural heritage with a strong emphasis on sustainability. Reinventing traditions and a new take on both materials and colours or shapes make the architect's ideas even more fascinating. While she has developed an expressive architectural language, all of her buildings are inviting and offer new sensual experiences. Remarkable features be it within interiors or outer textures, or the solutions for connecting inside and outside, are far from obvious and thus add a pinch of surprise to refresh our traditional way of looking at architecture.

Mandrup is famous for taking part in public debates, whether on the role of architecture today, sustainability, or gender equality, with her already famous statement "I am not a female architect. I am an architect". In addition to developing her practice she serves as Vice Chairman of the Louisiana Museum of Modern Art, is a member of the Historic Buildings Council in Denmark, and Adjunct Professor at The Royal Danish Academy of Fine Arts. The architect is herself the winner of many prestigious international architectural awards.

"I always look for
something that can
exist in a parallel way,
or make a supplement
to the place so that you
think that it should have
always been there and
it actually enhances the
area."

You founded your Copenhagen-based studio in 1999.
You remain responsible for design in all projects. What
does your creative process, the dialogue between you
and your team of 70, look like to make everything fall
into place while working on a new project?

It depends very much on the point of the process we're
in. I have a CEO taking care of all administrative work
and we have a business developer taking care of
acquisitions. I solely work on design and regularly take
part in different design meetings for various projects. The
way we work is very much teamwork. Everybody on the
team attends meetings at the beginning of the process
but then of course it depends on the directions we take.
We spend quite a lot of time on collecting data – history,
the site information, or aspects we like to look into, like
the economic profile of the district. Then we analyse
everything and try to find a departure point for the design.
When we do competitions, at least half of the time is
spent working on analyses but also on trying to look into
different concepts. We tend to keep away from shape for
a long time, just not to fall in love with any one idea. Then
we test a lot of different materials and systems. Partly we
work very analytically and partly experimentally and these
two come together. To us it's important that we can keep
a kind of personal attitude toward what's coming up in
the office.

Is your background in ceramics and sculpture
responsible for how sculptural your buildings become?

I guess so. It is a big interest of mine to work with
buildings as sculptural possibility. Together with materials
possibilities, this is where I like to work. To make a good
piece of architecture is to think about both aesthetical
and practical aspects.

What are your aesthetically adventurous structures
inspired by?

Mainly I get inspired by working on the site. Depending on
whether you work in an urban context or in a landscape
context, there is always 'something' there that can be
enhanced or explored. Either you work with contrast or
something that matches the context. Exposing 'what's there'
is very important to me.

Your architecture proves that you've mastered it,
especially when your buildings are surrounded by
stunning landscapes. How do you work out the context
and why are contextual considerations so important in
Scandinavian architecture?

I think partly due to the fact that we, Scandinavian
architects, are used to having a discussion about
contextual relationships, you always consider and discuss
various relations between buildings and the surroundings,
and how they work together. I think in Denmark (or in
Scandinavia) t it is very natural to have this discussion
and to think about this relationship. We're not brought
up to create some flashy objects. Part of the way the
assignments are given at school also taught us to
consider the context.

In our practice, it is a mixture of a lot of things depending
on where we build. When we work with stunning
landscapes, placing a building is about not being too
humble but also having respect for where you are: a kind
of balance between supplementing the landscape and
overtaking the place. I always look for something that can

exist in a parallel way, or make a supplement to the place so that you think that it should have always been there and it actually enhances the area. Those are the criteria of success when you work with a landscape. It is much more complicated in an urban context. Sometimes you need to explain your concept more and it is also not as picturesque as a rural landscape. Sometimes there should be more to the story and then you need to get to know the place better to be able to do that.

**Analogue models are essential in your practice, just like computer programmes are for more geometrically advanced ideas. Shaping means not only coming up with a proper figure to connect a building with a place but also selecting materials. How do you research your materials?**

My mother was a textile designer and I think textiles are very interesting, but it was always interesting for me to work with different materials. Especially with those that are not too expensive – how do you get something that has texture and quality without having a great budget. We test different materialities. Sometimes it is location connected, sometimes we wish to have something anonymous. It is always nice to try to push the notion of something. It's like trying to find a character through the material as well. When we did the Wadden Sea Centre, everyone was saying, so you used thatch and wood, but it was not about bringing back old traditions or original construction. It is always much more about looking at the materiality as an almost abstract thing.

**As you often stress, ideally, architecture should make spaces for better living and support the way people use buildings, or even be powerful enough to be able to change their everyday lives. What do you think are the biggest challenges of architecture today and tomorrow?**

There are many big challenges but something that is occupying me a lot is the notion of loneliness – the way we live and the way society is right now. It is easier not to be a part of society, pushed away because you don't have a job or you are not educated. In a way there is the core of society that works a lot and very hard, and the outskirts of society that is becoming bigger and bigger. There are many people who do not feel useful anymore and of course it's a political issue to change that but we can also influence it by the way we create architecture. We should be more inclusive. When designing living areas, it is important to decide how to make it possible to include people of different economic backgrounds or groups. Architects can change a lot when they are really open.

AMAGER CHILDREN'S CULTURE HOUSE
COPENHAGEN, DENMARK, 2013

The advisors for this fanciful project were the children themselves.
It seemed logical for the architect to consult with those who were
going to use the building. What evolved is a surprising corner
building, skilfully incorporated into the existing context and
perfectly expressing a childlike sense of fun and imagination. The
building has also been furnished with customized furniture, which
enhances creativity. The architect explains that "the roof and
façades are treated as the same, and the house does not have
a beginning and end as ordinary houses do. All interior spaces
are visually connected and are bound together by dynamic
circulation".

As the largest unbroken system of intertidal sand and mud flats in the world, the Wadden Sea is a UNESCO World Heritage site. To harmonize with the horizontal landscape of the coastal area, Mandrup designed a low yet extensive sculpturous building. The thatched roof and wooden façades are a homage not only to the regional material but also to traditional craftsmanship. Thanks to the tactile qualities of the materials, the natural colours, and the irregularly bent structure (as if shaped by puffs of coastal winds), it smoothly merges with the magnificent scenery of this national park. It is a great example of architecture conceived in a profound dialogue with nature.

THE ICEFJORD CENTRE
ILULISSAT, GREENLAND, PLANNED 2021

One of Mandrup's latest projects (with the completion planned for 2021) is also located in an UNESCO-protected area. The Icefjord Centre's statement describes "the framework of the building" as "covered by a gently sloping, curved wooden boardwalk that embodies the starting point of the World Heritage Trail and at the same time, acts as a gathering point, viewing platform, and informal seating area." Mandrup envisioned the gigantic curved construction to be partially submerged into the terrain and partially floating in the air. The spectacular aerodynamic shape also minimizes snow build-up. Its specific setting benefits from amazing views on one of the most active glaciers on the planet.

# NORMA MERRICK SKLAREK

New York–born Norma Merrick Sklarek (1926–2012) was the first African American woman to graduate from Columbia University School of Architecture and broke many historical barriers to pave the path in the discipline for generations to come. Despite the fact that Sklarek's education and skills were excellent, her application was rejected 19 times before she got her first job as a junior draftsperson in New York city's Department of Public Works. While working there, in 1954 she passed the exam to become a licenced architect in the state of New York. One year later Sklarek joined the Skidmore, Owings & Merrill practice, where she was responsible for large-scale projects.

At the same time, she also taught evening architecture courses at City College of New York. In 1959 the architect became a member of the American Institute of Architects (AIA), which honoured her with a fellowship in 1980.

Sklarek was most successful, however, after moving to California. In 1960 she began working at Gruen Associates and quickly became the firm's director of architecture. Starting in 1964 she worked as a licenced architect in California. Her responsibilities included hiring architects as well as coordinating the technical aspects of major schemes, like the California Mart, Pacific Design Center, San Bernardino City Hall, and the U.S. Embassy in Tokyo, which today are considered icons of modern American architecture. She collaborated on these projects with the firm's partner, Argentinean architect César Pelli. After two decades Sklarek decided to join the Los Angeles–based Welton Becket Associates as a vice president. The main and very successful realization of this stage of her career was Terminal One at Los Angeles International Airport. 1985 marked the bold move of Sklarek co-founding her own practice with two other female architects, Margot Siegel and Katherine Diamond. At the time it was the largest woman-owned practice across the U.S. Before retiring in 1992, Sklarek worked in one more firm.

Her remarkable professional career of more than fifty years was a successful path, yet filled with many challenges, which Sklarek faced with both courage and determination. The architect, known for being extremely efficient, hard-working, and active, devoted her retirement to engagement with public and professional service as well as lecturing at Howard and Columbia Universities. The architect used her experience as well as academic position to mentor and support minorities in the field of architecture, in particular women. Throughout her whole career, Sklarek contributed numerous texts to architectural journals and other publications, which all influenced the discipline. With her life's work she became a role model, one that she had never had in her career path. To honour her work, Howard University awards a scholarship in her name – the Norma Merrick Sklarek Architectural Scholarship Award.

SAN BERNARDINO CITY HALL
SAN BERNARDINO, CA, USA, 1973

Designed during Sklarek's time at Gruen Associates, the City Hall was designed in collaboration with César Pelli. The six-storey solid cube is entirely clad in glass. No fewer than six thousand tinted smoke glass windows make it impossible to see the interiors from the outside. This smooth and seamless shell emphasises the uniform shape of the building. The only section breaking the regularity is the entrance, raised above the ground on massive pilotis. Modern and functional, it is well suited to its surroundings within the San Bernardino Civic Plaza. The City Hall was selected as one of the Nation's Outstanding City Halls by the Library of Congress and the American Institute of Architects.

# MARTA PELEGRÍN

Spanish architect Prof. Dr. Arch. Marta Pelegrín (b. 1973) of MEDIOMUNDO ARQUITECTOS graduated from the prestigious ETSA in Seville and received her PhD in Architectural Design from the University of Seville. She chose the discipline because it links together culture, space, people, and design, but has also a specific technical approach. After working at Cruz y Ortiz Arquitectos where she realised the Rijksmuseum, among other projects, she teamed up with Fernando Pérez. In 2007 they co-established the firm MEDIOMUNDO Arquitectos to focus on large-scale projects including masterplans, public space design, and residential and educational architecture. Realising projects in various European countries, the studio

also works on commissions like exhibition and interior design, retail, and even product design. They describe their approach as "cooperative, hands-on and based on lateral thinking". As their statement continues, "the coherence of the firm's work is based on a distinctive way of working that deliberately supports the interaction of professional practice, research, and teaching, taking part in wider teams, which constantly enriches the principles of their work". The collaborative result versus one based on a single and all-controlling vision also matches the way they perceive the practice: they "understand architecture as a production instead of a product".

The duo see architecture as the background for other aspects of life, as well. They tend to describe the design process with numerous metaphors, like filling empty drawers. "We find the everyday moment appealing and appreciate the small gestures, the details that bring beauty into everyday life", they explain. "And what makes everyday life beautiful? Empty drawers are nothing special, but you can fill them, and then things get interesting". Their approach is driven by the preliminary stages. Some of the dominant aspects of their research are getting familiar with the site, making lots of sketches and exchanging ideas, and discussing needs and preferences with future users, as well as investigating the local manufacturers to have them produce locally. Based on the information they gather in these stages, they create directions for developing the future design. However, as they stress, "architecture begins when the building is inhabited". The users are always at the heart of the creative process and the final result. The architects, independently of the type of building, never forget about creating common spaces for meetings or entertainment, like spacious atriums or extensive roof gardens.

Discussing the biggest challenges facing women in architecture, Pelegrín reflects that "women are already proposing and involving different disciplines and agents to produce architecture. Our main challenge might be continuing being dreamful to achieve other results by means of other processes". The architect's philosophy is based on three pillars: thread, tissue, and confection, referring to architecture design and the spatial and materials aspects of the discipline. The first one, 'thread', represents concepts and ideas that form a framework for the practice developed through research, lectures, or discussions. 'Tissue' stands for knitting works together with the context, while Pelegrín explains 'confection' as "a series of [architectural] productions, which express, 'spatialize', and materialize the processual conceptual work that refers to 'thread' and 'tissue' ".

Designed as a meeting point for the local community, the Centre is recognisable among the dense fabric of taller residential buildings that surround it thanks to the red-lacquered steel exterior. Its accessible and easy-to-navigate interiors, which optimise the visual as well as physical connections of spaces, were crucial for the architects. The ground floor creates a wi-fi plaza below the building, with access to a small garden and a porch linked to a cafeteria and multipurpose rooms. On the higher level, there are computer labs, workshops, and offices. The free space of the roof terrace can be used for various events.

## SAN FRANCISCO MOVIE THEATRE
## VEJER DE LA FRONTERA, CADIZ, SPAIN, 2010

The design of this movie theatre involved the revitalisation of an existing but practically obsolete cinema in an old warehouse. To preserve the historical character of the building, the old facilities were renovated. The architects also proposed a process to recover the sociocultural surroundings of the building. "While the original cinema existed with its back to the urban setting, the new movie theatre opens onto the street in dialogue with its surroundings", they explain. For this function, the inviting double-height lobby along the façade offers a foretaste of how voluminous the whole building is. The new movie theatre is particularly spacious, with seats on two floors.



MARTA PELEGRÍN

FACULTY OF HEALTH SCIENCES
GRANADA, SPAIN, 2010

The complex volume of the Faculty of
Health Sciences sitting alongside the
University Hospital is 130 metres long and
19 metres wide, housing ten floors and three
floors, west to east. The architects explain
that they proposed "a building of simple
and immediate materiality". The well-
planned and maximally optimised spatial
arrangements allow for encompassing
auditoriums, classrooms, and patios, as
well as administration and deans' offices.
The white and textured concrete, visible
both on the outer shell and in the interiors,
is complemented with an inner coating in
black steel plates and epoxy paint, marking
the stairs and circulation spaces.

# CARME PIGEM

After graduating from the Olot School of Fine Arts, Spanish architect Carme Pigem (b. 1962) continued her studies at the School of Architecture in Valles (Escola Tècnica Superior d'Arquitectura del Vallès, or ETSAV), where she met Rafael Aranda and Ramon Vilalta. They all completed their architecture degrees in 1987 and established their shared practice, RCR Arquitectes, in their home city of Olot in the following year. In 1988, they received first prize in a competition by the Spanish Ministry of Public Works and Urbanism for the project of a lighthouse in Punta Aldea. It was not built, but the project defined the creative principles of the studio. Since then they have realised a number of projects, starting in their native province of Girona and other Spanish cities, later mostly in  France and Belgium, and recently in United Arab Emirates, Portugal and Taiwan. From housing to museums, from kindergartens to public open spaces, from wineries to swimming pools, the idiom they have developed earned them the Pritzker Prize in 2017. "They have compared us with a jazz trio that improvises. As in music it is the art of creating and executing something that has not previously been written and that arises spontaneously through a series of material," reflects Pigem. "Architecture is a language with rules that can be interpreted in many ways and in this lies the magic of jointly seeking a concept that will be the main thread of the project. This is what we call "shared creativity." We replace the "I" with the "we". In this sense, we discuss the main aspects of each project together," she emphasises. The studio pays special attention to two aspects – the inside-outside relation and features that affect feelings. The key task is here a study of the place. "Not only do we approach it from the usual criteria such as orientation, context, and topography, among others, but we also seek to understand what the place makes us feel and how to enhance what exists," explains Pigem. "Revealing the potentiality of the place that makes a unique architecture belonging to that place, establishing both a strong relationship between interior and exterior. This conjunction of objective and subjective responses are those that breathe soul into the project and feeling into the work. In this way, the place is interpreted in sensory keys that are then felt when the space is lived in. But we also understand that everyone will then feel the architecture with their body and their experience in a personal and unique way," she concludes.

The practice's team is 70% women and the founders have continually supported the presence of women in their projects. In addition, at least half of the participants of the studio's annual Summer Workshops have been women. "Of course there is still a lot to do, especially in matters of the profession and motherhood," acknowledges Pigem. "I myself have been fortunate to be able to work as an architect and be a mother. This has been possible because my partners have supported it as something natural and that is why I now represent the first woman with a Pritzker prize who has also had the opportunity to be a mother".

RURAL HOUSE
VALL DE BIANYA, GIRONA, 2007

Embedded in a hill, the Rural House becomes part of the
landscape. As the site is located between two fields, the
structure runs down the slope that connects them. The
entrance creates a connection with the lower level, while
the bedrooms' courtyards as well as the extensive pond
in front of the living room merge the house with the upper
field. Numerous glazed surfaces make the best of two
scenic views of a Romanic church and the Pyrenes. Despite
its clear geometry and rough steel, the construction does
not dominate the surrounding nature. Its private spaces are
designed flexibly and can open or close depending on
the needs of the inhabitants.

BARBERÍ SPACE
OLOT, GIRONA, 2008

Converted from the old Barberí foundry, from the beginning of the 20th century, this building serves as RCR Arquitectes' office. Some features, like smoke-laden walls were left unchanged and their combination with contemporary additions creates a striking mélange. The dialogue between the wood, stone, glass, and steel contributes to the unique spirit of this space with its past. It consists of three parts – the double-height library with a massive table is the main and common office; the workstation building faces the interior courtyard, with trees and a pavilion made of glass and iron columns. "Our world is established here," state the architects, "putting down roots and raising minds".

WAALSE KROOK MEDIATHEQUE
GHENT, BELGIUM, 2017

The complex of the Mediatheque truly incorporates many
functions, from a library and a centre for new media, to a
space for children and youth, as well as multi-purpose rooms.
Combining them all under one roof required elaborated
solutions, developed in collaboration with the local Coussée
& Goris studio. Located along the bank of the Krook canal the
structure takes an elongated form, defined by a composition
of vertical and horizontal elements. The intricate pattern on
the outer shell creates a play of light that softens the massive
shape. The square in front of the building meant for events is
roofed by the building's cantilevered façade. Due to the scale,
this shift in the top level looks rather powerful. The interiors,
planned as an open space, are all well connected and
furnished with custom-made furniture in solid steel.

# CARME PINÓS

"I see architecture as a trigger of relationships, a place of intersections and encounters. I design places where movements and routes intersect and exchange, spaces where people identify as part of a community, but also feel they belong to universality", explains Carme Pinós (b. 1954), describing her approach to the discipline. After graduating from the Escuela Técnica Superior de Arquitectura de Barcelona, the architect continued her studies, focusing on urbanism. She gained recognition while working in a partnership with Enric Miralles from 1982 to 1991 and spread her wings after 1992 when she established her own Barcelona-based practice. While her philosophy remained the same, the method of work naturally changed between these two periods. Initially all was born from a dialogue; today she likes to approach projects in solitude. Only when she has a scheme that meets the needs of the project and includes a clear idea for the structure does Pinós start working with her team. She works on projects around the world, from Spain to Mexico to Australia. Most of them come through competitions and range from public spaces to urban refurbishments. Housing, offices, and various facilities like a biomass boiler, underground station, and crematorium are also important additions to her impressive oeuvre.

Independent of the type or localization, the thread linking all of her projects is their visual complexity. Pinós plays with geometry in a most inspiring and poetic way. Her forceful buildings form striking intersections of volumes. Her interiors, which are just as vibrant, are spacious and filled with natural light. Despite the fact that her proposed structures are rather grand or massive, she manages to achieve well-balanced, yet dynamic, compositions that please – and at times challenge – the eye, both inside and outside. Pinós' buildings are spectacular and strongly present, yet they are far from being disconnected from the context. On the contrary, the architect takes the existing fabric into account, initiating a multi-perspective dialogue through the shapes of the structures as much as through their interior arrangements. As much as the rich structures she designs lead an interesting internal dialogue, at the same time they are always a response to their surroundings, especially – but not only – when they are located in the heart of historical cities. Pinós' creations, although perfectly practical, resemble sculptures that one can look at from various perspectives, without having a clearly defined façade.

Asked why it is so important to create architecture with urbanism in mind, she emphasises the importance of cities. The city is the place where society develops and where we feel most as a community, she remarks. The city as the repository of memory also retains our own history. "I never forget the human scale and I always try to be aware that we are not simply designing a building but weaving an urban fabric," stresses Pinós, adding that "when the context is not urban, we could say that we weave a landscape". In addition to working as an architect, Pinós teaches and delivers workshops internationally. She was named Honorary Fellow of the American Institute of Architects in 2011 and, two years later, RIBA International Fellow for her contribution to the discipline.

Standing out in the densely developed skyscraper district of Guadalajara, Cube II is an extremely sculptural form. The architect designed two parallelepiped volumes, supporting each other and juxtaposed at an acute angle, which as a result creates two triangles with a vertical connection in the middle. Thanks to this structural arrangement, the interiors are column-free. This dynamic yet perfectly balanced structure inclines towards the main street and resembles the bow of a ship. While none of the façades is parallel with the ground of the site, the rhythmic composition of windows is muted behind a mesh that envelopes the outer surfaces.

CAIXAFORUM CULTURAL EXHIBITION CENTRE
ZARAGOZA, SPAIN, 2014

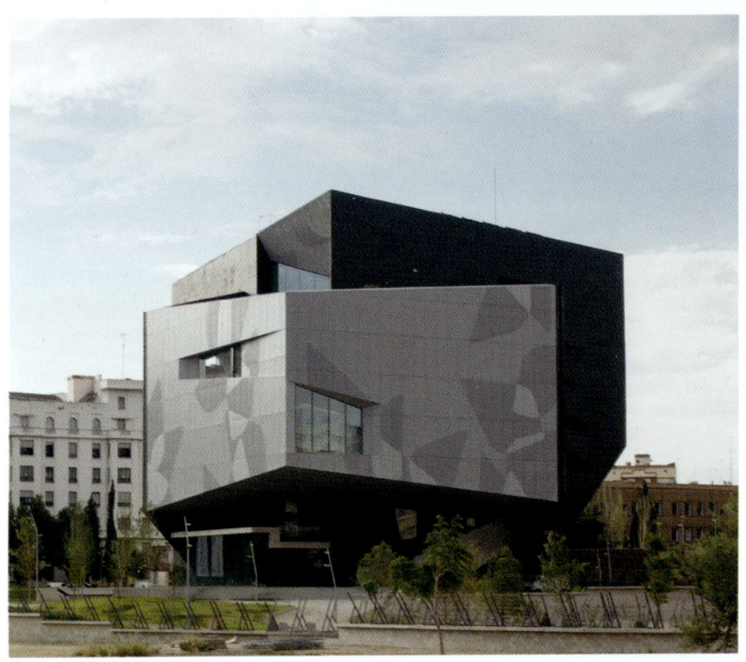

The architect's main goal was to design a building that feels like a city, a unique structure with public spaces. Typically for Pinós, it had to be designed to connect those who walk around and inside of it with various urban perspectives. The ground floor with the lobby and the store is the base for a massive level with two intersecting halls, suspended dramatically over the ground. The poetic composition of geometrical volumes is not the only surprise. An auditorium located underground, accessible through a foyer, has an exit via a semi-underground garden to link the building smoothly with its surroundings.

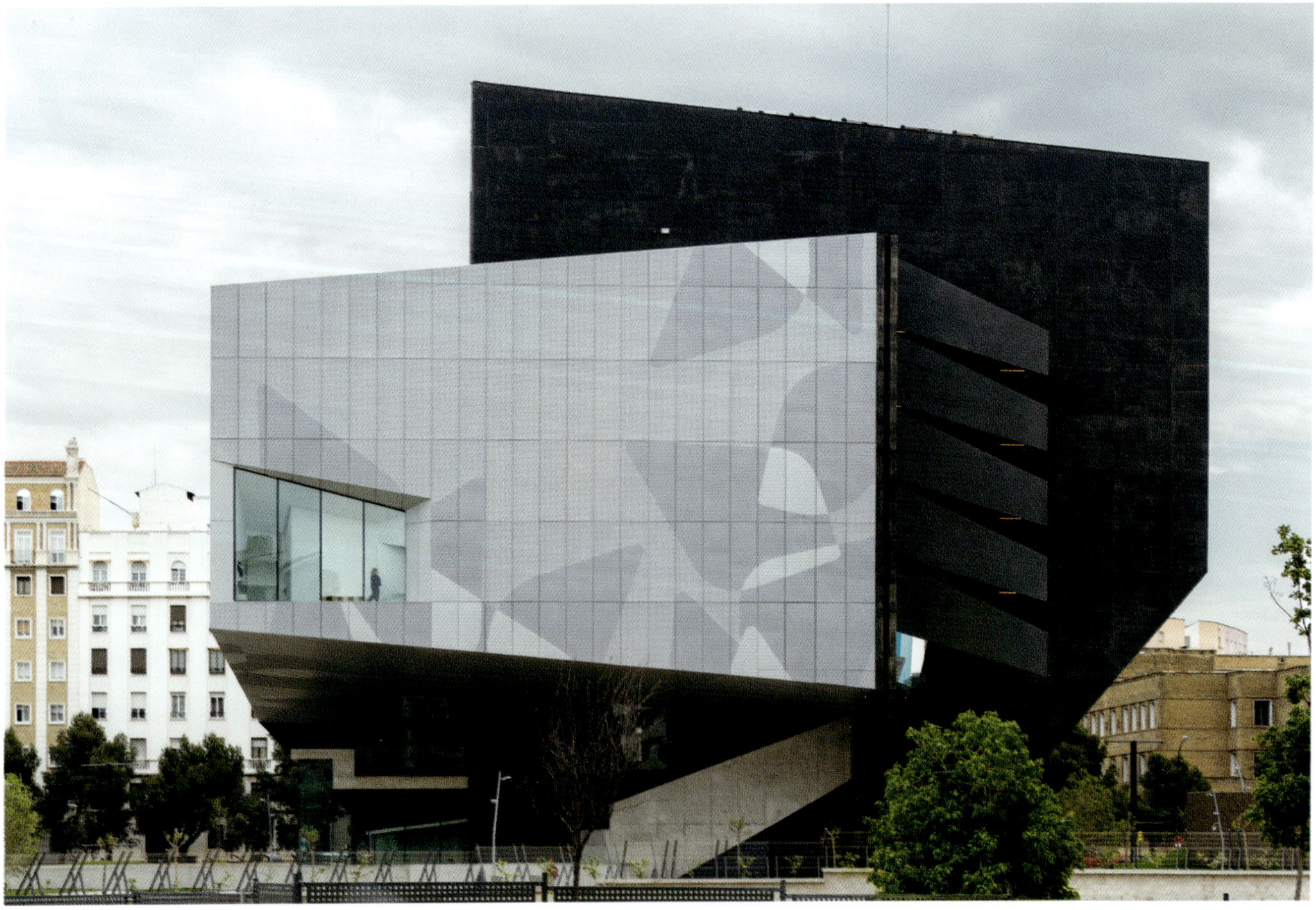

ESCOLA MASSANA, ART AND DESIGN CENTRE
BARCELONA, SPAIN, 2017

The multifaceted building of the
Massana School sits perfectly in the
heart of Barcelona, with various parts
connected visually with the streets
around Gardunya Square. Inside, the
sequence of shifting volumes offers
views towards different directions, while
outside it creates terraces, thanks to
which the massive structure does not
appear bulky. Weaving this sculpturous
structure into the historical urban
fabric was the architect's objective.
The numerous windows and glazed
walls fill the interior with light, which is
regulated through a brise soleil shell.
The regular pattern of this aesthetically
sophisticated solution enhances the
complex geometry of the structure.

# SAMIRA RATHOD

A graduate of the Sir J. J. College of Architecture in Mumbai, Indian architect Samira Rathod (b. 1963) completed her Master in Architecture at the University of Illinois at Urbana-Champaign. During her stay in the U.S. she collaborated with the California-based Don Wald and Associates studio. Upon returning to India, Rathod worked with Ratan Batliboi for several years for before establishing her own practice – Samira Rathod Design Atelier in 2000. Her practice's portfolio ranges from residential projects to office and school buildings. Following her passion for writing and theorising, in 2008 she founded a critical architectural publication focusing on Indian architecture called SPADE. Developing this activity, Rathod is the founder and director of SPADE India Research Cell, which is devoted to research on the condition and impact of design in India. The architect also devotes part of her time to teaching and is an adjunct faculty member at the Kamla Raheja Institute of Architecture in Mumbai.

"The essence of design lies in bringing poetry into the building through the surreal ideas of the esoteric", Rathod says of her creative process. With aspects like the function, programme, and site conditions setting the course of design, the concept is conceived through extensive research and group discussions. "An object, a word, a mood, an animal... any thought or idea is where the design begins. The idea is then thoroughly researched to grasp its complete potential so it can be developed into the language the design dictates", explains the design firm's statement. These ideas are then translated through numerous sketches. For the initial steps, the architect relies on drawings more than computer programmes (which dominate at a later stage of design). Sketching is also essential for light studies, as in many of Rathod's buildings the play of light and shadow plays a special role. Physical models, the following phase of the process, allow Rathod to study forms, volume, and geometrical relations, like scale and proportions. The last step is testing materials, which the architect puts a special emphasis on. She is always eager to explore new ideas and processes to recognise the attributes of materials and how they can be used in particular buildings.

Each aspect, even down to the smallest detail, is carefully considered as, for the architect, each project should be cohesive vision. "I want everything to have a certain connection that comes through deliberate design", explains Rathod. Her portfolio provides numerous examples of perfect combinations of materials and shapes that are adjusted to the context of the site as much as to the character of each building. Once completed, her creations are visually striking, with unique solutions, both visual and technical, and are coherent even if their structures are complex. Rathod is known for working extensively on the site. "While drawings communicate much of the design, the feedback from the design can be clearly articulated on the site", she reflects. Part of the architect's practice is the furniture and product design label the Big Piano. Rathod also takes interior design commissions. "As an architect, when I design interior spaces, my approach is more inclined towards the design of space and less towards styling", she remarks.

"When I design, I like to compose the presence of light, choreograph its movement into the spaces like one does staccatos, and when one strings these together in as seamless flow of experiences, there is a symphony that I call architecture."

Studies in light form a large part of your creative process – you do a lot of drawings at the studio, more than using computer programmes, which dominate at the later stages of design. In many of your buildings, a translucent effect plays a main role, producing a visually stunning game of shadows (particularly striking when juxtaposed with opaque elements). Why is light so important for you?

I like to see the world as a painting. I find compositions in everything; there are frames everywhere, like as if through a photographer's lens … In the most mundane I can see the exotic; the world and all its objects are in a still painting, changing hues as the light moves. I see the landscapes drenched in red wine through my sunglasses, I see the city draped in calming grey just before the first rains, I see pellets of light strewn on the floor through a perforated roof. There is music everywhere, if we can draw ourselves to listen… and what a wonderful world it is then, like a prelude to a musical composition.

I believe that we can see because of this light, and that light alone can play a dramatic role in our experiences of space, not only how we discern it but also how we perceive it; and how we feel about it impacts our behaviour and emotions.

For me as an architect and builder, light is a powerful material to elevate the mood of my users, to lure their attention from materialism to a higher state of being – where even the mundane becomes magical. I believe architecture to have that power. When I design, I like to compose the presence of light, choreograph its movement into the spaces like one does staccatos, and when one strings these together in as seamless flow of experiences, there is a symphony that I call architecture.

**In pursuit of innovation, but also for the sake of original aesthetic solutions, you are keen on experimenting with** both forms and materials with results that are often surprising. How do you research materials and which do you find most interesting?

If I could answer the question of "how do I research material?" with one word, I would say "serendipitously". It is a constant search, but not one with a specific agenda. Our research is not like that of a chemical laboratory with a given agenda.

We ask many questions: What could be done here? How could this material act differently? What are its attributes? Can one explore its other forms? Can this apply to architecture and building?

We dream the answers, and then try to manifest them. There is a lot of experimentation, which begins with a lot of mixing and dabbling, like a newly wedded wife, making a meal for her husband, with all her love and without any specific recipe; what may come of it may or may not be delicious, but it will have been cooked. This dabbling is then followed by research on durability, the behaviours of the materials, maintenance issues, and many such criteria that allow its qualification so that a new technique, idea, or material may be safely used. This is also followed by post-operative reports, to reinstate its regular use.

For me materials have no caste, religion, or hierarchy. They have attributes and work well in juxtaposition with each other. I like to think of materials as people in a crowd, in a group, in a room having different conversations.

**What has influenced your work the most?**

There are many influences. But – like they say, that a person's making is in his first 11 formative years – I think it would have to be my childhood, which I largely spent

with my grandparents, both paternal and maternal. This time that I shared with them, in a subliminal way, shaped my being.

Another big influence has been my studies in America, where I did my master's in architectural design, which reinforced my ideas of design. The two most influential teachers have been my art teacher in my secondary school, Mr. Ramakant Deshpande, and Professor James Miller, who taught me during my postgraduate studies in architecture in America. My art teacher taught me about compositions and reading paintings, and from that early on I developed a keen interest in the fine arts.

I am a close to avid reader, and love to literally surround myself with books. I like to read biographies, and am most moved by their lives, their struggles, their assiduous dedication to their work, and their fearless courage to express new ideas.

As such, I feel it is art, be it a poem, a painting, or a piece of music, that I would say, largely influences my work. Art helps me broaden my spectrum of thought and understanding. It brings solace and peace to my mind, and I truly find joy in it. Art has been a source of inspiration for my work and it is from here that I am able to construct its narratives.

**Following your passion for theorising and discussing architecture, you established SPADE, a biannual architectural journal and SIRCLE (Spade India Research Cell). Can you tell more about both initiatives?**

When SPADE first came into being, there were no serious design magazines in the country that actually dared to candidly discuss issues of design in India. Most tabloids were only offering silly bouquets and sycophancy to architects and their projects. None offered valuable criticism, or even investigated the real problems. SPADE emerged in that vacuum, and got its name from the work it was set up to do – call a spade a spade, and dig hard and deep in search of good design.

We came out with four issues of the journal, SPADE, each issue of which dealt with a word trigger for ideation and dialogue, though limited to design in India. They were: "politics", "reincarnation", "collage", and "opium".
But after that, it lost some steam, and instead of the journal, we went on to produce researched documents, on different subjects, under the aegis of SIRCLE (Spade India Research Cell).

Several publications are listed on the website. The latest one, called Museum of Trees, not only documents the 3000 trees in the Mumbai zoo, but really aims to look at each tree as an entity, with all its wonderful characteristics and attributes, and to draw attention to it when it is mostly taken for granted.

There is another publication that discusses the idea of dismantling and recycling buildings, one that looks keenly at South Indian architecture, and many other smaller and more narrowly focused research publications. All of these publications are still available, and can be ordered from the website.

**Is it difficult to run a practice in India as a female architect? What is the architectural scene like?**

I am not sure how much I would subscribe to this whole gender bias against women. It does exist and I would be naive to think otherwise. However, I don't think that, today, to run a practice as a woman in India is that difficult. To think that every failure is due to the gender bias would be self-annihilating. The key to running a practice, and a good one, is hard work with a strong, unflinching focus and integrity of purpose, whether it is run by a man or a woman. An architect must breathe and live for the one and only love of their life – DESIGN.

**What in your view are the biggest challenges for architecture today?**

I am going to draw my answer from the work one of India's most prolific artists, Jitish Kallat, whose intellectual understanding and ideas about our collective human state illustrate closest the threat of our collaborative annihilation. We are seeing the many wrongs of where we are headed, and there is enough evidence of the planet's extinction being near, both in body and ideas.

The biggest challenge, then, for us as architects, is in how to build or how not to build, with this full understanding, and whether the architecture can actually be a call, a symbol, or a philosophy that may be pledged by the larger mass in question, to simply delay this extinction.

ART GALLERY
BARODA, GUJARAT, INDIA, 2012

The Art Gallery was realised as an extension of a steel sculptor's workshop, located in a warehouse. Envisioned in the sculpturous form of a volume in sheet steel, it visibly stands out against the original brick building. Its solid shape is softened by numerous glass openings that let the light stream in to create an interesting play of shadows, particularly along the accordion-like staircase. "The programme was to be an annex-like gallery and café that invites passers-by into the artist's space, giving them a glimpse of his work and process", explains the architect. The gallery also exhibits other local artists.

## SHADOW HOUSE
SAHAN GAON, ALIBAUG, MUMBAI, INDIA, 2017

The Shadow House sits alone in the
middle of a vast landscape overlooking
hills and fields. It has been constructed
to provide the maximum amount of
shade and coolness in the heat, as well
as calmness. Inspired by houses typical
for southern India, with low slung roofs
and a central courtyard (here equipped
with a small pool), it is a complex
structure made of an interesting mélange
of steel, concrete, and wood that all
contribute to create an intriguing game
of shadows. The architect reflects that
with its numerous skylights, "the house is
designed like a sieve through which light
is filtered".

pages 175–177
BHADRAN SCHOOL
BHADRAN, GUJARAT, INDIA, 2020

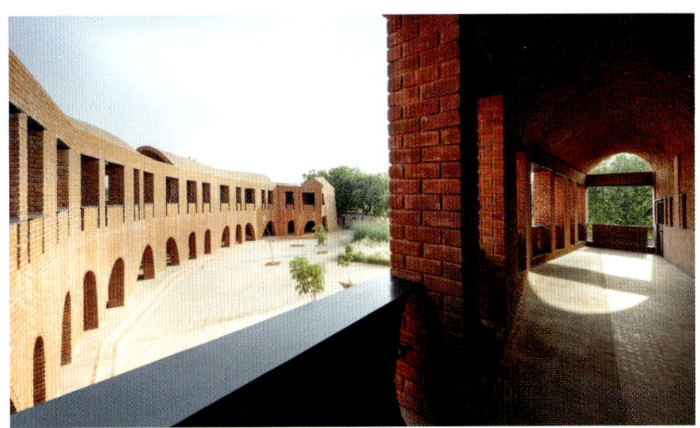

"A building, a school, where the play of hide and seek is perpetual" is probably the best introduction to the visually stunning school in Bhadran, with its numerous alcoves, niches, and bridges. Surrounded by a fruit orchard, the organically shaped complex made of terracotta bricks was conceived as a series of modular spaces. Each module was planned to have a pair of classrooms and a corridor with sinusoid vaults. Inspiring the imagination and inviting visitors to play around, the volume was conceptualised from a child's early scribbles, which resulted in a composition of playful arches.

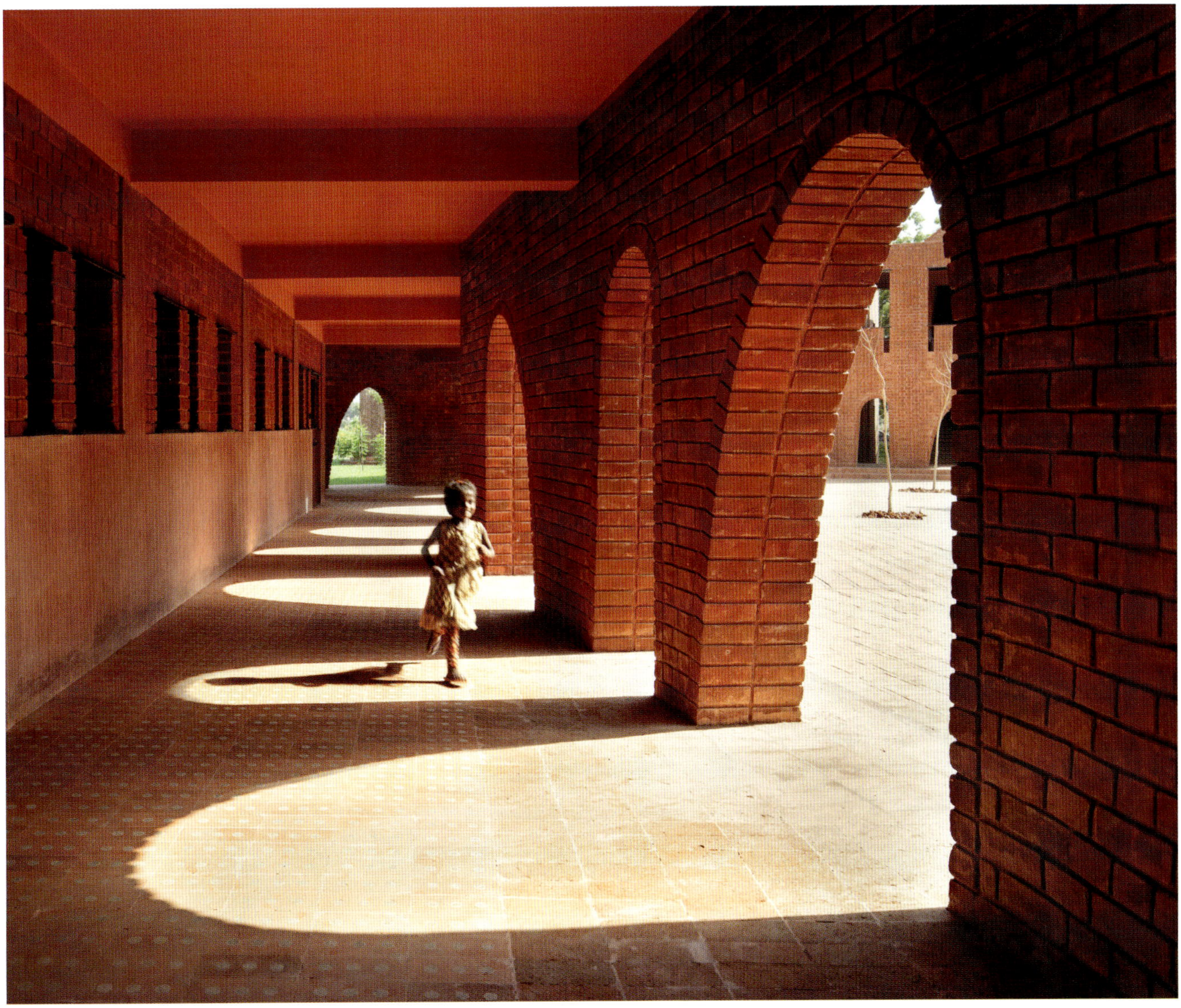

# SU ROGERS

Su Rogers (b. 1939) gained her Bachelor of Science degree in Sociology at the London School of Economics and continued studying Town Planning at the Yale School of Architecture. In the 1960s and early 1970s, she co-founded and partnered with several significant architectural practices. The first one, Team 4, was a joint collaborative gathering established in 1962 by the architect and her first husband Richard Rogers, along with the couple Norman and Wendy Foster. The quartet worked on a number of realizations, mainly in residential architecture. Their best known common projects were two houses in Cornwall commissioned by Su Rogers' parents, Marcus and Rene Brumwell. One of them was the modernist Creek Vean, currently a listed building, is built into the steep hill of a river bank. Its playfully arranged geometric volumes refer to the topography

of the plot. The house is visibly divided into two separate parts – private and social, which are subtly linked with a glass-roofed corridor that also functions as a gallery space. The stairs, partly overgrown by grass, create a smooth connection between the building and the surrounding garden. Partly hidden between the trees growing on the plot, all rooms of the villa have a panoramic view of the surrounding vegetation and the river. The purity of the two main materials, glass and concrete, creates a visually strong juxtaposition despite the small scale. The house was completed in 1966 and it happened to be one of Team 4's last common projects.

Su and Richard Rogers worked as a duo until around 1970 and continued to develop residential solutions, including their proposal for "The House of Today" competition. The Zip-Up House they envisioned at the time was never built, but the concept was largely employed for the 22 Parkside house in London that the couple designed for Richard Rogers' parents. In 1971 they teamed up with Italian architect Renzo Piano. Their collaboration started with their winning the competition for the design of the newly created Centre Pompidou with one of the most innovative and daring projects in the history of modern architecture. The Rogers split up shortly after.

Teaching was a very important part of Rogers' career. She taught at the Architectural Association from 1971 until 1977 and at the Royal College of Art from 1976 until 1985. From 1978 until 1985 she also ran the Project Office at the Royal College of Art, which allowed for students to have some experience of working in an office. In 1985, the architect got back to architectural practice and partnered with her second husband, John Miller, in Colquhoun, Miller and Partners, which became the John Miller + Partners firm four years later, and was active until 2011. The practice focused on large-scale projects like university amenities and art galleries, as well as affordable housing. They were responsible for the Royal Scottish Academy refurbishment (1999) and the Tate Britain Centenary development in London (2001) as well as several University buildings in Cambridge, East Anglia and Warwick or the Fitzwilliam Museum (2004), to name but a few major projects. Throughout her entire professional career, Su Rogers has also been teaching internationally at University College Dublin and Columbia University in New York City.

pages 179–181
CREEK VEAN
FEOCK, UK, 1966

Designed by Team 4 – Richard and Su Rogers and Norman and Wendy Foster – this modernist villa is incorporated into the context of the site. Sitting on a river bank, the house is split into two cubic volumes of different heights. Outside, these are divided by grass-covered stairs leading to the garden down the hill, yet they are connected inside with a gallery corridor on the ground floor level, covered with a glass roof. The lower volume creates an intimate space for a bedroom and study with a flat roof overgrown by vegetation. The two-level volume houses dining and living areas and its entirely glazed façade offers a panoramic view. The large transparent surfaces create a visually stark contrast with the pure concrete blocks used both on the outer shells and in the interiors.

# NATHALIE ROZENCWAJG

Nathalie Rozencwajg (b. 1975) graduated from the Architectural Association School of Architecture (AA) in London in 2001. After gaining experience in large architectural firms and realising projects in London, Beijing, and Athens, she pursued her professional career by co-founding RARE architecture studio, before setting up NAME. In the initial years of her practice, despite the fact that she was most often the only women at the table, Rozencwajg did not feel treated differently as a female architect. "However," she reflects, "the biggest challenge comes without a doubt with motherhood. The practice of architecture and heading a studio demands time, many hours of work and often travel. Architecture is a very demanding profession. I believe that its being a parent rather than only a woman that impacts my professional path.".

Her studio's statement explains their philosophy: "A name is an important act of creation. Naming is just the beginning of crafting a new identity, meaning and presence. Our philosophy at NAME architecture is to approach every project as a novel act of creation." With offices in London and Paris, NAME operates globally. Its diverse portfolio ranges from residential architecture, to shopping malls, to interior revamps. Rozencwajg's field of expertise is breathing new life into historic buildings in conservation areas. NAME has completed a number of notable refurbishment  projects with particular expertise in the hospitality sector. Her visually striking combinations of the existing fabric and her purely modern formal language creates interesting architectural dialogues, which help write new chapters of historical districts. Understanding and identifying the constraints of the site are important in the architect's creative process, as the boundaries actually enhance the design by pushing her inventiveness and resulting in original solutions, and sometimes unforeseen responses. The crucial aspect for Rozencwajg, however, is "to be inspired by the site, the building – to find the element that will initiate the story. The driving concept will then act as backbone to hold the many iterations that a design process inevitably encounters – be it due to client feedback, stakeholders, regulations, budget, etc... Designing and building is a long process, it lasts for years. Years during which as an architect you have to keep believing in your project while sometimes adapting it." She continues, "developing a strong concept from the outset helps me maintain the course and the essential ideas of a design". The architect believes in the enriching potential of collaborative work and for each new project, she forms bespoke collaborations with a trusted network of experts.

Discussing some of the biggest challenges for architects today, Rozencwajg mentions the globalisation of architecture, which, despite its many advantages, has created a disconcertingly homogenous situation. "In this context it is challenging to remain distinctive and linked to the place, to a cultural context. It is demanding of your creative process to remain somewhat detached and propose something singular," she believes, adding that "the next big challenge that architects are not yet fully measuring will be the impact of Artificial Intelligence on our practice. Functional layouts will increasingly be developed by software – we thus need to redefine and argue what will remain or become the role of an architect".

THE TOWN HALL HOTEL
LONDON, UK, 2010

RARE has transformed the old Bethnal Green Town Hall at the heart of London's East End into a luxury hotel with a restaurant and a bar. As the original early-20th-century building had fallen into disrepair, the project involved the restoration of the Edwardian and Art Deco elements and a new extension behind the existing structure. The building structure is wrapped in a laser cut powder-coated aluminium skin that is perforated with an abstract pattern inspired by historical motifs in the Grade II listed building. This aesthetically elaborated concept is also functional, protecting hotel guests' privacy and providing a sun shading device.

CASTLE LANE APARTMENTS
LONDON, UK, 2017

Due to its location in a conservation area in the vicinity of Buckingham Palace, the design of this high-end apartment building had to address stringent constraints and regulations. Rozencwajg explains that prioritising the historic and cultural importance of the locality was essential. As she elaborates, "we were inspired to create a contemporary continuation of the historic streetscape, using existing materials and features in a contemporary way". The project is defined by an innovative take on the classic bow window. Massive floor-to-ceiling windows take the form of protruding curved shapes that add both dynamism and poetry to the building while extending the interiors.

# DENISE SCOTT BROWN

After attending the University of Witwatersrand, Denise Scott Brown (b. 1931) studied architecture at the Architectural Association in London. She received master's degrees in architecture and city planning from the University of Pennsylvania. Her work as an architect, planner, and urban designer as well as a theorist and writer has had a significant influence on the whole discipline. For more than fifty years the architect worked in collaboration with her husband, Robert Venturi (1925–2018). The couple is widely regarded as the inventors of postmodernism. In their common practice, Venturi, Scott Brown and Associates (VSBA), she was involved in a wide range of architectural realizations. As Principle-in-Charge, she was responsible for urban planning, urban design, and campus planning. Successes in developing the interdisciplinary firm were enhanced by her teaching and research activities. Scott Brown held both architecture and planning professorships at numerous universities, like Harvard, Yale, and UCLA, to name but a few, and educated generations of architects through her numerous publications, like "Architecture and Decorative Arts, Two Naifs in Japan" from 1991 and "Architecture as Signs and Systems for a Mannerist Time" from 2004 (both co-authored by Robert Venturi), or "Urban Concepts" (1990) and "Having Words" (2009).

Another essential aspect of her work has been her research projects. The most famous, "Learning from Las Vegas" (1972; a revised version with Robert Venturi and Steven Izenour followed in 1977), which investigated the emerging automobile city, the relation of the social and physical in architecture, and lastly, symbolism and communication in architecture, was published as a book. Today it continues to be a must-read for architecture professionals and aficionados alike, as it has become an inspirational guide on how to conduct architectural research. The Las Vegas case study is also considered a quintessential example of the postmodern way of thinking, which, just as revolutionary in its time, caused many controversies and initiated heated debates among architects. It is truly impossible to name the long list of the architect's distinctions, awards, and public roles in the most prestigious bodies around the globe. It is crucial, however, to explore some of the key projects in the architect's fascinating and multifaceted career.

One of Scott Brown's first big projects was the plan for South Street in Philadelphia, which not only stopped controversial plans for the Crosstown Expressway but also introduced a series of ideas for how to revive the area, like the renovation and expansion of low-income housing. Based on the architect's photographic study of South Street and extensive research on the local context and inhabitants' needs, Scott Brown's concepts contributed to South Street's regeneration between the 1970s and 1990s. The architect also made plans for Miami Beach (Florida) and Memphis (Tennessee), among cities. Another focus in the architect's practice was campus master planning. In 1997, VSBA analysed and improved the strategic plan for the University of Michigan, which is an interesting case study of a variety of ways of thinking about the campus, including the principles for the location of buildings, the organisation of the landscape, and outlining the relationship between areas and buildings' functions. Another important realization from 1992, designed in association with Anderson/Schwarz Architects Hermet-Blanc-Delagausie-Mommens/Atelier A4, was the Département de la Haute-Garonne provincial capitol building in Toulouse, France. The extensive complex included offices, the assembly chamber, public services, and three-storey underground parking, as well as outdoor and indoor ceremonial spaces. It was envisioned as a massive volume of two slender six-storey wings, linked by two glass-clad building bridges with a monumental entrance with two columns that echoed a historic city gate. One year earlier Scott Brown completed work on one of London's major realizations at the time – the Sainsbury Wing of the National Gallery in the heart of Trafalgar Square.

pages 187–189
SAINSBURY WING
LONDON, UK, 1991

One of the best examples of European postmodern architecture,
the extension of the National Gallery in London is a successful
combination of styles and materials. Its contrasting elevations
elegantly adjust the volume to the existing urban context. The
entrance façade, facing Trafalgar Square, is a visual continuation
of the main gallery building with its rhythmic pillars. Gradually,
however, the forms are reduced to become purely geometric
just around the corner. At the same time, modern glass and
steel elements remain visible. This surprising yet well-composed
mélange echoes the eclectic nature of the metropolis. Presented
by three Sainsbury brothers – John, Simon, and Timothy – the
building was opened by Queen Elizabeth in 1991 and houses the
museum's renowned collection of early Renaissance paintings.

# CRISTINA SEGNI

Cristina Segni (b. 1974) studied architecture in Rome and Madrid before moving to London in 2000. Three years later the architect joined Foster + Partners and has been responsible for a wide range of projects, from a Milan Fair Masterplan to a residential complex in St. Moritz, to town hall buildings in remote locations like Riyadh or Buenos Aires. 2009 marked the beginning of a major realization in California of Apple Park, for which Segni has been one of the design leaders. In 2016 she moved to the U.S. to oversee the completion of the innovative project. The architect is currently based in San Francisco, where she is working on further projects.

In 2009, when Segni was made a partner at Foster + Partners, it was still unusual for a female architect to take such a high position. Discussing gender-based challenges in her professional career, she speaks about gaining respect in the traditionally male-dominated construction industry. "Sometimes, during my career, it felt a bit like being an outsider to a private members' club", she acknowledges. On a more positive note she believes that things are changing. "Many practices, like ours, support mentoring schemes for young female architects and promote several initiatives aimed at highlighting the issues faced by women in architecture as well as their valuable contribution to the industry. Each of these is a step in the right direction", Segni affirms. She also points out the necessity of understanding the fundamental differences in working as well as communication styles between men and women.

"For me, architecture is about people and the lived experience. It has a strong social purpose, in the sense that it can substantially improve everyday lives as well as help to create an identity for individuals and communities", she emphasises. Her approach to architecture has been highly influenced by her growing up in Italy, where she was surrounded by millennia of architecture literally everywhere. Her upbringing instilled in her a great appreciation for architecture of varying heritage and history and a passion for design. It also inspired her to understand architecture as a sense of permanence – on the one hand it represents the current world but it is also a means for shaping the future.

Segni's main goals are to create unique, innovative buildings that are an integral part of the landscape, whether in the city or surrounded by nature, where every detail, from the façade to the shape of the door handles, is designed specifically for the physical and spiritual well-being of the people who are going to experience it. Working on the Apple Park project meant pushing technology to its limits for every stage and component of the project. Upon its completion, Segni continues to push the boundaries of the discipline. "We used to say the sky is the limit, but even that has been transcended!", she observes. "We are now working on extra-terrestrial habitats for people on the Moon and Mars. Innovation in building materials, design technologies and construction tools has made it possible to realise projects that were previously thought impossible".

THE MUREZZAN
ST MORITZ, SWITZERLAND, 2007

Located in a scenic Swiss valley, The Murezzan combined two existing buildings from the beginning of the 20th century – the Albana Hotel and the Post Haus restaurant – as part of their refurbishment, along with the construction of the Chesa apartment building. The renovation of the historical hotels was based on their original plans and aimed at reversing some of the more recent alterations. The restoration of the detailed interiors and original proportions celebrates traditional alpine architecture. The new apartment building, with its striking wooden roof canopy over a double-height colonnade on the street façade, also houses retail spaces. The historical and modern buildings face each other across the street and are connected by an underground passage.

CIUDAD CASA DE GOBIERNO
BUENOS AIRES, ARGENTINA, 2015

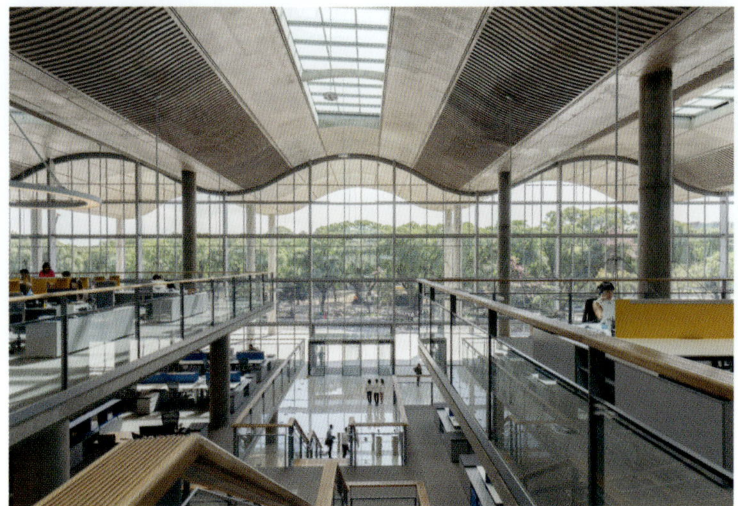

This vast city hall of Buenos Aires, defined by a massive flowing roof canopy resting on pillars, has an impressive four-storey-high atrium with a fully glazed façade. Every aspect of the scheme was designed in response to the local climate. The selection of materials was additionally inspired by the site's industrial past. As it spans an entire city block, the building is part of the whole district's revitalisation plan. In harmony with the building's park-side setting, the project, as the architects explain, "combines an environmentally efficient design with an innovative, highly flexible internal arrangement of terraced office floors".

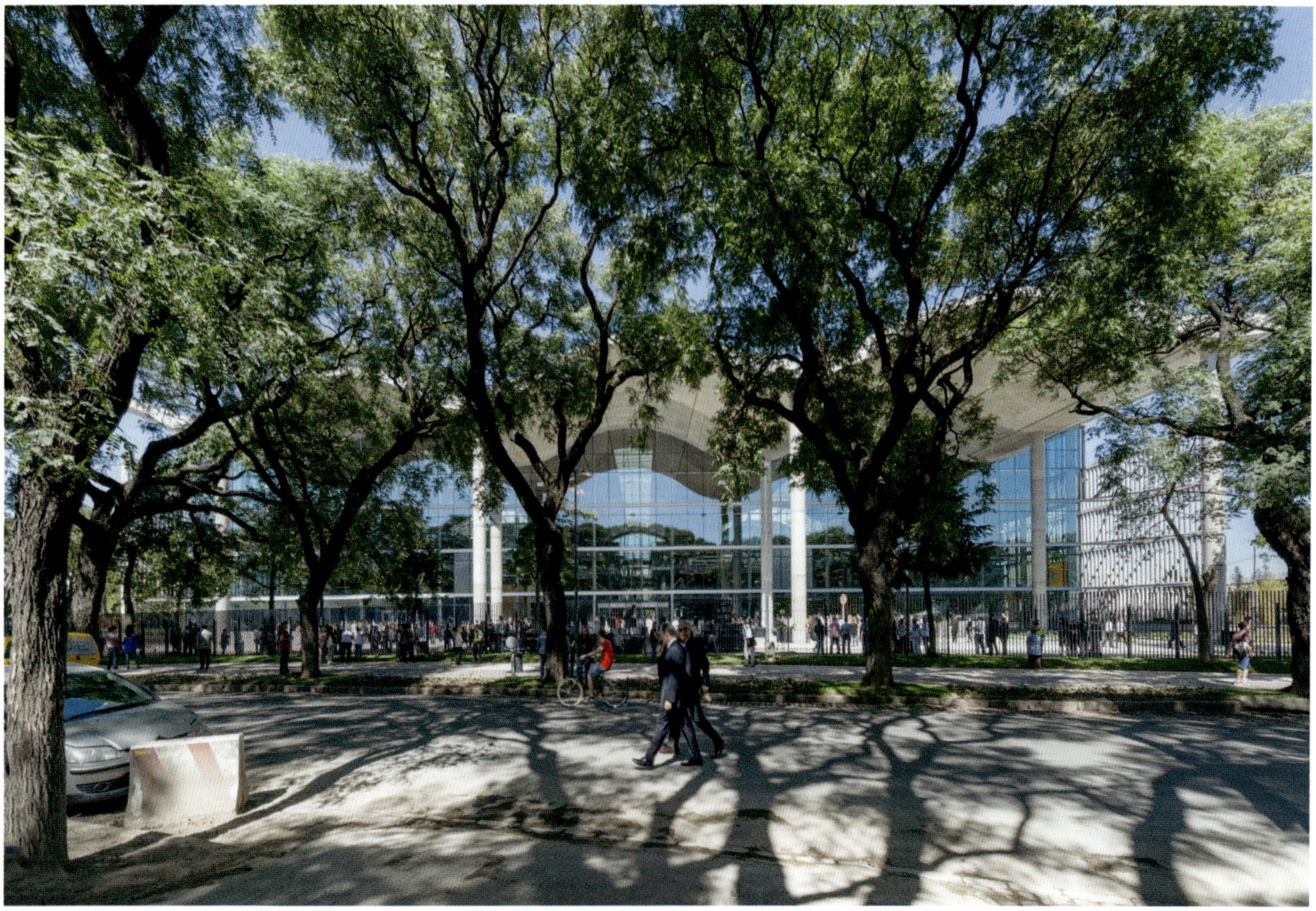

## APPLE PARK
### CUPERTINO, USA, 2018

This ultra-modern complex encompasses
the Ring Building, Steve Jobs Theater, Fitness
& Wellness Center, and Visitors' Center.
Sitting low in the extensive landscape with
more than 9,000 trees, meadows, sport
fields, terraces, and a pond, the campus is
powered by 100 percent renewable energy.
The advanced precast concrete structure
of the Ring Building has glazed perimeter
walkways featuring the largest sheets of
curved glass ever constructed. Full-height
atria entrances fill the interiors with light
at the eight cardinal axis points, and an
extensive restaurant, designed to encourage
interaction, occupies the Ring's entire
axis. Interestingly, one of its façades rolls
effortlessly on tracks despite its enormous
size (15 metres high and 55 metres wide!).

# KAZUYO SEJIMA

In her childhood Kazuyo Sejima (b. 1956) came across a picture of a house designed by the legendary Kiyonori Kikutake; her fascination with this image inspired her to study architecture and had an impact on her further work. Upon graduating from Japan Women's University, Sejima gained first professional experience at the office of the internationally renowned Toyo Ito, one of the most innovative Japanese architects at the time. In 1987, she established her own practice, which brought her recognition in Japan. International success and commissions all over the globe followed after 1995, when Sejima additionally

founded the Tokyo-based SANAA together with Ryue Nishizawa. While the duo also continue to work individually, their common studio numbering around 40 devoted members. For their work, Sejima and Nishizawa were chosen as the laureates of the Pritzker Architecture Prize in 2010.

In the same year, Sejima became the first woman to take on the directorship of the 12th Architecture Biennale in Venice in the event's history. In one of many interviews on this occasion she reflected: "I have a dream that architecture can bring something to contemporary society. Architecture is how people meet in space". This was also the theme of the Biennale – "people meet in architecture". The architect's main goal for the exhibition was to clarify contemporary values and understand possible new lifestyles for the 21st century. The idea was to help people relate to architecture, help architecture relate to people and help people relate to themselves. Sejima invited artists and engineers, not only architects, because she believes architecture to be a product of collaboration.

Some of the characteristics of Sejima's architecture are fluidity, lightness, and transparency. The perception of continuity is crucial for her aesthetics. "A room can have a connection to the outside or to another room", she remarks. "The quality of the relationships determines the quality of the space". The reduction of divisions in the interiors allows users to move freely and explore the space intuitively. The ultimate goal is a feeling of endless continuity through the volume. This relates to the inside and outside connection, designed to be as smooth as possible with all peculiarities of each site in mind. Physical models help Sejima's design team find the best proportions and spatial relations in each case. The buildings Sejima designs are thus often intertwined with nature and demonstrate a great sense of harmony on both levels – architecture with its context and with its users. Materials also play an important role in her practice, as they influence the way we perceive and enjoy architecture, no less than colours do. Both can enhance another crucial element, namely the way light travels through interiors, which Sejima believes should be generously filled with natural light, nearly transparent to reduce the border between the interior and exterior. Each design draws from its specific site, adjusted to its topography and reflecting the individuality of the location, while the significant scales initiate playful dialogues with their surroundings.

# "Architecture is how people meet in space."

In 2010, you were the first women to take on the directorship of the Architecture Biennale in Venice. Did the fact that you're a female architect influence your work?

The fact that I'm a woman influences my perspective to some extent, of course. But I think architecture is always teamwork rather than individual work. In this sense, I would say my gender doesn't really affect our designs.

On the occasion of the Biennale, you said: "I have a dream that architecture can bring something to contemporary society. Architecture is how people meet in space." You also often say that today it is museums that should become common meeting platforms. What is the recipe for a perfect public space in your view?

It is not about a perfect public space, but I have always tried to create architecture that is like a park. I want to make spaces where people can enjoy doing a variety of things, with a sense that they are with others, and with a respect for diversity.

Is there any project you dream of designing?

I would like to continue exploring the potential of public space, in many different forms.

Where do you draw your inspiration from and what does your creative process look like?

Sometimes a new idea just "comes to mind", but usually I draw inspiration from my experiences and what I see, as well as from conversations with others. Ideas grow bit by bit in my head.

NEW MUSEUM
NEW YORK, USA, 2007

Designed together with Ryue
Nishizawa, the New Museum
building in lower Manhattan
is visually striking with its
simplicity of concept and
creative take on geometric
forms. This combination,
given the volume's scale, has
impacted New York's urban
landscape. As a reference
to the district's traditional
square block architecture,
a pile of white cubes in
various sizes is wrapped
in a layer of anodised
aluminium mesh on top of
the white walls. Stacked up
asymmetrically, they play with
our perception. The building
encompasses an auditorium,
a four-storey gallery with
flexible exhibition space, an
educational centre, as well as
offices and a multi-purpose
room on the top floor.

KAZUYO SEJIMA

DIAMOND EQUIPMENT DAROMA RESTAURANT EQUIPMENT

SUMIDA HOKUSAI MUSEUM
TOKYO, JAPAN, 2016

The Sumida Ward district in Tokyo was home to acclaimed Japanese woodblock painter Katsushika Hokusai. This four-storey angular volume exhibits a collection of over 1800 of the artist's works including the iconic The Great Wave off Kanagawa, as well as a life-sized model of his studio. The geometric cut-outs in the monolithic structure are sources of light for the interiors, where walkways and apertures also take on triangular shapes. The museum not only celebrates the artist's creations but also functions as a cultural landmark for the local community. Although visually significantly different, the condensed form fits in well in the context of its surrounding buildings.

KAZUYO SEJIMA

OSAKA UNIVERSITY OF ARTS, ART
SCIENCE DEPARTMENT BUILDING
OSAKA, JAPAN, 2018

An addition to the university's
campus designed by Teiichi
Takahashi of Daiichi-Kobo
Associates, this new building
takes the form of three irregularly
undulating discs submerged
into the hilly site covered with
trees. Located at the forefront
of the campus, it houses a lab
and studio, lecture halls, and
faculty research labs, as well as
digital art galleries. Through its
organic shape, the three-level
construction made of ring-shaped
slabs initiates a dialogue with the
surrounding nature. The architect's
intention was to create a hill-like
roof that would correspond with
the natural topography and blend
into its environment. The light
structure also provides bright
and airy interiors with numerous
meeting spaces for students.

# ANNABELLE SELLDORF

Born and raised in Germany, Annabelle Selldorf (b. 1960) received a Bachelor of Architecture degree from Pratt Institute and a Master of Architecture degree from Syracuse University in Florence, Italy. Selldorf founded her New York–based practice in 1988. Running a studio as a female architect was not something she consciously thought about at the time but there was surely an impact. "I think it is difficult for architects of any gender to demonstrate and communicate what they do and its value, and if you are a woman practicing in a traditionally male-dominated field, it is going to be just that much harder to be understood and recognised," she reflects. Much has changed but there is still more to do to create true equity. Selldorf suggests that "one of the key issues is the number of women in leadership positions which is still lacking – often women drop out of the field when they begin to have children and find the structure and demands of practice incompatible with raising a family," adding that she is "very proud of the number of female partners (four of five) and project managers that we have here in the firm, as well as how many women have had a child and returned to work, or in several cases two children".

The studio designs a wide range of projects worldwide. From cultural institutions and university buildings, to multi-family residential realizations, to commercial galleries and retail spaces, as well as renovations and masterplans. Interestingly, Selldorf also designed the Sunset Park Material Recovery Facility, which is a new recycling facility and education centre on the Brooklyn waterfront – the largest of its kind in the U.S. The creative work of her 70-person team has a clear structure. Selldorf provides the design direction and leadership for every project. "I have two design partners who have been working alongside me for many years – Sara Lopergolo and Julie Hausch-Fen," she explains. "They divide the projects so that one of them is also involved in every project. They then work with the teams on a regular basis to advance the design and technical aspects of the project and we come together frequently as well. "While nine project managers are responsible for the day-to-day oversight, everyone gets the opportunity to work on any kind of project.

With a strong belief in the transformational power of architecture, which positively impacts both individuals and whole communities, Selldorf's practice develops context-driven concepts. Some of the architect's key principles are to draw inspiration from local materials and building traditions and from humanism for any scale and condition. The practical aspects of a building must be intertwined with the aesthetic ones. Her studio's statement reads, "a true piece of architecture must surpass the practical. With each project we strive to transcend the practical with the poetic, creating something with resonance and permanence". Asked about the biggest challenge in designing architecture today, Selldorf emphasises the need for a holistic approach, considering architecture's impact on the environment, and a commitment to creating sustainable cities.

DAVID ZWIRNER 20TH STREET
NEW YORK, USA, 2013

Drawing from the industrial spirit of the West Chelsea district, Selldorf designed a building of interesting visual contradictions. The exposed concrete, with its rough appearance,  is elegantly punctured by the teak storefront and windows. The regular layout of the façade echoes the neighbouring industrial structures but also creates a play between solid and transparent forms. The galleries are filled with natural light and have concrete and white oak flooring. The minimalistic concept here meets a monumental look. Designed to museum standards, the building houses exhibition and working spaces on five levels connected by a central staircase with a skylight.

## 347 BOWERY
## NEW YORK, USA, 2016

The juxtaposition of zinc panels on this apartment high-rise with the grey Kolumba brick on the retail space at its base clearly divides the two functionally different parts of the building. This 13-storey residential tower fills a corner with wide perspectives across Lower Manhattan. Numerous windows, starting with the glass storefront up to the upper floors, with floor-to-ceiling corner balconies on each floor, provide views and well-lit interiors. Four duplex units and a penthouse triplex are all designed around a central spiralling staircase. They also all have a suspended catwalk overlooking the living space and separating the master and secondary bedrooms.

ANNABELLE SELLDORF

LUMA ARLES
ARLES, FRANCE, 2018

Selldorf is a part of the team
working on the Luma Arles
multi-disciplinary art centre
located south of Arles' historic
city core. The architect is
not only contributing to the
overall master plans but is
also converting five original
structures of the ruins of a rail
depot. The renovated parts are
planned to house new exhibition
facilities, a hotel, a visitor centre,
a café, and a dance studio and
artists' residence. The industrial
structures with steel columns and
trusses are maintained yet are
well adjusted to new purposes.
Expanded and relocated
skylights provide natural light,
one of the main goals of the
project, along with its grand
proportions and clear circulation.

# ALISON MARGARET SMITHSON

British architect Alison Margaret Smithson (1928–1993) studied architecture at the University of Durham, where she met her husband Peter Smithson (1923–2003). Upon graduating, the couple joined the architectural department of London County Council, which at that time was in charge of city planning and council housing among other roles projects. In 1950 they established their common architectural practice and co-signed all architectural projects as well as written works.

The Smithsons became leading representatives of British New Brutalism, a term that was used in the 'Architectural Design' feature on one of the couple's unbuilt houses and was quickly adopted in discussions of the architecture of the era. Their first competition was for a secondary school at Hunstanton, where they employed surprising and innovative elements,

like the welded steel frame and exposed pipework. Later, the dominant materials in their radical ideas were concrete, bricks, or timber. Unplastered internal walls and ceilings, as well as visible service conduits, would become common in their projects. As advocates of modular buildings that are low cost and of the purity of the materials, they significantly influenced the decades to come, and are considered post-war Britain's most radical architects. Their radical ideas were highly innovative and sometimes even shocking at the time. In particular, the rough quality of their buildings, owing to the stark presentation of structure and materials, led to heated discussions. They aimed to develop architecture that would suit changing times, both aesthetically and functionally. They believed that buildings were supposed to reflect the needs of inhabitants, an approach that intensified after their trip to Japan in 1960. A great example is the Garden Building of St. Hilda's College of the University of Oxford. Constructed between 1968 and 1970, it provided accommodation for the students. The square plan with chamfered corners features three façades, dominated by large windows, that overlook a garden with a preserved beech tree. The layered outer shell is an interesting juxtaposition of glass and a timber trellis running between levels. The fourth, entrance façade combined brick and glass. Pre-cast posts and beams along with concrete panels create the supporting structure of the building. The well-lit interiors are spacious and furnished with wood. All rooms have a full-height door, fitted cupboards, and a mini dressing room for intimacy and corridor noise reduction. The Economist Buildings at St James's Street in London remain the couple's most recognisable realization. This well-proportioned complex of three individual buildings is visually bound by its homogenous external form. Distinctive as it is, it also works well within the historical architectural context of the site.

The couple realised relatively few buildings; however, their unbuilt projects were widely publicised to share their visionary concepts. The architects also produced remarkable town-planning projects with innovative ideas for high-level roads and pedestrian walkways. Additionally, the Smithsons authored many theoretical writings which were as influential as their architecture. In the 1950s they published their projects in the 'Architects' Yearbooks' and between 1955 and 1975 were contributors for 'Architectural Design'. Alison Margaret Smithson was also a novelist – in 1966 she wrote a novel titled "A Portrait of the Female Mind as a Young Girl".

## THE ECONOMIST BUILDING
## LONDON, UK, 1964

Considered one of London's most impressive modern spaces, it is Alison and Peter Smithson's largest realization. Built on the premises bombed during the war, the new Economist complex included three buildings: a 16-storey office tower, a residential block, and a bank, gathered around a small irregularly shaped piazza with underground parking below. The volumes are based on square plans with canted corners and have a uniform external shell dominated by concrete, grey enamelled metal, and glass. In 1990 the complex underwent refurbishment, with changes such as remodelling the office's lobby and transforming some of the office's levels from a series of two-person units into open-spaces.

# BENEDETTA TAGLIABUE

Milan-born Benedetta Tagliabue (b. 1963) graduated with a degree in architecture from the Istituto di Architettura di Venezia (IUAV) in Italy. She also studied in Switzerland and New York. In 1991, Tagliabue started collaborating with her husband Enric Miralles (1955–2000), with whom, four years later, she established an international architecture studio, Miralles Tagliabue EMBT. The Barcelona-based practice has realised numerous architectural projects, both in Europe and China. The scope of projects in

the studio's portfolio is truly wide and ranges from schools, markets, and pavilions, to metro stations and even a parliament building. "The majority of the EMBT projects are commissioned by public clients with special emphasis on urban space and the coherence between the built environment and the public space", explains the architect. Over the years the practice has expanded its fields of activities to also work on landscape architecture, conversions, and both interior and product design. In 2010, Miralles Tagliabue EMBT opened a second office in Shanghai.

Tagliabue has said in an interview: "The intention of my work is to do something that helps people. Helps seeing everything differently. Helps making people comfortable, feel familiar". Her curious and open mind draws inspiration from various creative fields. At the core of her design process is experimenting in pursuit of finding new materials and exploring new ways of doing things. Tagliabue's architecture is characterised by its light yet complex structures, transparency, and richness in texture. As her studio's statement explains, "our philosophy reflects the belief of changing the environment by observing and respecting the site, its history and culture". Always attentive to the site's context, she aims to create unique and dynamic designs that relate to their surroundings, where they are inserted into the existing fabric. In her view, equally important as integrating buildings into the site is bringing nature into the designs – quite literally but also by means of an organic architectural language. Her creative process often begins with creating collages made of photos and objects from the site and from the brief. Put together, these are key to her understanding of the complexity of the site.

Discussing the situation of women in architecture, Tagliabue refers to her challenging experiences of becoming the head of a studio and the process of being accepted mainly by the male-dominated construction sector. At the same time, she reflects: "I am certain that, in architecture, women have a lot of different ways of approaching the profession and that women's capabilities, and the subtle differences women can interpret, are very useful in society". In addition to the architectural practice, Tagliabue regularly lectures at numerous universities around the globe, and has been a visiting professor at Harvard University and ETSAB in Barcelona. She is also part of the Pritzker Prize jury, and is the head of the Enric Miralles Foundation, promoting experimental architecture in the spirit of her late husband and partner.

pages 207-209
KÁLIDA SANT PAU CENTRE
BARCELONA, SPAIN, 2019

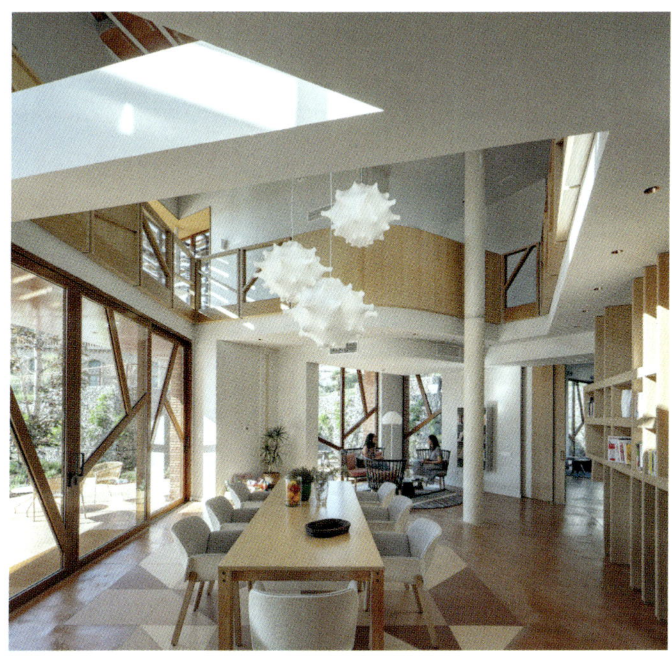

Part of Maggie's Centre Network, this building is designed to support patients diagnosed with cancer and is surrounded by green area that adjoins the clinical hospital. Envisioned as a welcoming space filled with light, the interiors are a mélange of open and private areas. The multifaceted volume refers to the concept of a garden pavilion, where a good inside-outside relation is crucial. Hence, the lower level, conceived as a sequence of flexible spaces, opens to a garden protected by walls and pergolas. The complexity of the structure is enhanced by the richness of the façade's texture, made of bricks with glazed ceramic insertions.

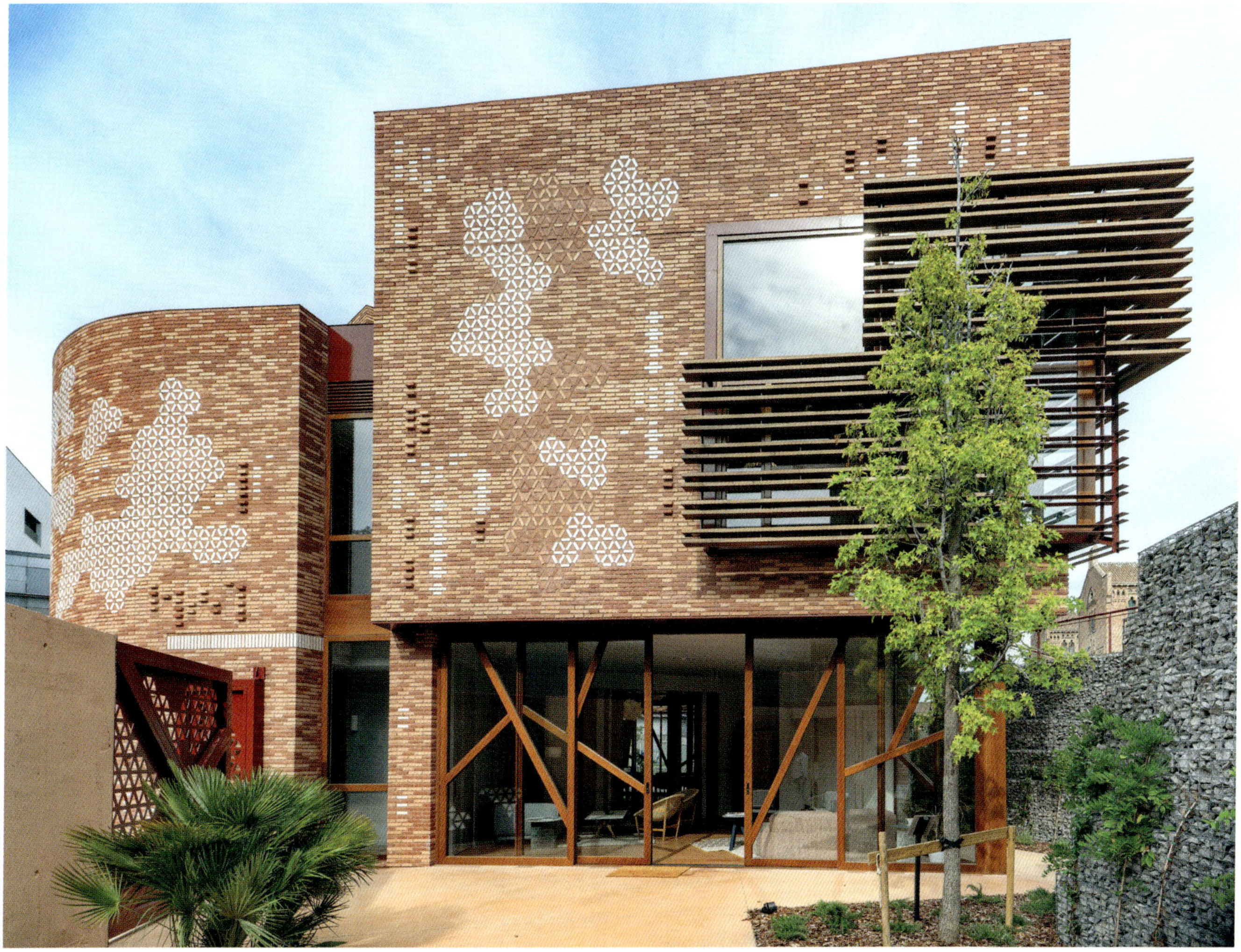

The project includes a system of ramps, stairways, and catwalks that connect different levels and bring people closer to the water. Realised in the framework of a revitalisation and development of the shores of the River Elbe in the heart of Hamburg, the project activates the area along the water in three ways. At the water level, extensive platforms offer access for small boats; 4.5 metres higher, a promenade overlooks the river; and the street level serves as an inviting space, with pedestrian and play areas. The ingeniously planned steps, terraces, and playgrounds for children provide space for visitors to enjoy the city views and relax within a busy urban environment.

Located in a high-rise district, the tower takes the form of a curved shape, initiating a dialogue with surrounding buildings. "Since the beginning of the project, the main idea was the symbiosis between the fragmentation and re-composition of nature and the buildings as pine trees", explains the studio. Referring to a pine tree forest, the building undergoes a transformation vertically – from the ground floor, with structural elements, just like tree trunks, that create the construction of the tower, which then gradually disappears into the sky. The façade is based on an interplay between tree drawings the holes between the trees.

# XU TIANTIAN

Xu Tiantian (b. 1975) is said to be the first Chinese female architect to found a practice without a male partner. She received a Bachelor's degree from Tsinghua University in Beijing and her Master of Architecture in Urban Design from the Harvard Graduate School of Design. After her studies, Tiantian worked at a practice run by her professors in Boston before moving to Rotterdam for one year to work at the Office for Metropolitan Architecture (OMA). Upon her return to China, encouraged by dynamic changes in the country, her early work was mainly in collaboration with the artist Ai Weiwei on the Jinhua Sculpture Park. Eventually Tiantian established her own architectural office DnA_Design and Architecture in Beijing. The first major project was the commission for a new, contemporary version of an artists' village, a combination of an arts centre, a gallery, and artists' studios.

Her interdisciplinary practice realises a number of different projects including art museums, cultural and sport centres, factory facilities, theatre buildings, urban revitalizations, and housing. "Our approach to projects starts with research and discussion of the context, programme, and their interaction, which we believe are the fundamental elements, or the DNA, that will define the design and architecture, to adapt, engage, and contribute to our society of multiplicity and complexity," reads the studio's statement. Shape-wise, the structures Tiantian envisions are unique, due, in part, to her selection of perfectly adjusted materials. Both the geometry and materiality of her buildings demonstrate her knowledge about the site's heritage, which she references subtly. The architect also develops her projects in close collaboration with the local community as much as local workers.

Tiantian has gained particular recognition for the revitalisation of many villages in the rural region of Songyang. In the process of transforming the landscape of the Chinese countryside, the architect invented a method that she describes as architectural acupuncture. "Architectural acupuncture is a strategy that helps to open up an area. In acupuncture we want to increase blood flow, not just treat a single, specific area as in surgery," she explains. As the term comes from Chinese medicine, it is easily understandable; villagers thus know that they can expect small, regenerating interventions that will serve to unblock the potential of declining villages. The architect's goal is to help such communities recover. Respecting the identity and context of each place, Tiantian always looks for what is unique and attractive about each particular village. Working across different locations, the architect attempts to create connections between them, through common attractions or collaborations. As an example, the architect describes a village in which "a porcelain factory is founded. There you can make bottles for products such as brown sugar or rice wine from the other villages. In this way an economic cycle is created". These revitalisations have a much bigger effect beyond their architectural impact. New buildings have the power to improve their users' lives and are hence transformational for the whole community and the way it functions. For her deeply contextual projects, executed with conviction, and for working in a sustainable way with an entrepreneurial spirit, Tiantian was awarded the Moira Gemill Prize for Emerging Architecture at the Women in Architecture Awards in 2019.

pages 213-215
SONGZHUANG ARTIST COMMUNE
SONGZHUANG, BEIJING, CHINA, 2009

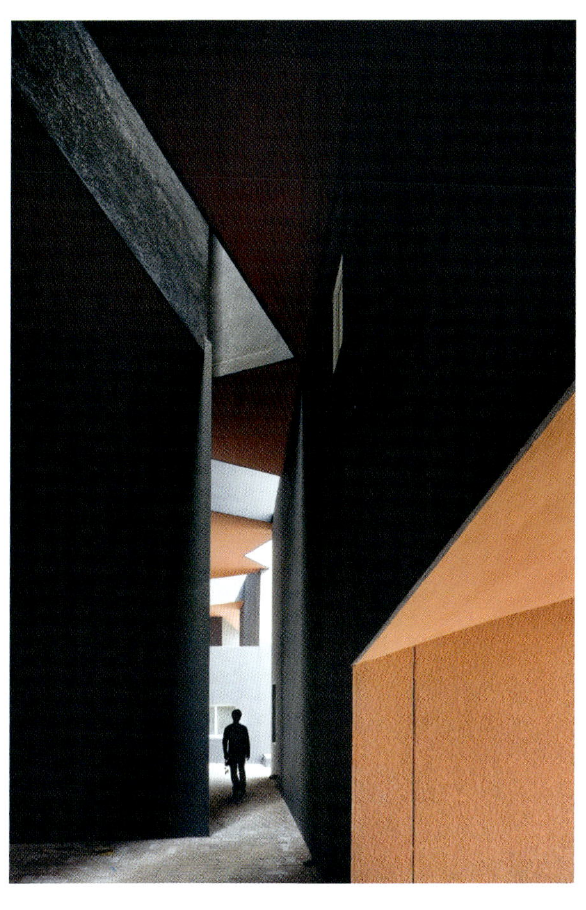

This commune is an answer to the expansion of the artist population in the Songzhuang Artist Village at the East Sixth Ring Road of Beijing city. This 20-unit artist residence in a former outdoor storage lot is a spectacular composition of geometric shapes. Stacked up, the volumes resemble containers, which refers to the site's history. The 6-metre-high box-like studios are combined with 6-metre-high living volumes, including a bedroom, kitchen, and toilet, that take more complex forms, whether on one or two levels. The multifaceted structure of the complex creates a visually powerful interplay between volumes and voids, light and shadows, with outdoor community spaces.

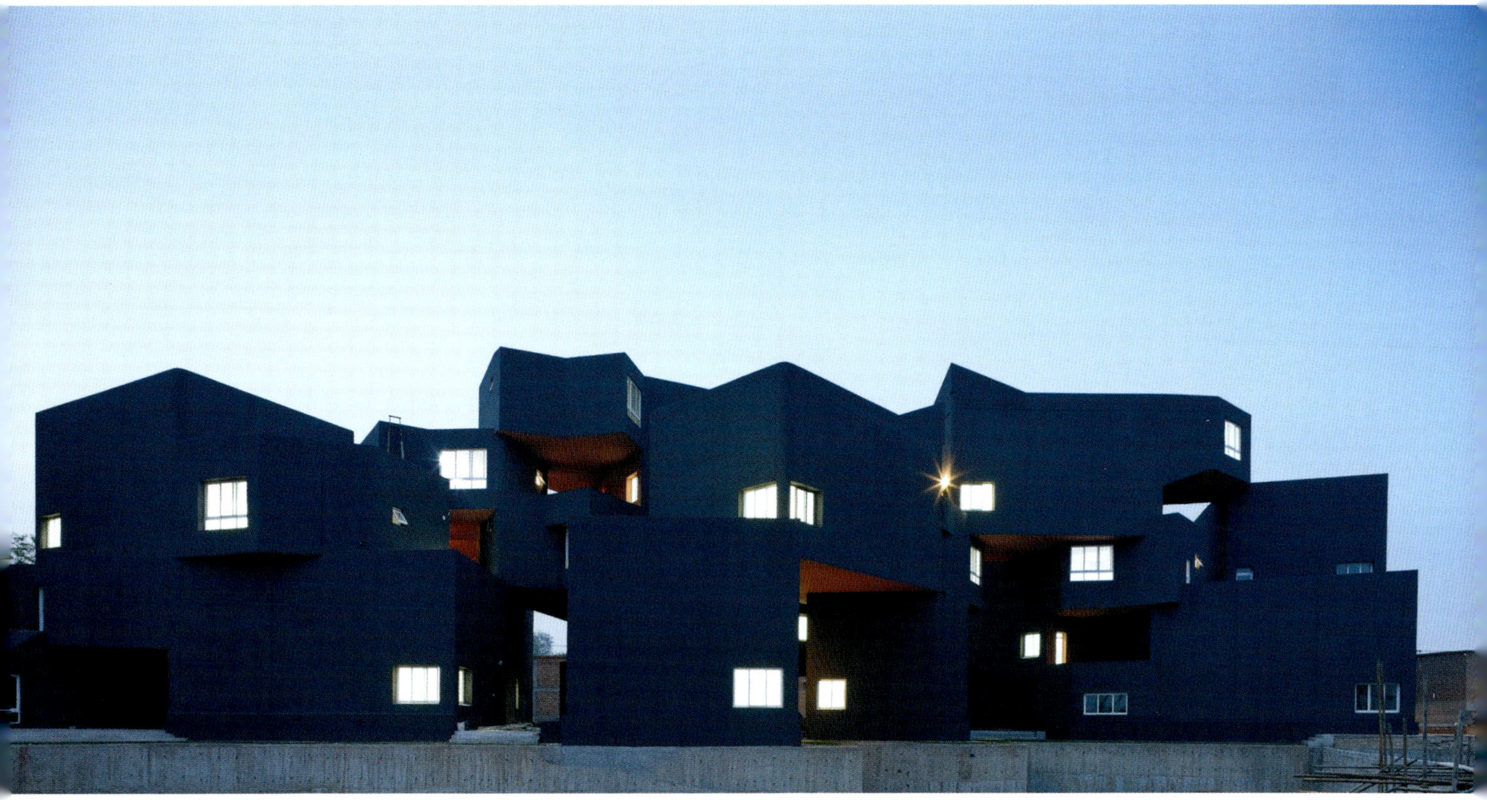

SONGYANG DAMUSHAN TEAHOUSE
SONGYANG DAMUSHAN TEA VALLEY, LISHUI, ZHEJIANG PROVINCE, CHINA, 2015

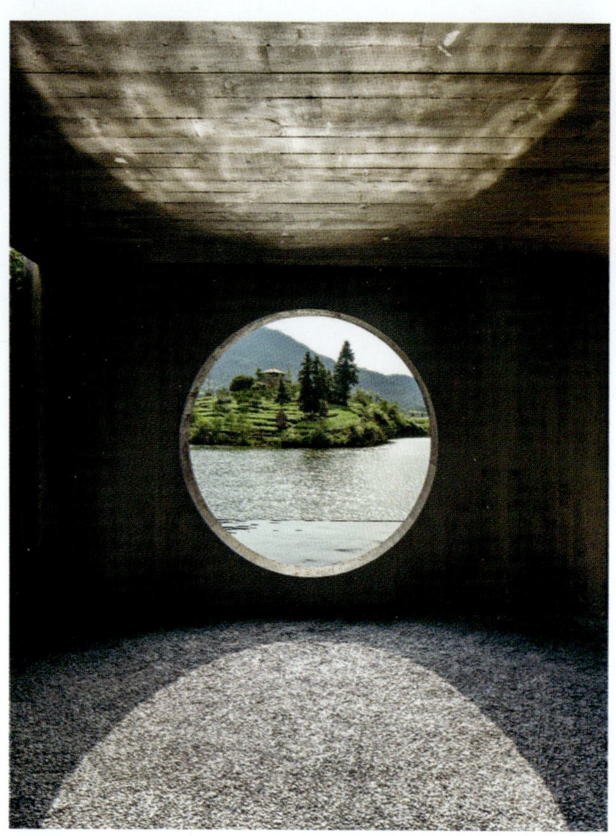

Sitting in the middle of a tea plantation along the shores of an irrigation reservoir, this teahouse was planned as a long corridor made entirely of concrete. It consists of several spaces; the main one is a two-storey open space with a skylight and glass front, facing a shaded plaza, followed by two rooms for private tea ceremonies and a meditation room with a circular opening in one wall. The contemplation of nature is enhanced by the spectacle of light reflected on the surface of the water and penetrating the interior. This sequence of spaces is enhanced by small courtyards offering views towards the surrounding landscape.

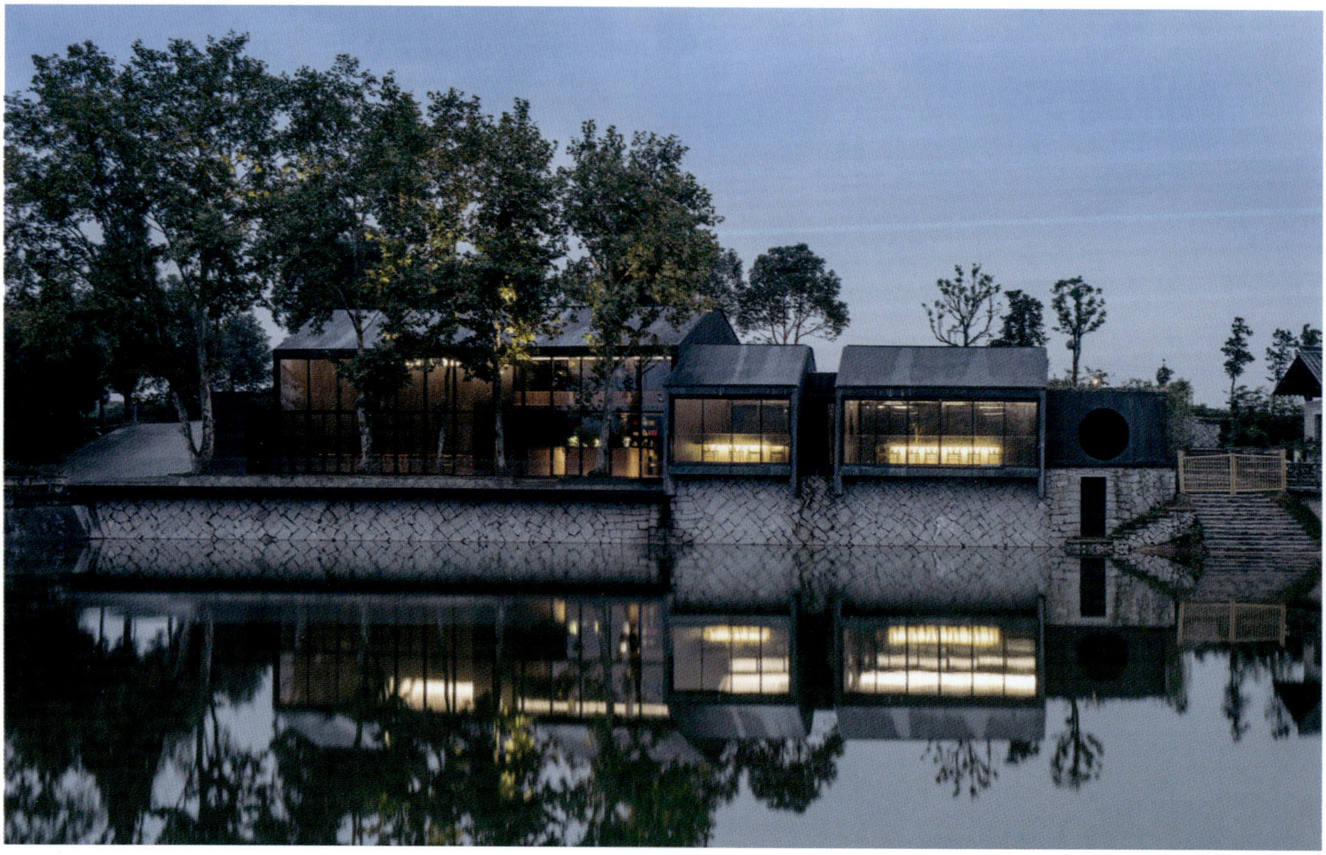

BROWN SUGAR FACTORY
XING VILLAGE, ZHANGXI VILLAGE,
SONGYANG COUNTY, LISHUI,
ZHEJIANG PROVINCE, CHINA, 2016

Located in a village famous for its brown sugar production, this new factory has been divided into four parts. The building not only includes sugarcane storage space and a main production area but also a village public space, dedicated to cultural events and a leisure part for locals and visitors. Light steel construction is used to cover the production area and the equally large leisure space. These two are divided by a glass transparent partition to allow observations of the factory at work, which is particularly absorbing as elements like the space layout, lamps, and uniforms are all carefully choreographed.

# MONICA TRICARIO

constantly pursuing dialogue and attention to details," explains Tricario. Both the studio founders and their collaborators come from different backgrounds, which ensures a continuous and stimulating exchange that enhances the design process. Drawing from and finding constant references in nature, culture, and music, as well as art and history, they pay special attention to the function and the pre-existing area. Whether it is a contemporary, bustling building in the middle of a historical district or a refurbished space combining the original fabric with new architecture, Piuarch's designs demonstrate an astounding coexistence of all elements. "When approaching a new project, we usually attempt to preserve the context, studying its exceptional features, in order to bring out its inner soul," notes Tricario. "Considerable effort is put into reclaiming and improving its former morphology, materials, nature, social, and cultural features. We look for the artistic and historic movements which it went through, in order to interpret it in the best way and reflect it in every interstice, detail, and view of the building," she concludes. For the studio, the ultimate goal is to find an accurate balance between tradition, the special nature of a place, and modernity. What binds all of their projects is the use of the highest quality, technologically advanced materials and bold geometric forms. Their work, characterised by their very rhythmical, complex, well-thought-out, and visually stunning solutions, is in large part inspired by the 20th century movements, from geometric abstraction to kinetic art, as Tricario emphasises. Due to their hectic schedules the whole team rarely works on the same project, as they used to do at the outset. However, all big decisions are discussed together as a team. Their projects are always the result of collaboration, a sum of several voices and ideas, which becomes a joint vision.

As the only woman among four founders, Tricario observes that "architecture-wise, I do not think one's gender influences the design process. I think that it might be more linked with personal features and facets of an individual, as creativity, skills, and experiences." Piuarch has valued the power of the team and its cohesion, which has deeply shaped their design process reflecting their plurality. "However," Tricario mentions, "women have a natural inclination for gathering people, harmonising, and smoothing all situations, also criticalities. I think that within our group of four partners and founders, my duty has always been to balance all personalities, to keep cohesion and to find the perfect synergy among our different attitudes".

Italian architect Monica Tricario (b. 1963) of Piuarch studied architecture at Polytechnic University of Milan and while there she collaborated in the field of industrial design with Achille Castiglioni. Between 1988 and 1996 she worked at Vittorio Gregotti's architectural firm in Milan, where she met Francesco Fresa, Germán Fuenmayor, and Gino Garbellini. Together they cofounded the Piuarch studio in 1996. As a group of personalities and joint skills with a single vision, they lead a team of forty professionals based in the Brera district of Milan. "Here we develop projects in work groups which create synergies according to the personalities involved in them,

QUATTRO CORTI
SAINT PETERSBURG, RUSSIA, 2010

Located in the heart of Saint Petersburg, this new business centre was designed in the frames of the historical façades of two buildings previously occupying the plot, and it is barely visible from the street perspective. Four internal courtyards, incorporated into the new structure by a metal roof, are a source of light for the interiors but can also become gathering spaces and host events or art exhibitions. Their transparent façades are multifaceted compositions of reflective coloured glass panels, in gold, green, azure, and white. As they are set at different angles, they create a vibrant spectacle of reflections depending on the rays of sun.

PORTA NUOVA BUILDING
MILAN, ITALY 2013

With its sinuous form inscribing perfectly into the curved outline of the Piazza Gae Aulenti, Porta Nuova is a visual delight, not only because of its dynamic shape. Its façade that embraces the street is covered by a system of louvers at regular intervals, while the one facing the square forms a gigantic wall creating a rhythmical pattern of windows. The building consists of the commercial space located on the ground floor, five levels of offices above, and a system of internal patios with coloured walls. As part of the urban redevelopment of the square, it creates a link between the historical fabric and the newly built skyscrapers.

MONICA TRICARIO

pages 221–223
GUCCI HUB
MILAN, ITALY, 2016

This revamp of the old Caproni aircraft
factory, dating back to the 1920s, has
resulted in a new headquarters for the
acclaimed fashion label. The abandoned
red-brick and low-level warehouses have
been turned into an extensive complex
with offices, a show room, and spaces for
fashion shows, as well as a canteen and
a restaurant. The only new building, a six-
storey tower, fuses with the historical fabric.
With façades enveloped with sunscreens
creating a regular pattern, this vertical
element dominates over the horizontal
order of the renovated part. All volumes are
connected with pedestrian paths, green
spaces, and interior plazas.

# NATHALIE DE VRIES

Dutch architect Nathalie de Vries (b. 1965) graduated from Delft University of Technology and started her architectural career at Mecanoo. In 1993, together with Winy Maas and Jacob van Rijs, she co-founded the Rotterdam-based MVRDV, an inter-disciplinary studio working at the intersection of architecture and urban planning. The practice has gained recognition for its innovative and experimental approach based on thorough research and demonstrated by a wide range of scales and building types, from office buildings to housing, to masterplans for cities with a global scope. MVRDV also engages in revitalisations of Dutch monuments, like the Stedelijk Museum Schiedam and Buitenplaats Koningsweg in Arnhem. Reusing and redeveloping spaces is a common practise in the Netherlands, which influences the architects' approach to creating new places.

As suggested by De Vries, landscaping a building plays a crucial role, as a way of negotiating the relationship between the interior and exterior as well.

Whether converting old structures or designing new ones, they favour the direction of investigating new approaches rather than following particular schemes. "We take a perfectly normal thing, that's been done very often in a certain way, and we start to question that", says De Vries. "Why on earth should we make every new shopping mall, or office or tennis court in the same way?", she adds.

The main mission of the practice is to "enable cities and landscapes to develop towards a better future". At the core of the design process are collaborative and research-based methods, which allow the architects to find innovative solutions. The ultimate goal is to make buildings as inclusive as possible, and make the architecture flexible enough to meet any needs the future may bring. "We can create a new generation of architecture and urban design, and turn buildings into containers carrying an unknown – but nevertheless limitless – future," explains De Vries. The firm has also established an independent think tank and postgraduate research institute, Why Factory, which is run together with Delft University of Technology and develops ideas for the city of the future. "This research leads us to deal with issues ranging from global sustainability in large-scale studies, such as Pig City, to small, pragmatic architectural solutions for devastated areas, such as New Orleans", comment the studio.

De Vries draws inspiration from various disciplines, including design, technique, and fashion. Architecture allows her to drawn on all of these fields of interest to come up with ideas for new designs. She also enjoys the challenge of embracing the complexity of architectural projects. "What interests me is the challenge to fit all the different aspects and disciplines of the project together, like a complex jigsaw puzzle", she reflects. Parallel to designing architecture, De Vries is a Professor of Architectural Design at her alma mater and lectures internationally. To promote her studio's design philosophy, the architect has co-published a publication and curated an exhibition looking into the firm's typologies. Between 2015 and 2019, she was also the Chair of the Royal Institute of Dutch Architects. In her role as the Chief National Railroad Architect, De Vries has developed transport infrastructure in the Netherlands.

VILLA VPRO
HILVERSUM, THE NETHERLANDS, 1997

MVRDV's inaugural project (designed by all three found-ing partners) was realised for the VPRO Broadcasting Company, which commissioned a new headquarters. "The proposal departs from traditional cellular office environments by inviting occupants to transition seamlessly from one floor to the next through an undulating and stepped concrete landscape", explains the studio. To obtain transparency and fill the interiors with light and air, the architects based the structure of the villa on a grid of columns and stabilising props. Additionally, storey-high apertures offer access and views to the garden, patio, and terraces. The spatial arrangement of the interiors is far from obvious; all levels are fluidly connected by ramps, steps, or rises.

pages 231-233
HOUSE IN FROGS HOLLOW
NIAGARA ESCARPMENT, CANADA, 2010

Situated among gentle, eroded clay hills near protected
watershed zones and covered with native grasses and a
dense field of hawthorn, the house takes the form of a robust
geometric body. The architect carved it partly into a long slope,
integrating it in a way that also refers to the owners' strong
connection to the landscape. The environmental footprint of this
country retreat is kept low thanks to several design elements:
Heating is provided by radiant floor loops that supplement
the passive winter heat gain from south-facing windows. No
mechanical cooling is used – only operable windows that
facilitate passive ventilation, drawing cool air from the shaded
exterior areas. Last, the design also incorporates natural
materials and pigments, as well as a small square footage.

With housing offices, underground parking, retail space, and a panorama restaurant, Bałtyk (the building takes its name from a legendary cinema formerly located on the same plot) is visually striking with its twisted form. As it sits at one of the city's main communication roundabouts, it can be seen from various perspectives, which the architects used in a playful way. It looks quite different from each of the four sides. "The façade is floor-to-ceiling glass with vertical louvres of glass fibre concrete softening the impact of the sun without losing the vistas", explains the architect. Co-designed with Natkanies/Olechnicki Architekci, the building also creates a cosy square with surrounding buildings.

# BETSY WILLIAMSON

Ontario-based Betsy Williamson pursued architecture starting in high school, when she figured out in an architectural design course that it might be a great way to combine her skills in mathematics with her love of art history. With a Master of Architecture from Harvard University and a BA with Honours in Architecture from Barnard College, she co-founded an architectural design studio together with her husband Shane in 2008. "My studio is run collaboratively, between myself and my partner as well as amongst the entire staff", she explains. "I have found that collaboration allows every person in the studio to be invested in the design process which encourages the best work. You never know where the best idea will come from – and to make a great project you need the best ideas. Shane and I have our hands in everything, and I would hope that everyone in the studio could say the same thing," continues Williamson. She is involved more specifically in the detailing and, interestingly, in the on-site construction of the work. As much as design and building have their own unique sets of challenges, Williamson enjoys the complexity of construction and working with the building team. Her main ambition is to create buildings that will be both beautiful and long lasting, a goal which is impossible without her involvement in each part of the process.

As an eager advocate for equality in architecture, Williamson has been involved in a number of equity-based groups over the years, starting from when she was a graduate student. She also co-founded BEAT (Building Equality in Architecture Toronto), which focuses on creating events and web content, and providing mentorship and networking, for women in the field. "BEAT has exceeded my expectations in how effective it has been to create awareness," she says. "Many Toronto firms are now considering the issue of equity in their offices for the first time. As it has been for decades, there are equal numbers of women and men in schools of architecture and early in practice; however, women in leadership are still underrepresented in Canada", she says, emphasising that "it is important to focus our work on creating leadership opportunities for the next generation". Another field of the architect's activity is her engagement in and contributions to the urban development of Toronto, particularly as the vice-chair of the Waterfront Toronto Design Review Panel.

When discussing the biggest challenges of architecture today, she points to the complexity of the discipline: "it is always hard to build, to translate a conceptual idea into a beautifully detailed project that provides value for the client and addresses the responsibility we have to the environment while also participating in architectural discourse". She reflects that "architecture is our primary visual culture that affects how we engage with and see the world. It is not just the marriage of art and science, but also participates in the ethics of building socially and environmentally. This is a tall task and is surely our greatest challenge."

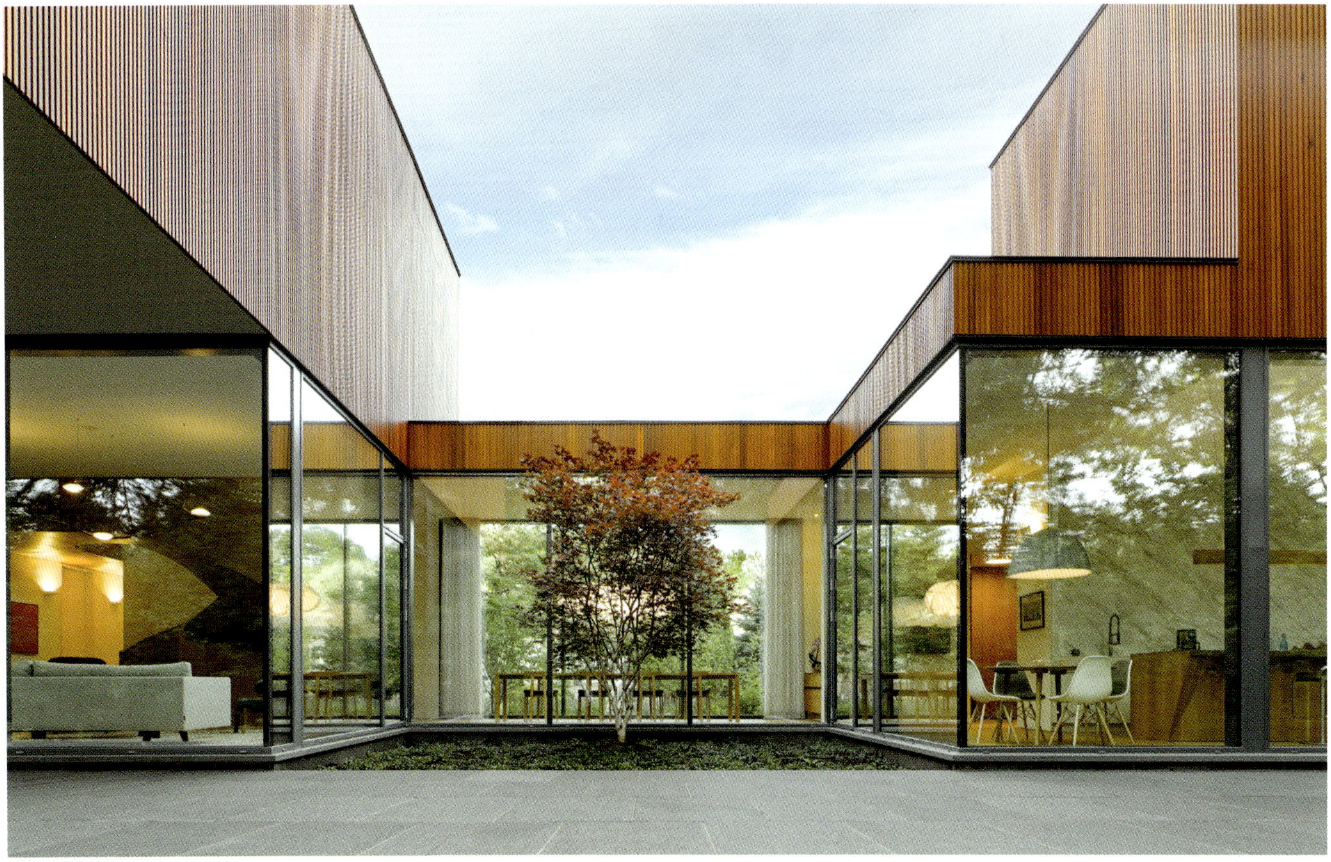

HOUSE ON ANCASTER CREEK
HAMILTON, CANADA, 2016

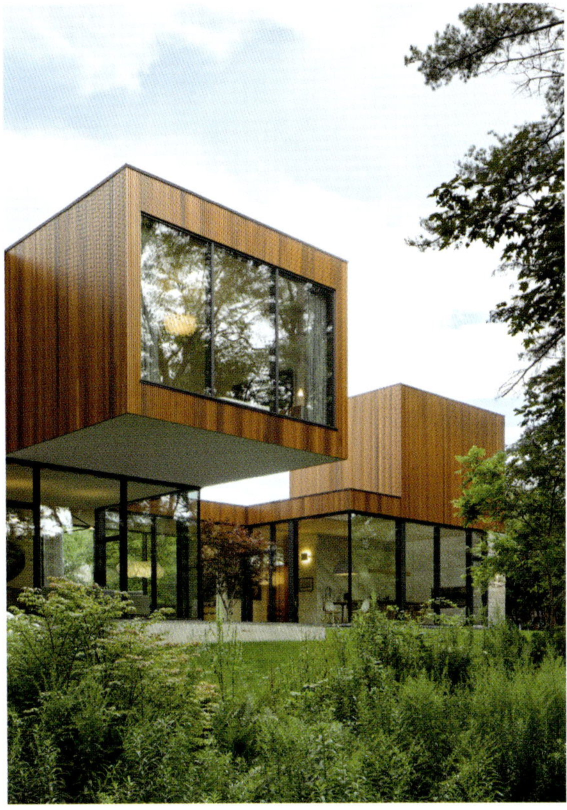

Designed for multigenerational family of aging parents to live with their adult children , this house creates a "scenario for living that allows for autonomy while mutually benefiting from proximity". Envisioned as a horizontal combination of two distinct residences, both are shaped as linear bars that sit perpendicular to each other, creating a courtyard and stacking at the corner. The social spaces, like the dining, living, and outdoor areas, are shared by both families. A dominant element dynamically connecting both floors is a spectacular laminated plywood spiral staircase in the living room. The aesthetically sophisticated and light structure made of glass and honed limestone on the ground floor contrasts with the flat-sawn cedar top level. The architect uses local materials and sustainable solutions.

## HOUSE ON BALA LINE
### TORONTO, CANADA, 2016

The Bala line, like many of Toronto's unused historic rails, is located on a steep slope and offers an upper plateau for residential architecture with a view overlooking a wooded valley below. This family house sits on one of several quite densely inhabited plots, with numerous windows to take in the landscapes. The intriguing combination of forms and materials on the outside evolves into a series of terraced spaces, echoing the cascading topography of the surrounding landscape. A massive double-cantilever open corner is designed as a counterbalance for the 'carved' front façade but also smoothly links the living room with the outdoor area.

BETSY WILLIAMSON

# ADA YVARS BRAVO

Spanish architect Ada Yvars Bravo grew up in Barcelona, where she had been influenced by great buildings since she was little and had wanted to become an architect as a child. Upon completing her studies at ETSAB (Escola Tècnica Superior d'Arquitectura de Barcelona) in her home city, Yvars Bravo first gained professional experience at Carlos Ferrater Architects in Spain, and later by working in London for Florian Beiger

Architects, Pierre D'Avoine Architects and David Chipperfield Architects. After a couple of years, she and her partner Ali Mangera decided to start their own architectural office, Mangera Yvars Architects (MYAA), to provide architecture, interior, landscape, and masterplanning services internationally. What appears to have been a springboard for their practice was a commission for the Qatar Faculty of Islamic Studies, which gave them the opportunity to expand. Realising projects in the Middle East was like opening a new chapter for the studio.

"We made a conscious decision to work over there based on the belief that we could shape countries and make big buildings", she explains. "We wanted to work somewhere that we could really make a difference", adds Yvars Bravo. Their work ranges from large-scale designs, like a stadium and an airport, to private residences, cultural institutions, seafront schemes, and creating a whole new city district. "As architects working in the public and private sector", the MYAA statement reads, "we strongly believe in the principle that good architecture and urban design can contribute to better societies". With two main offices in London and Barcelona, they create architecture that is based on in-depth social and cultural analysis supported by research and data. The social and historical context of a site always plays a significant role in shaping the final design.

For Mangera and Yvars Bravo, architecture is not merely a stunning visual form but also a thoughtful reference to local traditions and society's needs. Depending on the nature of the project, the approach can be swiftly adjusted. "Our purpose is not only to provide exceptional architecture to our clients through innovation and value, but to ensure that our approach leads to better, more inclusive and sustainable cities that provide a benefit to all", emphasise the architects. Sustainability is yet another important issue in MYAA's practice and it is understood "not simply in terms of needs and obligations but in terms of human, cultural, social, and economic development". One of their innovative concepts is developing sustainable housing prototypes for mass housing using energy-efficient production technology.

AVONDALE PARK PAVILION
LONDON, UK, 2010

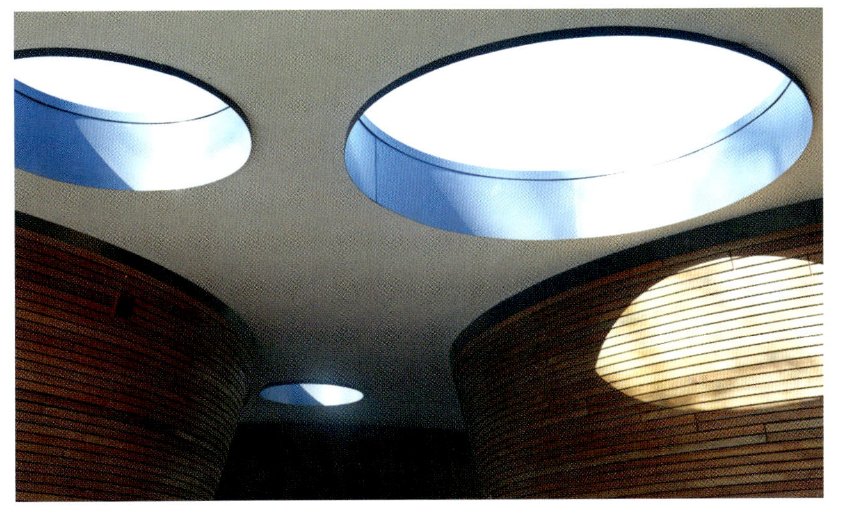

The Pavilion, located in one of the parks in the Notting Hill district in London, is a complex of four volumes. "The conical forms are related to the historic kiln and potteries which used to be located in the Avondale Park area", explains the architect. All elements have different functions and are connected only through an organic roof, which extends to cover part of the exterior picnic space. The curvaceous shapes, together with the porous texture of the outer shell, blend into the surroundings. A ground source heat pump, photovoltaic cells and circular green roof discs make it a very sustainable building.

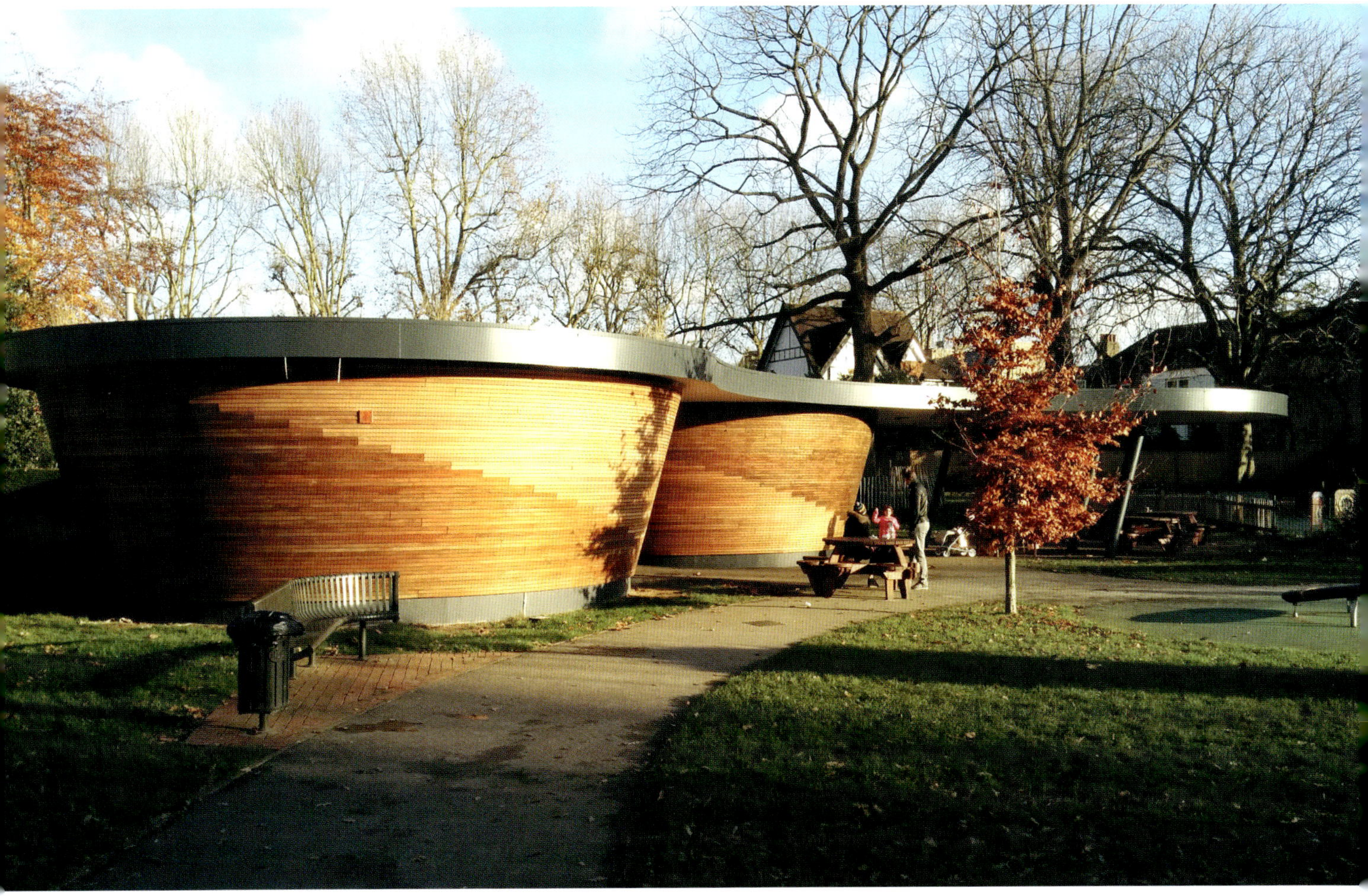

## QFIS UNIVERSITY
## DOHA, QATAR, 2015

Located in the Educational City Campus, the Qatar Faculty of Islamic Studies (QFIS) is planned as a spiral arrangement and encompasses a library and classrooms, as well as faculty offices. The building, meant by the architects to be a social-condenser, community building, and a university, is accessible to students and the local community. "Uniquely for the Muslim World, the scheme gives male and female students parity by providing co-educational, non-hierarchical space where men and women have equal consideration", stress the architects. With two 90-metre-high minarets symbolising "knowledge and light" on one side, this visually impressive volume is bound with the mosque through a four-storey ablution cascade around undulating stairs.

GATEWAY
ANTANANARIVO, MADAGASCAR, ONGOING

Constrained by a narrow triangular plot between a canal and the main road, Gateway is an eight-storey building combining several functions. Commercial spaces take up the ground level, the middle section is devoted to office space, and the upper floors are designed as residential space. While the angular form resembles traditional housing typologies from Madagascar, the geometric cladding panels of the outer shell, punctured by irregular elongated windows, draw from the traditional national board game called Fanorona. The building initiates a larger residential and commercial development.

# CAZÚ ZEGERS

Cazú Zegers (b. 1958), a Chilean architect based in Santiago, has been working independently since 1990. Her practice's mission is to develop expressive architecture that is, as she describes, closely related to Chile, and its territory, landscape, and traditions. "As an architect, my life task has been to find a Latin American Architecture contemporary language that has to do with this relation with the landscape and local and vernacular processes," explains Zegers. Her poetic architectural dialogue with the South American landscape is based on finding a balance between being absorbed by it and competing with the natural beauty of the place. Zegers came up with the concept that "the territory is to America what monuments are

to Europe", which defines the relation she thinks that architecture should have with the landscape in South America. "For me the challenge is how we build and develop territories without demystifying the land," she explains. "One of the clues is to understand the landscape as a Natural Monument, so every building that we build has a respectful relation with it, in a way that the natural monument enriches the building and the building is enriched by the landscape," she emphasises.

Achieving this in her practice translates into the process of intense sketching at the site. Her drawings become a way to understand the place, and its structure, sounds, colours, and textures. The architect also notes that her designs are always very discreet, so the landscape can show itself. On yet another level Zegers' architecture also engages in a dialogue with past traditions, like her wooden architecture that reprises the vernacular construction models and uses a traditional process. Interestingly, she suggests that the work developed by her firm be considered a "work in progress" rather than a "finished work", which, as she notes, involves a poetic reflection about the way we inhabit the territory.

Discussing the situation of women architects in Chile, she remarks that it is still difficult to get important commissions, which is the reason women have usually worked on small-scale projects. Her own portfolio, however, includes a wide spectrum of realizations, ranging from housing to a cultural centre, to a chapel and hotels. At the same time, Zegers praises women's in-depth and complex thinking. "Architecture is an art that develops in space and consequently is three-dimensional. I believe that we women architects work in a field of "n" dimensions in which the senses play a role of indisputable importance", she suggests in one of her interviews, "the work therefore becomes a focus of multiple relationships that respond to the client's requirements in a poetic and original fashion". By establishing the "El Observatorio Lastarria Foundation" ("a place to observe Chile"), Zegers has initiated research on Chilean women in art and architecture with a series of workshops to counterbalance their invisibility. The architect continually advocates that "women and indigenous communities are fundamental to come into the cultural discussion as equals to balance life and development." In addition to running her practice, Zegers also teaches and lectures both in Chile and internationally.

TIERRA PATAGONIA HOTEL
TORRES DEL PAINE, CHILE, 2011

"The gesture of the building arises from the shapes drawn by the wind, a natural element characteristic of the area", states the architect. The picturesque setting of the national park and the shores of Lake Sarmiento with amazing views all around required a project that would fuse with the site without destroying the natural harmony of the place. The low, extremely long, and dune-like shape emerging from the land looks like an ancient fossil of a prehistoric animal stranded on the shore of the lake. Made in wood and stone, the building becomes a visible but not invasive addition to the landscape.

## SOPLO HOUSE
### LO BARNECHEA, CHILE, 2011

The architect's own pavilion-style house located at the foot of Manquehue hill in Santiago has two completely different faces. While the access from the street is formed by a sequence of curved walls, inspired by experiencing Richard Serra's sculptures, the opposite façade opening to the landscape is entirely glazed. Parallelly, the interiors are designed as an open space with a double circulation in the back and through a corridor along the landscape, with none of the rooms touching the façade windows. To contribute to the thermal efficiency of the house, the roof is covered with a deck and flowers.

LLU HOUSE
FUNDO CARRÁN, CHILE, 2018

The complex, yet well-connected spaces arranged on a single floor create a home for four generations of the same family. The Region of Los Ríos in the south of Chile is known for its rainy weather conditions, which inspired the tent-like structure that is able to evacuate loads of water. Through the shapes, numerous openings, and materials, the house is in a constant dialogue with the nature on site. The interiors are visually striking, with their continuous walls and all-present wood. By lifting some of the volumes up onto a steel pillar construction, the architect gained outdoor space that is partly roofed.

# INDEX

OLAJUMOKE ADENOWO – AD CONSULTING
**B. 1968, BASED IN LAGOS, NIGERIA**
GUIDING LIGHT ASSEMBLY //
  LAGOS, NIGERIA, 2002
AD STUDIO // LEKKI, LAGOS, NIGERIA, 2014
REEVE ROAD // LAGOS, NIGERIA, 2018
PP. 8–13

AMALE ANDRAOS - WORKac
**B. 1973, BASED IN NEW YORK, USA**
KEW GARDENS HILLS LIBRARY //
  QUEENS, NEW YORK USA 2017
MIAMI MUSEUM GARAGE // MIAMI, USA, 2018
RHODE ISLAND SCHOOL OF DESIGN
  STUDENT CENTER // PROVIDENCE, USA, 2019
PP. 14–17

GAE AULENTI
**1927–2012, BASED IN ITALY**
MUSÉE D'ORSAY // PARIS, FRANCE, 1986
PP. 18–21

SANDRA BARCLAY – BARCLAY & CROUSSE
**B. 1967, BASED IN LIMA, PERU**
PARACAS MUSEUM // PARACAS, PERU, 2012
UNIVERSITY FACILITIES UDEP //
  PIUNA, PERU, 2016
REGIONAL GOVERNMENT HEADQUARTERS
  // MOQUEGUA, PERU, 2018
PP. 22–25

DEBORAH BERKE
DEBORAH BERKE PARTNERS
**B. 1954, BASED IN NEW YORK, USA**
MARIANNE BOESKY GALLERY //
  NEW YORK, USA, 2007

48 BOND STREET // NEW YORK, USA, 2008
CUMMINS INDY DISTRIBUTION
  HEADQUARTERS // INDIANAPOLIS, USA, 2017
PP. 26–29

TATIANA BILBAO - TATIANA BILBAO ESTUDIO
**B. 1972, BASED IN MEXICO CITY, MEXICO**
BIOINNOVA // CULIACÁN, MÉXICO, 2012
ACUÑA SUSTAINABLE HOUSING // ACUÑA,
  COAHUILA, MEXICO, 2015
LOS TERRENOS // SAN PEDRO GARZA
  GARCÍA, MEXICO, 2016
PP. 30–35

LINA BO BARDI
**1914–1992, BASED IN BRAZIL**
SESC POMPÉIA // SÃO PAULO, BRAZIL, 1986
PP. 36–39

CAROLINE BOS – UNSTUDIO
**B. 1959, BASED IN AMSTERDAM,
THE NETHERLANDS**
BRAINPORT SMART DISTRICT //
  HELMOND, BRANDEVOORT, THE
  NETHERLANDS, ONGOING
ARNHEM CENTRAL STATION //
  ARNHEM, THE NETHERLANDS, 2015
PP. 40–43

ALISON BROOKS
ALISON BROOKS ARCHITECTS
**B. 1962, BASED IN LONDON, UK**
QUARTERHOUSE // FOLKESTONE,
  UNITED KINGDOM, 2009
THE SMILE // LONDON,
  UNITED KINGDOM, 2016

EXETER COLLEGE COHEN QUAD //
  OXFORD, UNITED KINGDOM, 2017
PP. 44-49

SARAH CALBURN
SARAH CALBURN ARCHITECTS
B. 1964, BASED IN JOHANNESBURG,
SOUTH AFRICA
LITTLE CLIFF HOUSE // CRAIGHALL PARK,
  JOHANNESBURG, SOUTH AFRICA, 2006
COCOON HOUSE // ILLOVO,
  JOHANNESBURG, SOUTH AFRICA, 2011
ROEDEAN SCHOOL. CENTRE FOR
  MATHEMATICS EXCELLENCE //
  HOUGHTON, SOUTH AFRICA
PP. 50-53

FERNANDA CANALES – FERNANDA CANALES
ARQUITECTURA
B. 1974, BASED IN MEXICO CITY, MEXICO
ELENA GARRO CULTURAL CENTRE //
  MEXICO CITY, MEXICO, 2012
PORTALES HOUSING //
  MEXICO CITY, MEXICO 2016
CASA BRUMA // VALLE DE BRAVO,
  MEXICO, 2017
PP. 54-59

LUCÍA CANO - SELGASCANO
B. 1965, BASED IN MADRID, SPAIN
SELGASCANO OFFICE // MADRID, SPAIN, 2007
MÉRIDA FACTORY YOUTH MOVEMENT //
  MÉRIDA, SPAIN, 2011
PLASENCIA AUDITORIUM AND CONGRESS
  CENTER // CARTAGENA, SPAIN, 2017
PP. 60-63

ODILE DECQ - STUDIO ODILE DECQ
B. 1955, BASED IN PARIS, FRANCE
FRAC BRETAGNE // RENNES, FRANCE, 2012
SAINT-ANGE RESIDENCY // SEYSSINS,
  FRANCE, 2015
LE CARGO // PARIS, FRANCE, 2016
PP. 64-69

ELIZABETH DILLER
DILLER SCOFIDIO + RENFRO
B. 1954, BASED IN NEW YORK, USA
THE HIGH LINE // NEW YORK CITY, USA, 2014
THE SHED // NEW YORK CITY, USA, 2019
THE MUSEUM OF MODERN ART //
  NEW YORK CITY, USA, 2019
PP. 70-75

JANE DREW
1911-1996
THE UNIVERSITY OF IBADAN //
  IBADAN, NIGERIA, 1949–60
PP. 76-79

FRIDA ESCOBEDO - FRIDA ESCOBEDO
B. 1979, BASED IN MEXICO CITY, MEXICO
LA TALLERA // CUERNAVACA, MEXICO, 2012
GSB STANFORD // PALO ALTO, CALIFORNIA,
  USA, 2016
MAR TIRRENO // MEXICO CITY, MEXICO, 2019
PP. 80-83

YVONNE FARRELL & SHELLEY McNAMARA
GRAFTON ARCHITECTS
B. 1951 & 1952, BASED IN DUBLIN, IRELAND
SOLSTICE ARTS CENTRE // NAVAN,
  CO. MEATH, IRELAND, 2007

UNIVERSITY LUIGI BOCCONI – SCHOOL
  OF ECONOMICS // MILAN, ITALY, 2008
TOWN HOUSE KINGSTON UNIVERSITY
  LONDON // KINGSTON UPON THAMES,
  UK, 2019
PP. 84-89


**DORIANA FUKSAS – FUKSAS**
**B. 1955, BASED IN ROME, ITALY AND PARIS,**
**FRANCE**

ARMANI 5TH AVENUE //
  NEW YORK, USA, 2009
SHENZHEN BAO'AN INTERNATIONAL
  AIRPORT – TERMINAL 3 // SHENZHEN,
  CHINA, 2013
NEW ROME - EUR CONVENTION CENTRE
  AND HOTEL 'THE CLOUD' //
  ROME, ITALY, 2016
PP. 90-93


**JEANNE GANG - STUDIO GANG**
**B. 1955, BASED IN NEW YORK**
**AND SAN FRANCISCO, USA**

ARCUS CENTER FOR SOCIAL JUSTICE
  LEADERSHIP // KALAMAZOO, MI, USA, 2014
WRITERS THEATRE // GLENCOE,
  ILLINOIS, USA, 2016
SOLAR CARVE // NEW YORK, USA, 2019
PP. 94-97


**EILEEN GRAY**
**1878-1976, BASED IN FRANCE**

E-1027 // ROQUEBRUNE–CAP-MARTIN,
  FRANCE, 1929
PP. 98-101


**ZAHA HADID – ZAHA HADID ARCHITECTS**
**1950-2016, BASED IN LONDON, UK**

LOIS & RICHARD ROSENTHAL CENTER
  FOR CONTEMPORARY ART // CINCINNATI,
  USA, 2003
MAXXI: MUSEUM OF XXI CENTURY ARTS //
  ROME, ITALY, 2009
HEYDAR ALIYEV CENTRE // BAKU,
  AZERBAIJAN, 2012
PP. 102-105


**ITSUKO HASEGAWA - ITSUKO HASEGAWA**
**ATELIER**
**B. 1941, BASED IN TOKYO, JAPAN**

SHONANDAI CULTURAL CENTRE //
  FUJISAWA, KANAGAWA, JAPAN, 1990
YAMANASHI FRUITS MUSEUM //
  YAMANASHI, JAPAN, 1995
FUJINOKUNI SENBONMATSU FORUM /
  PLAZA VERDE // NUMAZU, SHIZUOKA,
  JAPAN, 2013
PP. 106-109


**ANNA HERINGER - ANNA HERINGER**
**B. 1977, BASED IN LAUFEN, GERMANY**

METI SCHOOL // DIPSHIKHA,
  BANGLADESH, 2005
DESI TRAININGCENTER //
  RUDRAPUR, BANGLADESH
THREE HOSTELS // BAOXI, CHINA 2016
PP. 110-113


**FRANCINE HOUBEN – MECANOO**
**B. 1955, BASED IN DELFT, THE NETHERLANDS**

MONTEVIDEO RESIDENTIAL TOWER //
  ROTTERDAM, NETHERLANDS, 2005

LIBRARY OF BIRMINGHAM // BIRMINGHAM,
UNITED KINGDOM, 2013
NATIONAL KAOHSIUNG CENTRE FOR THE
ARTS // KAOHSIUNG, TAIWAN, 2018
PP. 114–119

ROSSANA HU – NERI & HU
B. 1968, BASED IN SHANGHAI, CHINA

THE WATERHOUSE // SOUTH BUND,
SHANGHAI, CHINA, 2010
LE MERIDIEN ZHENGZHOU //
ZHENGZHOU, CHINA, 2013
ARANYA ART CENTER // QINHUANGDAO,
CHINA, 2019
PP. 120–125

LOUISA HUTTON – SAUERBRUCHHUTTON
B. 1957, BASED IN BERLIN, GERMANY

IMMANUEL CHURCH AND PARISH CENTRE //
COLOGNE, GERMANY, 2013
M9 MUSEUM DISTRICT // VENICE, ITALY, 2018
EXPERIMENTA // HEILBRONN, GERMANY, 2019
PP. 126–129

KRISTIN JARMUND - KRISTIN JARMUND
ARKITEKTER
B. 1954, BASED IN OSLO, NORWAY

RAHOLT SECONDARY SCHOOL //
EIDSVOLL, NORWAY, 2004
NORWEGIAN EMBASSY // KATHMANDU,
NEPAL, 2008
TORGBYGGET // OSLO, NORWAY, 2018
PP. 130–133

AMANDA LEVETE - AL_A
B. 1955, BASED IN LONDON, UK

MAAT (MUSEUM OF ART, ARCHITECTURE AND
TECHNOLOGY) // LISBON, PORTUGAL, 2016
CENTRAL EMBASSY // BANGKOK, THAILAND,
2017
VICTORIA & ALBERT MUSEUM EXHIBITION
ROAD QUARTER // LONDON, UK, 2017
PP. 134–139

INÊS LOBO - INÊS LOBO ARQUITECTOS
B. 1966, BASED IN LISBOA, PORTUGAL

HOUSE IN MAGOITO, AZENHAS DO MAR //
SÃO JOÃO DAS LAMPAS, SINTRA,
PORTUGAL, 2009
ART AND ARCHITECTURE FACULTY //
ÉVORA, PORTUGAL, 2010
PUBLIC LIBRARY AND ARCHIVE LUÍS DA SILVA
RIBEIRO // ANGRA DO HEROÍSMO, AZORES,
PORTUGAL, 2016
PP. 140–143

ELLEN VAN LOON – OMA
B. 1963, BASED IN ROTTERDAM,
THE NETHERLANDS

DE ROTTERDAM // ROTTERDAM,
THE NETHERLANDS, 2013
BLOX / DAC (DANISH ARCHITECTURE CENTRE)
// GEN, DENMARK, 2017
AXEL SPRINGER CAMPUS // BERLIN,
GERMANY, 2019
PP. 144–149

DORTE MANDRUP – DORTE MANDRUP
B. 1961, BASED IN COPENHAGEN, DENMARK
AMAGER CHILDREN'S CULTURE HOUSE //
   COPENHAGEN, DENMARK, 2013
WADDEN SEA CENTRE //
   ESBJERG, DENMARK, 2017
THE ICEFJORD CENTRE // ILULISSAT,
   GREENLAND, PLANNED 2021
PP. 150–155

NORMA MERRICK SKLAREK
1926–2012, BASED IN THE USA
SAN BERNARDINO CITY HALL //
   SAN BERNARDINO, CA, USA, 1973
PP. 156–157

MARTA PELEGRÍN - MEDIOMUNDO
ARQUITECTOS
B. 1973, BASED IN SEVILLE, SPAIN
SOCIAL CYBER CENTRE MACARENA TRES
   HUERTAS // SEVILLE, SPAIN, 2009
SAN FRANCISCO MOVIE THEATRE //
   VEJER DE LA FRONTERA, CADIZ, SPAIN, 2010
FACULTY OF HEALTH SCIENCES //
   GRANADA, SPAIN, 2010
PP. 158–161

CARME PIGEM – RCR ARQUITECTES
B. 1962, BASED IN OLOT, SPAIN
RURAL HOUSE // VALL DE BIANYA,
   GIRONA, 2007
BARBERÍ SPACE // OLOT, GIRONA, 2008
WAALSE KROOK MEDIATHEQUE //
   GHENT, BELGIUM, 2018
PP. 162–165

CARME PINÓS – ESTUDIO CARME PINÓS
B. 1954, BASED IN BARCELONA, SPAIN
CUBE II OFFICE TOWER //
   GUADALAJARA, MEXICO 2014
CAIXAFORUM CULTURAL EXHIBITION //
   CENTRE ZARAGOZA, SPAIN, 2014
ESCOLA MASSANA, ART AND DESIGN
   CENTRE // BARCELONA, SPAIN, 2017
PP. 166–169

SAMIRA RATHOD – SRDA
B. 1963, BASED IN MUMBAI, INDIA
ART GALLERY // BARODA, GUJARAT,
   INDIA, 2012
SHADOW HOUSE S // AHAN GAON,
   ALIBAUG, MUMBAI, INDIA, 2017
BHADRAN SCHOOL // BHADRAN,
   GUJARAT, INDIA, 2020
PP. 170–175

SU ROGERS
B. 1939, BASED IN LONDON, UK
CREEK VEAN // FEOCK, UK, 1966
PP. 178–181

NATHALIE ROZENCWAJG
NAME ARCHITECTURE
B. 1975, BASED IN LONDON, UK
THE TOWN HALL HOTEL //
   LONDON, UK, 2010
CASTLE LANE APARTMENTS //
   LONDON, UK, 2017
PP. 182–185

DENISE SCOTT BROWN
B. 1931, BASED IN PHILADELPHIA, USA

SAINSBURY WING // LONDON, UK, 2011
PP. 186–189

CRISTINA SEGNI – FOSTER + PARTNERS
B. 1974, BASED IN SAN FRANCISCO, USA

THE MUREZZAN // ST MORITZ,
   SWITZERLAND, 2007
CIUDAD CASA DE GOBIERNO //
   BUENOS AIRES, ARGENTINA, 2015
APPLE PARK // CUPERTINO, USA, 2018
PP. 190–193

KAZUYO SEJIMA – S A N A A
B. 1956, BASED IN TOKYO, JAPAN

NEW MUSEUM // NEW YORK, USA, 2007
SUMIDA HOKUSAI MUSEUM // TOKYO,
   JAPAN, 2016
OSAKA UNIVERSITY OF ARTS, ART SCIENCE
   DEPARTMENT BUILDING // OSAKA, JAPAN,
   2018
PP. 194–199

ANNABELLE SELLDORF – SELLDORF
ARCHITECTS
B. 1960, BASED IN NEW YORK, USA

DAVID ZWIRNER 20TH STREET //
   NEW YORK, USA, 2013
347 BOWERY // NEW YORK, USA, 2016
LUMA ARLES // ARLES, FRANCE, 2018
PP. 200–203

ALISON MARGARET SMITHSON
1923-2003, BASED IN LONDON, UK

THE ECONOMIST BUILDING //
   LONDON, UK, 1964
PP. 204–205

BENEDETTA TAGLIABUE – MIRALLES
TAGLIABUE EMBT
B. 1963, BASED IN BARCELONA, SPAIN

KÁLIDA SANT PAU CENTRE //
   BARCELONA, SPAIN, 2019
HAFENCITY PUBLIC SPACES //
   HAMBURG, GERMANY, 2020
CHINATRUST TOWER // TAICHUNG,
   TAIWAN, 2020
PP. 206–211

XU TIANTIAN – DNA
B. 1975, BASED IN BEIJING, CHINA

SONGZHUANG ARTIST COMMUNE //
   SONGZHUANG, BEIJING, CHINA, 2009
SONGYANG DAMUSHAN TEAHOUSE //
   SONGYANG DAMUSHAN TEA VALLEY,
   LISHUI, ZHEJIANG PROVINCE, CHINA, 2015
BROWN SUGAR FACTORY // XING VILLAGE,
   ZHEJIANG PROVINCE, CHINA, 2016
PP. 212–217

MONICA TRICARIO – PIUARCH
B. 1963, BASED IN MILAN, ITALY

QUATTRO CORTI // SAINT PETERSBURG,
   RUSSIA, 2010
PORTA NUOVA BUILDING //
   MILAN, ITALY 2013
GUCCI HUB // MILAN, ITALY, 2016
PP. 218–223

NATHALIE DE VRIES – MVRDV
B. 1965, BASED IN ROTTERDAM,
THE NETHERLANDS
VILLA VPRO // HILVERSUM,
  THE NETHERLANDS, 1997
BAŁTYK // POZNAŃ, POLAND, 2017
PP. 224–227

BETSY WILLIAMSON
WILLIAMSON WILLIAMSON
BASED IN TORONTO, CANADA
HOUSE ON ANCASTER CREEK //
  HAMILTON, CANADA, 2016
HOUSE ON BALA LINE //
  TORONTO, CANADA, 2016
HOUSE IN FROGS HOLLOW //
  NIAGARA ESCARPMENT, CANADA, 2010
PP. 228–233

ADA YVARS BRAVO – MYAA ARCHITECTS
BASED IN BARCELONA, SPAIN
AVONDALE PARK PAVILION //
  LONDON, UK, 2010
QFIS UNIVERSITY // DOHA, QATAR, 2015
GATEWAY // ANTANANARIVO, MADAGASCAR,
  ONGOING
PP. 234–237

CAZÚ ZEGERS – CAZÚ ZEGERS
B. 1958, BASED IN SANTIAGO, CHILE
TIERRA PATAGONIA HOTEL //
  TORRES DEL PAINE, CHILE, 2011
SOPLO HOUSE // LO BARNECHEA,
  CHILE, 2011
LLU HOUSE // FUNDO CARRÁN, CHILE, 2018
PP. 238–243

# ARCHITECTS' WEBSITES

OLAJUMOKE ADENOWO
AD Consulting / Lagos, Nigeria
**adconsultinglimited.com**

AMALE ANDRAOS
WORKac / New York, USA
**work.ac**

SANDRA BARCLAY
Barclay & Crousse / Lima, Peru
**barclaycrousse.com**

DEBORAH BERKE
Deborah Berke Partners / New York, USA
**dberke.com**

TATIANA BILBAO
Tatiana Bilbao Estudio / Mexico City, Mexico
**tatianabilbao.com**

LINA BO BARDI
**institutobardi.com.br**

CAROLINE BOS
UNStudio / Amsterdam, The Netherlands
**unstudio.com**

ALISON BROOKS
Alison Brooks Architects / London, UK
**alisonbrooksarchitects.com**

SARAH CALBURN
Sarah Calburn Architects /
Johannesburg, South Africa
**sarahcalburn.co.za**

FERNANDA CANALES
Fernanda Canales Arquitectura /
Mexico City, Mexico
**fernandacanales.com**

LUCÍA CANO
SelgasCano / Madrid, Spain
**selgascano.net**

ODILE DECQ
Studio Odile Decq / Paris, France
**odiledecq.com**

ELIZABETH DILLER
Diller Scofidio + Renfro / New York, USA
**dsrny.com**

FRIDA ESCOBEDO
Frida Escobedo / Mexico City, Mexico
**fridaescobedo.com**

YVONNE FARRELL & SHELLEY McNAMARA
Grafton Architects / Dublin, Ireland
**graftonarchitects.ie**

DORIANA FUKSAS
Fuksas / Rome, Italy and Paris, France
 fuksas.com

JEANNE GANG
Studio Gang / New York, San Francisco, USA
 studiogang.com

ZAHA HADID
Zaha Hadid Architects / London, UK
 zaha-hadid.com

ITSUKO HASEGAWA
Itsuko Hasegawa Atelier / Tokyo, Japan
 ihasegawa.com

ANNA HERINGER
Anna Heringer / Laufen, Germany
 anna-heringer.com

FRANCINE HOUBEN
Mecanoo / Delft, The Netherlands
 mecanoo.nl

ROSSANA HU
Neri & Hu / Shanghai, China
 neriandhu.com

LOUISA HUTTON
sauerbruchhutton / Berlin, Germany
 sauerbruchhutton.de

KRISTIN JARMUND
Kristin Jarmund Arkitekter / Oslo, Norway
 kj-a.no

AMANDA LEVETE
AL_A / London, UK
 ala.uk.com

INÊS LOBO
Inês Lobo Arquitectos / Lisboa, Portugal
 ilobo.pt

ELLEN VAN LOON
OMA / Rotterdam, The Netherlands
 oma.eu

DORTE MANDRUP
Dorte Mandrup / Copenhagen, Denmark
 dortemandrup.dk

MARTA PELEGRÍN
MEDIOMUNDO arquitectos / Seville, Spain
 mediomundo.es

CARME PIGEM
RCR Arquitectes / Olot, Spain
 rcrarquitectes.es

CARME PINÓS
Estudio Carme Pinós / Barcelona, Spain
 cpinos.com

SAMIRA RATHOD
srda / Mumbai, India
  **srda.co**

NATHALIE ROZENCWAJG
NAME architecture / London, UK
  **namearchitecture.net**

CRISTINA SEGNI
Foster + Partners / San Francisco, USA
  **fosterandpartners.com**

KAZUYO SEJIMA
S A N A A / Tokyo, Japan
  **sanaa.co.jp**

ANNABELLE SELLDORF
Selldorf Architects / New York, USA
  **selldorf.com**

BENEDETTA TAGLIABUE
Miralles Tagliabue EMBT /
Barcelona, Spain
  **mirallestagliabue.com**

XU TIANTIAN
DnA / Beijing, China
  **designandarchitecture.net**

MONICA TRICARIO
piuarch / Milan, Italy
  **piuarch.it**

NATHALIE DE VRIES
MVRDV / Rotterdam, The Netherlands
  **mvrdv.nl**

BETSY WILLIAMSON
Williamson Williamson / Toronto, Canada
  **williamsonwilliamson.com**

ADA YVARS BRAVO
MYAA Architects / Barcelona, Spain
  **myaa.eu**

CAZÚ ZEGERS
Cazú Zegers / Santiago, Chile
  **cazuzegers.cl**

# PHOTO CREDITS

pp. 2, 167 © Jordi Bernadó; 7, 54, 55 bottom, 58 top, 59, 81-83 © Rafael Gamo; 8, 11-13 © Olajumoke Adenowo, AD Consulting Limited; 14 © Amale Andraos; 15, 17 © Bruce Damonte; 16 © Miguel de Guzman; 18 © ARCHIVIO GAE AULENTI; 19 © Musée d'Orsay / Patrice Schmidt; 20 © pio3 / Shutterstock; 22 © Sandra Barclay; 23-25 © Cristobal Palma / Estudio Palma; 26 © WinnieAu; 27 © Eduard Heuber; 28 © CatherineTighe; 29 © Chris Cooper; 30 © Ana Hop; 33, 34, 61-63, 72-74, 105, 117 top, 213 bottom © Iwan Baan; 35 © Rory Gardiner; 36 © INSTITUTOBARDI / CASADEVIDRO; 37 © Douglas Damasceno / Stockimo / Alamy Stock Foto; 38-39 © Foto Arena LTDA / Alamy Stock Foto; 40 © Inga Powilleit; 41 © Plomp; 42-43, 47, 138-139 © Hufton+Crow; 44 © Mark Haddon; 45 © Dennis Gilbert; 46 © Paul Riddle; 48-49 © ABA; 50, 53 © Sarah Calburn; 51 © David Ross, 52 © Dustin Tusnovics ; 55 top, 56-57, 58 both images on the bottom © Sandra Pereznieto; 60 © SelgasCano; 64 © Franck Juery; 65-69, 103-104 © Roland Halbe; 70 © Geordie Wood; 75 © Brett Beyer; 76 © estate of J.S. Lewinski / National Portrait Gallery, London; 77-79 © Ruel Collection / Bridgeman Images; 80 © Carlos Torres; 84 © Alice Clancy; 85 © Ros Kavanagh; 86-87, 88 bottom © Federico Brunetti; 88 top © Alexandre Soria; 89 top © Dennis Gilbert; 89 bottom © Ed Reeves; 90 © Gianmarco Chieregato; 91 © Ramon Prat; 92 top © Leonardo Finotti_Shenzhen; 92 bottom © Archivio Fuksas; 93 top © Moreno Maggi; 93 bottom © Maurizio Marcato; 94 © Saverio Truglia; 95,96 © Steve Hall / Hall + Merrick Photographers; 97 © Nic Lehoux; 98 © Signal Photos / Alamy Stock Foto; 99 © Peter Cavanagh / Alamy Stock Foto; 100-101 © Olivier Martin Gambier/ARTEDIA/VIEW / Alamy Stock Foto; 102 © Steve Double; 106, 108 bottom © Itsuko Hasegawa; 107 top © Shuji Yamada; 107 bottom, 108 top © Mitsumasa Fujitsuka; 109 © Shinsuke Kera; 110 © Nina Rettenbacher; 111 © Kurt Hoerbst; 112 top © B.K.S. Inan; 112 bottom © Alexandra Grill; 113 ©Jenny JI; 114, 116 top © Mecanoo_Francine Houben; 115, 251 © Mecanoo photo by Ossip Architectuurfotografie; 116 bottom © Mecanoo photo by Harry Cock; 117 bottom, 118-119 © Mecanoo photo by Andrés Gallardo Albajar; 120 © Rossana Hu; 122-125 © Pedro Pegenaute; 126 © Valerie Bennett; 127 top © Annette Kisling; 127 bottom © Margot Gottschling; 128 © Alessandra Chemollo © Polymnia Venezia; 129 © Jan Bitter; 130 © Nadia Frantsen; 131 © Stian Wiik; 132 © Guri Dahl; 133 © Gitte Boge; 134 © Matt Holyoak; 137 top © Fernando Guerra; 137 bottom © EDP Foundation; 140 © Inês Lobo; 141-143 © Leonardo Finotti; 144 © Kristian Ridder Nielsen; 145 © Ossip van Duivenbode; 146-147 © Rasmus Hjortshoj; 148 © Richard John Seymour; 149 © OMA; 150 © Volker Renner; 152 © Torben Eskerod; 153 © Jens Lindhe; 154 © Adam Moerk; 155 © MIR; 156-157 © courtesy of Gruen Associates; 158-161 © MEDIOMUNDO ARQUITECTOS; 162 © RCR Arquitectes; 163-165 © Hisao Suzuki / nuaa; 166 © Wayne Taylor; 168 top © Estudio Carme Pinós; 168 bottom © Ricardo Santonja, 169 © Duccio Malagamba; 170-177 © Samira Rathod – srda; 178 © Norman Foster Foundation Archive; 179, 188-189 © Arcaid Images  / Alamy Stock Foto; 180-181 © Heritage Image Partnership Ltd / Alamy Stock Foto; 182 © Nathalie Rozencwajg; 183 top © George Rex; 183 bottom © Sue Barr; 184-185 © NAARO; 186 © Courtesy of Venturi, Scott Brown and Associates, photo by Robert Venturi; 187 © Lana Rastro / Alamy Stock Foto; 190 © Cristina Segni; 191-193 © Nigel Young / Foster + Partners; 194, 198-199 © Kazuyo Sejima & Associates; 196-197 © Dean Kaufram; 200 © Brigitte Lacombe; 201 © Jason Schmidt, Courtesy of Selldorf Architects; 202 top © Nicholas Venezia, Courtesy of Selldorf Architects; 202 bottom © Courtesy of Selldorf Architects; 203 top © C+D Architecture, Courtesy of Selldorf Architects; 203 bottom ©Hervé Hôte, Courtesy of Selldorf Architects; 204 © National Portrait Gallery, London; 205 © FP Collection / Alamy Stock Foto; 206 © Enrico Basili; 207-209 © Courtesy of Miralles Tagliabue EMBT; 210 © Courtesy of the HafenCity Hamburg GmbH; 211 © Yu Chen Tsao; 212 © Xu Tiantian / DnA_Design and Architecture; 213 top, 214-215 © Zhou Ruogu; 216 top, 217 © Ziling Wang; 216 bottom © Hao Chen; 218 © Delfino Sisto Legnani e Marco Cappelletti; 219-223 © Andrea Martiradonna; 224 © Erik Smits; 225 © MVRDV, photo by Rob 't Hart; 226-227 © Ossip van Duivenbode; 228-229 © Betsy Williamson; 230-233 © Bob Gundu; 234-237 © Mangera Yvars Architects; 238 © Cazú Zegers; 239-240 © Pía Vergara; 242 © Ana Maria Lopez; 243 top © Ian Hsu; 243 bottom © Ian Gildemeister

ACKNOWLEDGEMENTS

Writing this book was a wonderful adventure. I am extending my gratitude to all the amazing architects featured here. It was a great honour and pleasure to look into their practices and learn how passionately and inventively they contribute to architecture, which is a complex and fascinating discipline.

I would like to thank the team at Prestel, especially Claudia Stäuble and Sabine Schmid, who believed in this title from the very beginning and gave me the chance to become immersed into this absorbing subject. I'm extremely grateful for their support and this unique opportunity. A big thank you also goes to Allison Silver Adelman, who expertly copy-edited the texts for the book. And last but not least, I thank my husband Pierre for his continuous support.

I dedicate this title to my beloved daughter Emilie, who is about to celebrate her third birthday as I'm completing the book. She is an amazing girl – extremely inventive, eager to learn, and wonderfully curious about the world around her. It will be interesting to see what she decides to do in her adult life, but whatever it is, I hope the architects' portraits gathered here will be for her, and for all readers, a source of great inspiration for finding creative outlets, thinking outside of the box, and pursuing their dreams.



Front cover photo: © Iwan Baan
Back cover photo: © Ros Kavanagh

Library of Congress Control Number is available; a CIP catalogue record for this book is available from the British Library.



Editorial direction: Claudia Stäuble, Sabine Schmid
Texts, design and layout: Agata Toromanoff
Copy-editing: Allison Silver Adelman
Production: Andrea Cobré
Separations: Schnieber Graphik, München
Printing and binding: DZS Grafik, d.o.o., Ljubljana
Paper: 150g Profisilk

Penguin Random House Verlagsgruppe FSC® N001967

Printed in Slovenia

ISBN 978-3-7913-8663-8

www.prestel.com